"No one captures the magic, delight, struggle, and triumphs to be found in middle school like Phyllis Fagell. She knows middle school inside and out, and her advice is some of the best available for students, parents, and teachers."

—JESSICA LAHEY, author of *The Gift of Failure*

"I love, love *Middle School Matters*! Phyllis Fagell has done a stupendous job! *Middle School Matters* gives parents of middle school boys and girls an essential guide to walk alongside their children as they go through middle school. The book is filled with just the right combination of research and common sense strategies that only a middle school counselor in the trenches could deliver. With this book, parents don't need to dread the middle school years. Instead they can be prepared and informed so they can do best by their kids. I wish I had had this book when my boys were in middle school!"

—ROSALIND WISEMAN, author of *Queen Bees and Wannabes* and founder of Cultures of Dignity

"Middle school parents: help is finally here! This is the book parents have been waiting for since . . . forever. Parents have long been socialized to fear the middle school years as a time of great turmoil and never-ending drama, but Phyllis Fagell opens our eyes to the modern middle school student by sharing a powerful combination of current research, anecdotes from actual middle schoolers, and her own expertise as a middle school counselor. *Middle School Matters* is packed with helpful tips and actionable strategies to help your middle school student thrive instead of simply survive."

—KATIE HURLEY, LCSW, author of *No More*
Mean Girls and *The Happy Kid Handbook*

"Middle school does matter! And, parents matter during these years . . . as much as you ever have, maybe more. As young people strive to answer, 'Who am I?' they need you to stand solidly in their corner reminding them that they are perfect just as they are. Phyllis Fagell has created a masterpiece here—an actionable guide filled with the skill sets you'll need to support your child through these critical life-shaping years."

—KEN GINSBURG, MD, MS Ed, author of *Raising*
Kids to Thrive and *Building Resilience*
in Children and Teens, Parentandteen.com

"*Middle School Matters* is a must-read for parents, educators and anyone else seeking guidance through the transitions of this critical developmental period, with all its psychological, physical, social and academic challenges. Fagell writes clearly and concisely, offering practical suggestions and engaging anecdotes to illustrate her points. The conversation starters are excellent!"

—MARY K. ALVORD, PhD, psychologist and coauthor
Conquer Negative Thinking for Teens, and *Resilience*
Builder Program for Children and Adolescence.

"As a lifelong educator and the parent of two teens and a tween, I cannot recommend this book enough! I just wish *Middle School Matters* had been written when I was a superintendent and led a middle school transformation effort, as the ideas, advice, and practical guidance are invaluable. Phyllis Fagell has done us all a great service by breaking down the middle school years into easily understood concepts that parents and educators can use to work with early adolescents in any setting. Phyllis presents simple strategies and approaches to help students—and adults— navigate an amazingly complex and exciting time in their lives. I highly encourage teachers, principals, parents, policy makers, and anyone interested in using the middle school years to lay the foundation for success in the teenage years and beyond to read and apply the lessons of this book now!"

—Joshua P. Starr, EdD, Chief Executive
Officer, PDK International

"Parents of middle schoolers, rejoice! In Phyllis Fagell you get a triple threat: a veteran counselor who's seen it all, a wise parent, and an excellent writer who knows her research and has talked with every expert you don't have the time to read. This book is your middle school wingman, a clear, smart read you can pick up whenever you need it, to guide you through whatever curveball your child decides to throw your way."

—Rachel Simmons, author of Odd Girl Out
and Enough As She Is

"This book is an indispensable tool for anyone who parents or works with middle schoolers. It's extremely well-researched, smart, readable and empathetic. The chapters on healthy sexuality, preparing for love and helping boys connect with others give these critical, often-overlooked, topics the lip service they—and young adolescents—desperately need."

—Andrew Reiner, educator, writer,
and masculinity researcher

"This brilliant book will make you rethink everything you imagined about the middle school years Phyllis Fagell's love for this tween/teen breed abounds as she convinces us that emotions and drama may be high, but the growth and change happening is actually wildly exciting. We need to see it as an opportunity, and enjoy it a bit. These kids aren't a mess—they are open, sponges. Sure they fail, but they are learning resilience. The best part of this book is, instead of simply identifying and analyzing what's happening, Fagell gives parents really practical, specific tips on everything from meltdowns to bullying to social media. The hardest part of being a parent is we need a script! We can read book after book and understand what's going on in those mushrooming teen brains, to some extent, but when faced with a kid writhing on the floor about a perceived slight, we need some actual language in the moment. Fagell hands the script over, and it's laced with humor and wisdom. She makes getting through these years seem not only possible, but full of some joy as well!"

—CLAIRE SHIPMAN, journalist and author of
Confidence Code and *Confidence Code for Girls*

Middle School
MATTERS

Middle School MATTERS

The 10 Key Skills Kids Need to
Thrive in Middle School and Beyond—
and How Parents Can Help

PHYLLIS L. FAGELL, LCPC

LIFE
LONG

Copyright © 2019 by Phyllis Fagell
Cover design by Georgia Feldman
Cover image Verónica Grech
Cover copyright © 2019 Hachette Book Group, Inc.

Da Capo Press
Hachette Book Group
1290 Avenue of the Americas, New York, NY 10104
www.dacapopress.com
@DaCapoPress

Printed in the United States of America
First Edition: August 2019
Published by Da Capo Press, an imprint of Perseus Books, LLC, a subsidiary of Hachette Book Group, Inc.

The Hachette Speakers Bureau provides a wide range of authors for speaking events. To find out more, go to www.hachettespeakersbureau.com or call (866) 376-6591.

The publisher is not responsible for websites (or their content) that are not owned by the publisher.

Print book interior design by Linda Mark

Library of Congress Cataloging-in-Publication Data has been applied for.

ISBNs: 978-0-7382-3508-0 (trade paperback); 978-0-7382-3509-7 (ebook)

LSC-C

10 9 8 7 6 5 4 3 2 1

FOR STEVE, BEN, EMILY, AND ALEX

CONTENTS

Foreword   *xi*

Introduction   *xv*

Chapter 1   WHAT'S THE BIG DEAL ABOUT MIDDLE SCHOOL?   1

VALUES AND INTEGRITY
"It's easier to lie than deal with all the drama." 8

Chapter 2   MAKING RESPONSIBLE, HEALTHY,
AND ETHICAL DECISIONS   11

Chapter 3   FOSTERING HONESTY   24

Chapter 4   ENCOURAGING KINDNESS AND EMPATHY   35

Chapter 5   EMBRACING DIFFERENCE IN SELF AND OTHERS   49

SOCIAL SKILLS
"I feel judged and ignored." 65

Chapter 6   MANAGING SHIFTING FRIENDSHIPS   67

Chapter 7   DEALING WITH BULLYING   79

Chapter 8   COPING WITH GOSSIP AND SOCIAL TURMOIL   91

Chapter 9   GROWING UP SEXUALLY HEALTHY   103

Chapter 10   PREPARING FOR LOVE   120

LEARNING
"Everyone is getting A's except for me." 129

Chapter 11   ENCOURAGING BALANCE AND
SETTING REASONABLE EXPECTATIONS   131

Chapter 12   TACKLING HOMEWORK   141

Chapter 13   INTERVENING WHEN SCHOOL IS A STRUGGLE   151

EMPOWERMENT AND RESILIENCE
"There are all sorts of people in the world, and we'll all find our place." 163

Chapter 14   CONNECTING WITH BOYS AND
HELPING THEM CONNECT WITH OTHERS   165

Chapter 15   RAISING STRONG, EMPOWERED GIRLS   179

Chapter 16   TAKING RISKS IN A WORLD OF NO'S   193

Chapter 17   MANAGING SETBACKS AND SHORING UP RESILIENCE   205

Chapter 18   PREPARING KIDS FOR A CHANGING WORLD   219

Conclusion   MOVING FORWARD: "Make mistakes,
model self-compassion, and grow alongside your child."   231

Parent Discussion Guide   237
Educator Discussion Guide   249
Resources   257
Acknowledgments   281
Index   283
About the Author   298

FOREWORD

I GIVE PRESENTATIONS TO THOUSANDS OF PARENTS AROUND THE world, and their biggest concerns always revolve around middle school—everything from shifting friendships to character development to learning and preparing kids for an unknown, changing world. Parents may ask me how they can help their kids recover from social rejection or bullying, or how they can instill honesty, empathy, responsibility, and kindness. You may wonder: When is the best time to give my child a phone, let them use social media, or take public transportation alone? How much should I be helping them with homework, monitoring their online behavior, or communicating with their teachers? What are the signs that my child could have a learning or attentional challenge? And just how much stress, moodiness, and anxiety is normal for a middle schooler? You may have heard that focusing on grades and test scores won't create happy, successful, thriving kids, but it's a confusing message. You might be thinking, "Okay, but what am I supposed to be doing instead?"

Well, take a deep breath and relax. What you have in your hands is golden. Phyllis is the perfect person to address these questions and to write this book. She's an extraordinary middle school counselor with many years of experience. I've watched her in action with students, and she has rapport, competence, and compassion. She gives wonderful, profound, spot-on advice to help kids solve whatever issues they're facing. Because she's in the field working with children every day, she's privy to thoughts the rest of us don't often hear, and she's able to help you make sense of your child's feelings and behavior. She helps you see them through a different lens so you can leverage their strengths and stay close. You may not be able to use the same strategies that worked when your child was six or eight, but Phyllis gives you all the tools you need to make the most of these make-or-break years. This is a book that will allay any fears you have about your power as a parent.

Phyllis not only has advised thousands of parents in her capacity as a counselor, therapist, writer, and speaker, but she's also the mother of three children, including two teens and a tween. She's steeped in the phase, presenting at national conferences and schools and interviewing educators, students, and parents across the world. As a result, she's been able to identify the most pressing, key issues for middle schoolers today. One thing is clear: We're not the only ones concerned about this age group, and Phyllis's advice applies to kids everywhere.

There are many reasons I'm delighted to be writing this foreword, and many reasons why I think this is the best book out there on middle school. For starters, Phyllis's advice is not only practical and proven, but it's grounded in breaking new studies. She's a constant reader, and I can guarantee you that you're reading the most cutting-edge research available. She turns evidence-based ideas into common sense, reassuring, and concrete advice. She's always up to date, and she knows how to empower middle school–age kids. She doesn't just provide tips on how to deal with issues such as bullying, cliques, or poor grades. Her writing is far more nuanced, she digs deep to find the real issues at hand, and she contextualizes information so she can offer targeted advice. For example, she doesn't force social media into its own category. Instead, she addresses the topic anywhere it would crop up in a middle schooler's life, including in relation to sleep, self-regulation, homework completion, gossip, and sexting.

What also sets *Middle School Matters* (MSM) apart is that it translates kids' needs and concerns into simple, direct, easy interventions that have a big impact. Too often, we make parenting more complicated than it needs to be. MSM offers everything—conversation starters, stories, examples, statistics, resources, tips from experts, news stories, and anecdotes—so you can handle all kinds of scenarios. It's a road map for raising a healthy, happy, resilient, and ethical child.

At the heart of the book are middle schoolers themselves. There's an accumulation of student voices throughout the book that lend authenticity. Those voices are also a reality check. We read about kids' worries, wins, fears, insecurities, and dreams for the future. We hear glorious stories of big-hearted, courageous kids making a difference, and get a glimpse into what they want from us, their parents. We learn about possible gaps in their knowledge, and we begin to grasp just how different their world is from the one we remember. We also learn how to connect with our child without violating their desire for privacy. The underlying message is clear: this isn't a phase to dread or the time to back off. In fact, these are years to cherish.

One of my favorite sections—and I bet it will be one of your favorites as well—is the final chapter. The book shares the advice recent middle school graduates would give themselves, their parents, and current middle schoolers. One teen said, "Parents need to ask a lot of questions. Just sit down and talk about life, about their social drama, about academics, about whatever is on their mind, and let them know you hear them. Tell them you get that it's difficult, and maybe Mary Jo isn't being the best friend right now—but don't just jump in and give advice." The ideas they share parallel what Phyllis has been saying all along, but we get to hear it from a different set of voices.

Parenting is a work in progress; we're all constantly trying to get better, there's no instruction manual, and guilt and shame have no place in advice. MSM reaffirms this idea and encourages parents to help their child identify and take pride in their hidden superpowers. Above all, MSM wants you to be an unwavering source of support for your child and to stay optimistic and open-minded through their inevitable ups and downs. If you take MSM to heart, a couple of things will happen. You'll be a better parent, and you and your child will become kinder, better, more resourceful, inclusive, ethical people. And isn't that what we're all trying to do? We all want to raise a good, strong person who wants to improve the world and who can do so because we've empowered them. This is the way to grow and evolve alongside your child. After reading this book, I know you'll be able to make the most of these years, and I bet you'll even enjoy them!

—Dr. Michele Borba, author of
UnSelfie: Why Empathetic Kids
Succeed in Our All-About-Me World

INTRODUCTION

Mention the words "middle school" and most adults groan. I get it. Even if we handled the phase with grace, we're wired to remember the bad and downright awkward moments. I have my own mental catalogue: succumbing to pressure to weigh myself at a sleepover. Getting tossed out of classes for giggling uncontrollably and passing notes. Eking by with a D in seventh-grade math. Creating a "slam book" with friends so we could describe one another's flaws in detail. That seemed like a perfectly reasonable idea at the time, but the comments stuck. (It was thirty years before I cut my bangs again.) At twelve, peer approval was everything.

Kids are navigating a different world today, but middle school is equally memorable. No one gets out unchanged. Middle school is a stew of simmering hormones, shifting relationships, and increased expectations. Mere months separate elementary from middle school, but the shift is seismic. Suddenly, kids are yanked out of childhood and tossed into adolescence. They have to master locker combinations, multiple courses, and new routines. There's an influx of new students and greater academic demands. All of this is exciting, but leaves them feeling unmoored when they most want to belong and fit in.

This is why middle school can seem like an endless soap opera featuring complicated characters, from the thirteen-year-old girl who takes pictures of herself in provocative poses and shares them with complete strangers, to the twelve-year-old boy who does his homework every night but refuses to turn it in. A mature eighth-grade boy may baffle his parents by sticking his head in a toilet for fun on social media. A once-easygoing fifth grader may lash out at anyone who looks at her the wrong way in sixth grade. A seventh-grade soccer player may shut down when he gets cut from the school team. As painful as this is for them to experience, it can be even more excruciating to witness. Your kids may seem unrecognizable to you and feel like strangers to themselves.

Your child's lack of life experience exacerbates already heightened emotions. Adults tend to look back on that phase and remember only the intensity, but kids can emerge from this vulnerable period feeling happy, competent, and prepared for high school and adult life. Missteps are inevitable and shouldn't be seen as disasters. It feels counterintuitive, but those slips actually build resilience. It's tough to strike the right balance between supporting kids and impeding their emerging autonomy.

When I graduated from junior high school in 1987, I never imagined that someday I'd work in one. It took me a while to find my way back, but I've now been through middle school three times: as a student, as a parent, and now as a counselor. I started my career as a journalist writing about health and science. After the birth of my second child, I decided to change careers, becoming a licensed therapist and professional school counselor. Little did I know that my oldest son would start middle school the same year I began working in one! The following year, my daughter started sixth grade. (For the record, as of this writing, that's two kids down, one to go.) On top of that, I was seeing middle school kids and their parents in private practice.

Not surprisingly, I've become a little obsessed with this age group. Shortly after I started working as a middle school counselor, I began writing for the *Washington Post* about the stuff that keeps me fired up at night: busting myths, stereotypes, and outdated beliefs about learning, gender differences, mental health, and communication. Rethinking how we foster autonomy, teach self-regulation, and frame success. Instilling honesty, kindness, and resilience. I've looked to other fields from character education to technology for inspiration. I've spent the past few years interviewing psychologists, teachers, writers, researchers, students, physicians, parents, entrepreneurs, administrators, consultants, and maker educators. Along the way, I've developed and honed my own approach. One thing is clear: we need a new middle school mind-set.

As a counselor, I've vicariously experienced so much anxiety, but even so, I've started to question the cliché about middle school as an unavoidable period of misery that must be endured. After working with hundreds of kids and parents, I believe we've got the paradigm all wrong. Yes, middle school is messy, dramatic, and confusing at times, but it's also the perfect time to proactively build character and confidence.

I've seen this happen so many times. When I first started working with a sixth-grade girl named Rebecca, she was obsessed with her grades. Every night, she'd dissolve into tears, terrified that she had bombed a test. Her parents and I worried that she'd buckle under the increased pressure of high school. For the next two years, we worked together to teach Rebecca relaxation strategies, encourage balance, and help her avoid catastrophizing. By eighth grade, she was back on an even keel. The high school transition ended up being a non-event.

Joey, an eighth-grade ringleader, took school in stride but felt little empathy for classmates. He'd roll his eyes when someone got a wrong answer. He'd whisper to friends about other kids' lack of athleticism. When the gym teacher would ask him to cut it out, Joey would say he wasn't there to make friends. One weekend, Joey started a group text chain, telling a bunch of friends that a girl in their class had been hooking up with boys at other schools. It wasn't true, and when the girl's parents found out, they complained to school staff and other eighth-grade parents.

Joey was furious that adults were "badmouthing" him to one another instead of addressing him directly. He accused them of acting more like middle schoolers than grown-ups. He may not have seen the irony, but he took on gossip as his personal cause. He led a gradewide discussion about conflict resolution and respect. As a result, he improved the social dynamics for everyone.

These types of wins are the reason I love kids this age. They're flawed, curious, impressionable, and receptive to new ideas. They're sensitive to injustice, empathetic, and attuned to one another's needs. They'll tell me if a girl is cutting herself with a pair of nail scissors she's carting around in her pencil case. If a boy is skipping meals or his mood plummets abruptly, I'm likely to hear about it. When kids are instructed to tell an adult, that often means the school counselor. I frequently hear things that others don't, and I take that responsibility seriously.

As a counselor, I also hear from parents and guardians, who have asked me all kinds of questions, from the practical to the philosophical. Should they pay their children to get good grades? Should they make them stick with activities they hate? Is there a way to ensure they make good relationship choices? They question their instincts because this isn't the world they grew up in, when good grades and a slew of extracurricular activities set students up for the "right" college and successful careers. Parents are equally mystified by their kids' online social lives. It's a whole new era with many unknowns, and that can feel scary.

Understandably, parents want to control whatever variables they can. It's discombobulating to realize how much is beyond their reach, from their kids' shifting friendships to their interests and passions. While there's no magical parent who holds the secret to connecting with teens or launching them on the right path, no one should be throwing up their hands. The parent of a tantrum-prone two-year-old doesn't say, "You know, this kind of sucks, so I'm just going to hang back. When he's three, I'll teach him how to use his words." Similarly, parents of middle schoolers can't afford to sit this phase out.

Middle schoolers are young enough to be unjaded, but old enough to grasp sophisticated concepts. They can experiment, grow, and veer off course while the stakes are low. It's the ideal time to impart strategies, teach social-emotional skills, and foster integrity and healthy risk-taking. Rather than merely helping our kids to survive these years, we should look instead to set them up to thrive. If we get it right, we'll equip them to manage social turmoil, maintain reasonable academic expectations, and make well-considered decisions throughout their lives. Contrary to conventional wisdom, kids can emerge from middle school stronger and wiser for their struggles. Adults can and should play an active role in that process.

The good news is you aren't helpless. You add value by sharing both your positive and negative life experiences, offering unconditional love, modeling critical thinking, and giving them tools to manage setbacks. I'll provide a road map and outline concrete strategies for a wide range of scenarios, from "getting fired" by friends to managing a learning or attention issue. I'll also debunk many of the persistent myths about middle schoolers. By the time you finish this book, I want you to feel empowered to handle any middle school situation—and to see it as the once-in-a-lifetime opportunity it is for your child.

CHAPTER 1

WHAT'S THE BIG DEAL ABOUT MIDDLE SCHOOL?

"I've always loved middle school because kids are intellectually growing so much and discovering what they're passionate about, but still young and not too obsessed with whether they're cool. You can still capture that little kid part of them, but they're ready to go intellectually. It's that combination that's magical."

—SALLY SELBY, FORMER PRINCIPAL OF
SIDWELL FRIENDS MIDDLE SCHOOL

WHAT SETS MIDDLE SCHOOLERS APART? MIDDLE SCHOOL IS when life begins to get more complicated for kids, but it's not just the setting that makes it different. The psychologist G. Stanley Hall first identified early adolescence as a unique phase in 1904. By the 1950s, pioneering Swiss psychologist Jean Piaget had built on Hall's research and was working on developmental stage theory. We now know much more about these unique years of early adolescence—and why we should give them special attention.

These years are a time of incredible growth; the only other time in a child's life when they changed this rapidly was between birth and age two. Your middle schooler is changing physically, intellectually, morally, socially, and emotionally. Their prefrontal cortex, the part of the brain that handles executive functions and making decisions, is still developing. Adolescent developmental pediatrician Ken Ginsburg explains, "Brain development is occurring at a heightened pace; your ability to experience and interpret emotions is very, very high; you're beginning to imagine yourself as an independent being; and you're trying to figure out how you fit in." Ginsburg, the codirector of the Center for Parent and Teen Communication at Children's Hospital of Philadelphia and the author of *Raising Kids to Thrive*, wants parents to understand that adolescents' fundamental questions are "Who am I?" "Am I normal?" and "Do I fit in?"

Kids are starting to think abstractly, engage in moral reasoning, and look for meaning. They're tuned into fairness and equity, and they're starting to solidify the beliefs and values they'll hold for life. Social-emotional maturity is still a work in progress, and sorting out relational drama is a time-consuming task. Many are in the throes of puberty and becoming moodier, more self-conscious, and less self-assured. The great paradox of middle school is that kids can simultaneously feel judged and ignored. As they toggle between wanting to form their own identity and fit in with peers, they may withdraw or rebel.

Michael Gordon, a middle school principal for forty years, shared with me that both the fun and the challenge of middle school is that on different days, the same kid may present as thirteen going on thirty or thirteen going on three. "It often seems that two distinct versions reside simultaneously within the body of each student," he told me. "One is a wide-eyed, open, and happy child who will follow you anywhere with excitement and is amazed by almost anything well-presented. The other is more emotional and cerebral, capable of doing many things and synthesizing involved concepts."

When you consider what's happening to their brains and bodies, it's no wonder that the shift from elementary to middle school can be bumpy. By 1966, educators started advancing the need for a separate middle school model that could respond to the distinct characteristics of ten- to fifteen-year-old children. Still, there's reason to believe the traditional middle school/junior high model isn't ideal. In a study published in the *American Educational Research Journal*, investigators looked at 90,000 sixth through eighth graders in New York City and found that the social and academic benefits of being "top dog" are strongest in sixth grade. Kids seem to learn and achieve more in schools with longer grade spans, whether the school serves grades K–8 or 6–12. In another study published in the *Journal of Early Adolescence*, researchers tracked 6,000 students from kindergarten through eighth grade. They concluded that starting a new school in sixth or seventh grade negatively impacts kids' motivation and feelings about their academic ability.

There are many different iterations of middle school. High Rock School in Needham, Massachusetts, for example, has a separate school that's just for sixth graders. The city's public middle school serves the town's seventh and eighth graders, which mirrors my own junior high experience. By the time I felt like I'd adjusted, it was time to leave. Other schools, such as Sidwell Friends Middle School in Washington, DC, run from fifth through eighth grade. That model allows the fifth and sixth grades to function as an upper elementary program within the middle school. I met with the school's principal, Sally Selby, shortly before her retirement. "The sixth graders benefit from the interdisciplinary nature of instruction, the home-room model, and the real connection to one adult," she told me, adding that the oldest students benefit, too. "There's a refuge in having eighth grade in middle school that allows them to keep baking. They don't have to take on the weight of the responsibility of high school—the seriousness of, 'Oh my god, grades count.'"

Some educators are innovating to help students make a smoother transition to middle school. Robert Dodd, a principal in Maryland, collaborated with Johns Hopkins University faculty to assess whether sixth graders do better with less departmentalization. Dodd implemented the program, called Project SUCCESS, in two middle schools in his district and found that students have higher levels of achievement and social engagement when they spend half of each school day with one teacher and an intact peer group. It's an approach that more closely resembles the kids' elementary school experience. "The data is ridiculous," he told me. "These kids are more likely to feel that their teachers value and care about them and their peers want to help them."

I've been a counselor in both a huge, public 6–8 school and a small, independent K–8 school with a separate middle school program. In my experience, one school model might soften the journey more than another, but the developmental phase seems to define the experience more than the setting. Whether or not a student is "top dog," children in early adolescence require sensitive educators who can address their unique needs.

It can be a tough transition. Suddenly, kids are expected to act a lot older than they were just a few months earlier. On top of juggling increased academic demands, they're navigating a more complex social world. The expectations are higher academically, socially, and even athletically. Students' performance and motivation often slide during this transition, and as the American Psychological Association notes, this can lead to self-doubt. They're also discovering their academic identity. This is when you might hear a child start saying, "I'm not a math person," or, "I'm terrible at art." We need to preserve their creativity and confidence, because middle school is around the time when both take a nosedive. (This is especially true for girls. A Ypulse study found that between their tween and teen years, girls' confidence that other people like them falls from 71 percent to 38 percent—a 46 percent drop.)

Middle school can leave the most self-assured parents full of self-doubt, too. Your child may test your last nerve or pull away, but don't be fooled. They all crave acceptance. If you're frustrated, baffled, or in need of an empathy boost, remember what it felt like to be twelve. Try to appreciate how exhausting it is for your child to manage supercharged emotions every single day.

The Ten Key Skills Kids Need to Thrive in Middle School and Beyond

No matter where your child is developmentally right now, my goal is to ensure they emerge from this phase with the following ten key skills, which range from the social and emotional to the logistical.

1. **Make good friend choices.** In middle school, shifting friendships are a given. The ability to make good choices in friends comes on the heels of making some questionable ones. Kids will figure out

quickly which friends instill a sense of belonging and which make them feel uncomfortable. Some will still insist on hanging out with the ones who make them feel terrible, and it can take a long time for them to realize they're sacrificing themselves. I'll cover everything from gossip to bullying, providing specific strategies to help kids manage social turmoil.

2. **Negotiate conflict.** Kids this age must cope with increasingly complex social interactions. They need to learn how to resolve conflict, whether they choose to go several rounds in the ring with a friend or walk away from a toxic relationship. They also must learn how to work with peers. Not many students get through middle school without feeling like they had to carry the load on at least one group project. Teamwork provides a window into kids' grit, flexibility, self-awareness, and resiliency. They might be hampered by clumsy social interactions or an inability to collaborate. I'll outline a range of ways to bolster their ability to work well with others.

3. **Manage a student-teacher mismatch.** Kids can learn from a teacher they don't like. It's a chance to practice working with someone they find difficult. This is a life skill they'll need in the workplace, and it requires understanding themselves. I'll offer strategies to help kids manage these types of situations so they won't feel powerless.

4. **Create homework and organization systems.** Ideally, children, not teachers or parents, take ownership of homework and grades. Kids may say they don't care, but they don't have to be invested in a particular outcome to change their behavior. After all, people who hate exercise can still choose to lift weights. They need to be able to create and tweak their organization systems and learn to monitor and take responsibility for their own work. If you care about this more than they do, why should they worry? They need to learn to carry the burden and experience the connection between preparation and performance. Conversely, if they're perfectionists, they need to know they can survive and manage the disappointment of a low grade. I'll give tips on raising independent, curious, motivated, and resilient learners.

5. **Consider others' perspectives.** If we want kids to accept their uniqueness and embrace differences in others, they must build their self-awareness. They also need to develop the ability to step into someone else's shoes. I'll describe how parents can build kids' empathy, foster their positive self-concept, and help them cope with setbacks by transcending the self.

6. **Self-advocate.** This is hard for adults, let alone kids, but it's imperative in a world full of people who'll tell them "no." By middle school, kids should be mastering how to ask teachers for help or clarification. To get them to a point where they can do that, we need to encourage them to take risks and manage fear. I'll describe how parents can help them progress from meek to direct so they don't fall through the cracks.

7. **Self-regulate emotions.** Children often need assistance labeling strong emotions before they can regulate them. It's not easy for middle schoolers to make connections between thoughts, feelings, and behaviors. They may be stuck in all-or-nothing thinking or be consistently self-critical. Unlike adults, they lack the benefit of life experience or perspective. I'll share how parents can help kids manage their stress, whether they feel bad about themselves, concerned about a specific situation, anxious about events in the news, or worried about their own future.

8. **Cultivate passions and recognize limitations.** When children are fired up about something, it's important to let them run with it. Even if their chosen interest doesn't seem exciting to parents, they're identifying their strengths and figuring out what drives them. They're also discovering where they struggle. This is useful information. No one needs to be good at everything, and school isn't one-size-fits-all. By honoring who they are and giving them appropriate outlets for their talents, parents can position their kids to feel competent and make a difference.

9. **Make responsible, healthy, and ethical choices.** Kids need to know how to respect and take care of their bodies and make safe, healthy decisions. It's equally important that they understand how to avoid

putting others at risk. I'll offer strategies to keep the lines of communication open as you tackle issues such as sexting or self-harm.

10. **Create and innovate.** Our changing world needs imaginative creators and divergent thinkers. When children think outside the box, it builds their confidence. As your kids do their homework, read required texts, and take standardized tests, they may not understand that these benchmarks are not the only ways to measure success. To be prepared for the innovation era, they'll need to be able to make connections across courses and to build, write, invent, and experiment. When parents foster an inventor's mentality, they heighten their kid's resourcefulness. For many adults, this requires a mind shift, so I'll offer specific tips.

If we want kids to master these ten crucial skills, we need to start with the basics. If you use the strategies outlined in this book, you'll set your child up to thrive in high school and beyond. I'll use a key at the beginning of each chapter to illustrate how different strategies help kids acquire these competencies. The book is divided into four domains: values and integrity, social skills, learning, and empowerment and resilience. Let's start from the inside, with values and integrity. To morally and ethically negotiate challenges, kids need a solid sense of self and empathy for others. Chapters on smart decision-making, honesty, kindness, and embracing differences are all about building kids' character.

The second section covers social skills. Chapters on shifting friendships, bullying, gossip, sex, and love will help you teach your kids to identify healthy relationships and cope with social turmoil.

The third section focuses on learning. To help kids take responsibility for their own learning, parents need to foster intrinsic motivation and set reasonable expectations. In chapters on grades, homework, and learning challenges, I'll talk about how to capitalize on kids' strengths and interests and address their weaknesses.

The final section is on empowerment and resilience. Chapters on staying connected to your sons and daughters and nudging them out of their comfort zone will help you teach them to self-advocate, connect with others, and communicate effectively. This section also offers techniques to help kids manage setbacks, prepare for a changing world, and think flexibly and outside the box. Of all the skills on my Top Ten list, this one might be the most critical to their future career.

Parents' primary job is to love and honor their children, and this is especially important in middle school. The wider the gap between who kids really are and who they think you need them to be, the more they'll struggle. If they learn to embrace what makes them unique at an age when they most want to fit in, they'll be more accepting of others. Even as they establish boundaries, they need you now more than ever. You're the role model and safety net as they try on new identities and attitudes. I hope that you'll experiment with your kids, testing different approaches to academic, social, and emotional issues while the risks are small and the rewards are big.

VALUES AND INTEGRITY

"It's easier to lie than to deal with all the drama."

CHAPTER 2

MAKING RESPONSIBLE, HEALTHY, AND ETHICAL DECISIONS

KEY SKILLS

1—Make good friend choices
2—Negotiate conflict
5—Consider others' perspectives
6—Self-advocate
7—Self-regulate emotions
9—Make responsible, healthy, and ethical choices

"Is it safe to vape water? What about pot? How much alcohol is too much?"

"I hate Katherine, so I got her Google password from her planner and deleted the TV script she'd written."

"I lost a bet, so I had to drink hot sauce. I got really sick."

SHELBY, QUINN, AND SAMARA HAD BEEN POSTING VIDEOS ON-line for months. They'd carefully choose their outfits and songs, then spend hours crafting elaborate routines. One Friday night, they decided to record a video while dancing in bikinis. They set a timer so they could shoot the video hands-free, ensuring that everyone would be visible. After they picked a filter, they added the hashtag #sexy8thgradegirls and shared the video publicly. Shelby's mother, Maureen, recalls hearing the girls singing as she cooked downstairs. She was glad they were having fun. She had no idea they were about to get hundreds of creepy, unwanted propositions from middle-aged men.

At first, Shelby, Quinn, and Samara thought the attention was kind of funny, but the sheer volume of lewd comments started to scare them. They decided to involve Maureen, who was shocked to discover their settings were public. Ironically, they'd just attended an assembly at school about the dangers of posting provocative images online. Maureen realized the messages hadn't sunk in. They had to experience the fallout firsthand to really get it. The girls tried to minimize the damage by taking down the video and deleting their accounts. Maureen also called the other girls' parents, and they met to discuss privacy and safety. As the girls processed with their parents, the #sexy8thgradegirls hashtag suddenly felt particularly ill-conceived. Maureen says the talk was just a start. "If they can strip for the world while I roast chicken downstairs, this clearly can't be a one-and-done conversation."

"Parents often think their adolescents, who look like adults, are more mature than they are," says Dr. Joanna Cohen, associate professor of pediatrics and emergency medicine at Children's National Medical Center in Washington, DC. Remember that underdeveloped prefrontal cortex? Middle schoolers are prone to increased risk-taking and sensory overload and may fail to think through consequences. Although they're starting to take a more sophisticated interest in moral and ethical decisions, they can backslide into more childish behavior. It can be hard for middle schoolers to push the "pause" button and delay their desire for immediate rewards, especially when they think they have anonymity online.

This challenge can be easy for parents to forget. Kids at this age often demonstrate great insight, particularly once they hit eighth grade. But while kids make a big leap from sixth grade to eighth grade, there's no such thing as an average middle schooler. There can be vast differences even among students in the same grade. One eighth grader might be worrying about playing truth or dare, while his sexually active classmate is asking for information about condoms. Life and family experiences also play an important role. A seventh-grade boy who'd been sexually abused throughout childhood and early adolescence shared with me that he feared he might already be a father. Meanwhile, another boy the same age wanted to know if it was legal to take a sip of his father's beer.

Almost all middle schoolers have one thing in common. They're getting exposed to darker information than the high schoolers I counseled a decade ago. Perhaps it's not surprising, then, that they're more anxious, too. On top of academic and social pressure, they're worried about how their choices will impact their future.

Yet, developmentally they're still middle schoolers. They need help anticipating and interpreting events, and guidance making smart, ethical decisions. The goal should be to teach your child these skills now, before they find themselves (or put others) in confusing or dangerous situations. High school will bring more pressure and greater exposure to drinking, sex, drugs, and vaping.

Adolescents are "super learners," pediatrician Ken Ginsburg explains. "They're wired to seek novelty and sensations, and the middle school years are full of social disruptions and excitement." He urges parents to talk through peer negotiation strategies with their children that are aligned with their values. This conversation helps kids navigate difficult circumstances even when their peers make risky decisions.

To understand the decisions your child may have to confront now and in high school, consider a few telling statistics from Monitoring the Future, an ongoing study at the University of Michigan involving about 50,000 American students. In 2017, 8 percent of eighth graders reported nicotine vaping, and about 9 percent of eighth graders said they smoked cigarettes. It's important to know if your child is trying e-cigs. Researchers from the University of Pennsylvania and the University of Southern California found that fourteen-year-olds who tried e-cigs were three times more likely to try marijuana than students who hadn't tried them.

None of those statistics include sixth and seventh graders, but no news may be good news. Laurence Steinberg, a psychology professor at Temple University and author of *You and Your Adolescent*, told me that while some younger middle schoolers do try marijuana, he'd be surprised if many experimented with more than alcohol.

The 2015 Youth Risk Behavior Survey found that anywhere from 5.2 percent to 12.6 percent of middle schoolers have had sexual intercourse.

When the researchers looked at risk-taking behaviors among older teens, they found that 56.9 percent of sexually active high school students hadn't used a condom the last time they had sex, and 41.5 percent of high school drivers had texted while on the road. In other words, now is the time to teach your child how to anticipate and respond to various scenarios, before they endanger themselves or anyone else.

Don't assume your child can problem-solve like adults.

I invite my seventh graders to leave me notes whenever they have social concerns. I once received the comment, "I'm so sick of everyone blaming their undeveloped prefrontal cortex for their stupid decisions." While I empathized with that girl, it happens to be a valid excuse! The last parts of the brain to connect are the frontal and prefrontal cortices, where insight, empathy, and risk-taking are controlled. That doesn't happen until around age twenty-five.

This means that very smart kids may impulsively do stupid things. Add in limited life experience and mood swings, and you begin to see why your middle schooler still needs you to guide them and serve as their safety net. Remind your child that their brain is still growing and they're vulnerable to poor judgment. They may know that cheating or shaming someone is wrong, but then make an in-the-moment bad call. This is true even for sweet, straight-A, even-keeled children.

Brain development aside, whether they're fourteen or forty-four, smart people can make stupid decisions. Research published in the journal *Thinking Skills and Creativity* shows that critical thinking more strongly predicts life events than intelligence. The good news is that these skills can be taught. Expose your middle schooler to other people's way of thinking and expand their worldview. Encourage them to participate in activities that require collecting and evaluating information, such as joining a debate team or writing for their school paper. Pose thought-provoking questions, such as, "Should school be year-round?" or, "Should eighteen-year-olds be allowed to vote?" You also can pose more-general questions. "Would you rather be considered kind or successful? Would you rather be the best person on the worst team, or the worst person on the best team?" Ask them to defend their belief, then switch and adopt the opposing viewpoint.

Don't jump in to solve every dilemma, but debrief with your child once they've tried. If they mention they got in a fight with an administrator, for example, ask them how they intend to solve it. If they can't come up with any ideas, suggest good and bad options and ask them how they think they'll turn out. If they share that a student at another middle school got suspended for drinking, flesh out the story. Ask, "Do you think the punishment was reasonable?" Model flexibility in your own thinking.

Make a point of teaching media literacy skills, too. Kids are highly attuned to the concept of "fake news," but they don't necessarily understand how to determine whether a source is reliable. You can explain the distinction among news, editorials, and advertising; between a peer-reviewed study and anecdotal evidence; and between a national news source and a personal blog.

Help them formulate a plan for tricky situations.

Over the years, my students have ranged from sheltered to precocious. One might ask, "How will I know if it's peer pressure?" Meanwhile, another may wonder, "Is it safe to vape pot if I only do it a few times a week?" They all like to anticipate situations. They've asked questions such as, "How much alcohol is too much?" "If the police show up at a party, am I better staying there or running away?" They admit to very little experimentation, but they'll readily share stories of middle schoolers at neighboring schools who've been suspended for everything from bringing a knife to school to having sex in a stairwell. They're not always sure where the truth ends and urban legend begins.

Come up with hypothetical scenarios. Ask, "What can you do if you feel pressured to do something you don't want to do?" My students have brainstormed set phrases, including, "That stuff makes me sick"; "I'm not into that, thanks"; and, "My parents would kill me if they found out." It's not always intuitive to say "no." Remind your child that they're in charge of their body and no one can make them drink or do drugs. Point out that they should surround themselves with friends whose judgment they trust. Help them formulate a plan for getting out of sticky situations. "Code Word" is now part of popular culture, but Ginsburg originated the term. Come up with a word, such as "reboot," that only you and your child know. Then, when they need you to extricate them from a bad situation, they can call or text you the code word. Make sure they know you'll rescue them with no questions asked.

Debrief with your child after an incident. When my two older kids were in middle school, I let them use a ride share service together a few times. Once, a man tried to pick them up in a battered car with no license plate. When my kids told the driver they felt uneasy about getting in, he screamed at them to take the ride. That night, my husband and I asked our kids why they didn't walk away immediately, and we reminded them to always trust their instincts. They may never find themselves in that specific situation again, but I suspect they'll never forget how scary it felt to ignore their gut.

It's normal for adolescents to seek fun and novelty, and they're going to be exposed to negative choices in middle school. To help your child resist unhealthy pressures, make sure they have opportunities to stretch, experiment, and even experience safe thrills. That might mean inviting a classmate to a dance, trying out for a team, or auditioning for a play.

— Idea for Educators —
Present Ethical Dilemmas During Advisory

If you have advisories, morning meetings, or homeroom periods, use that time to walk kids through ethical dilemmas. What would they do if they knew a classmate had cheated on a test, or if they witnessed a friend steal makeup at the drugstore? If they knew a classmate had created a website to rank classmates based on their appearance, would they tell anyone? Why or why not? If a classmate confessed to them that they'd been cutting themselves, but made them promise not to tell anyone, what would they do? Once my eighth graders get the hang of this exercise, I let them take over. They pair up to write and present their own ethical dilemmas.

Instill healthy sleep and self-care habits.

Self-care leads to better decision-making, so be sure your kids are getting enough sleep, exercise, and good nutrition. According to pediatric emergency physician and senior medical director at PM Pediatrics Christina Johns, children between ages ten and twelve need nine to twelve hours of sleep, while thirteen-, fourteen-, and fifteen-year-olds need eight to ten hours each night. Sleep-deprived kids may have trouble making decisions, solving problems, getting along with others, paying attention, or controlling their emotions. The National Institutes of Health has reported that sleep deficiency is also tied to depression, suicide, and risk-taking behavior.

Social media use can contribute to the problem. Aside from wreaking havoc on sleep schedules, middle-of-the-night texting or Instagramming sets kids up for trouble. Bored, irritable kids are more likely to overshare or post something hostile at 2 a.m. than at 5 p.m. You can tell your child they have to "check in" their electronics at a specific time, or forbid them from using them in their bedroom. You can test ideas, too. Brendan Boyle, a partner at IDEO and founder of its Toy Lab, once put his son's cell phone in a sealed envelope. "He could keep it, but he just couldn't open it for a set amount of time," he told me, adding that running experiments can be more effective than setting tons of rules.

Middle schoolers need whatever support you can give, including help setting boundaries with peers. When a friend texts them late at night to the point of annoyance, for example, they might feel rude dropping out mid-conversation. Explain that their friends' needs don't trump their own, and encourage them to block anyone problematic. You can't shield them entirely, so be a mentor. Teach them the skills and habits they need to maintain balance. If you sense that your child is using social media to self-soothe, help them identify relaxation strategies. Some kids like to listen to music, while others need to break a sweat. When they know how to regulate their emotions, they'll be less likely to act impulsively, whether or not they're sleep-deprived.

Given the developmental stage, it's not surprising that your child won't always make well-considered decisions. Christina Johns has seen the many ways things can go wrong. Whether kids drink too much or make a suicide attempt after cheating at school, she's identified patterns. More often than not, she told me, one or both parents had a hunch that things weren't headed in the right direction. Maybe their son had become increasingly brash and obstinate, or their daughter had become more withdrawn. Follow your instincts. If you notice an increase in risk-taking behaviors, declining attention to schoolwork, or changes in sleeping and eating patterns, reach out to a trained mental health professional. (For more signs that it's time to seek help, see Chapter 17.)

Start from a place of trust, but expect mistakes.

Be consistent and make sure your child understands that trust and freedom are earned, and that their actions have natural and logical consequences. When you're known for consistent follow-through, your child will ponder decisions with a little more care. That said, there's never a reason to treat them like a lesser being. When I spoke to Michael Gordon, who worked as a middle school principal for forty years, he kept returning to this theme. "If an eighth grader goes to a party and is supposed to be home at 11 p.m., and they come in at midnight without calling, the first thing you do is hug them and say, 'I'm glad you're safe.' Tell them you're going to talk about why they didn't call in the morning, after they've had a chance to think about it. That gives everyone a chance to calm down."

The next morning, discuss what happened and come up with a consequence together. Your child may settle on a harsher punishment than you do. In this case, one outcome might be that they can't go to the next party because they've demonstrated that they're unable to handle the responsibility. When kids participate in rule-generation, they're more likely to cooperate. Sarah Rottenberg, associate director of the Integrated Product Design program at the University of Pennsylvania, thinks they often have better ideas, too. When she got her twin sons cell phones this year, the family brainstormed rules together. "They came up with no using the phones after school on weekdays, which was much stricter than we would have been," she told me.

Recognize the power of your expectations. If your child feels trusted, they won't want to let you down. That doesn't mean you should bury your head in the sand. As you'll discover in the next chapter, middle schoolers have all kinds of reasons for bending the truth. But you get what you give, whether it's trust or respect. Nothing will bug your child more than being falsely accused of misbehavior. If you have a good sense of how they're spending their time, and they're generally staying out of trouble, give them the benefit of the doubt.

Plus, research has shown that trust can be a self-fulfilling prophecy. In a study published in *Child Development,* participants were asked to judge how trustworthy kids' faces appeared to be. The more trustworthy they looked, the more their peers accepted them, and the more those children behaved in a kind, trustworthy manner. In other words, social expectations may lead kids to become more trustworthy. You can't control how strangers will perceive your child, but you can send a clear message about your own high expectations.

That said, acknowledge that it isn't always easy to make the "right" call. If your child stands up for someone who's getting bullied, they could become the target. If they report someone cheating, they could get a reputation as a snitch. Validate their concerns and acknowledge that they have something to lose. Then try to shift their perspective. Point out when they're overly focused on the downside. In a study in *Biological Psychiatry,* researchers found that anxious kids in particular may struggle with decisions that carry the potential for loss or social risk. As you walk your child through scenarios, emphasize the benefits of making smart, ethical choices. If they take a wrong turn anyway, do a post-mortem. Ask, "What did you learn? Are there any unexpected upsides to the situation?" Whether they got in a fight because they spread a rumor or failed a quiz because they were caught cheating, encourage introspection.

Talk about real and hypothetical events.

There are many real-world examples parents can use to underscore the importance of thinking before acting. For example, at least ten admitted Harvard students in the class of 2021 had their offers rescinded after they exchanged racist and sexually offensive Facebook messages. In another case, a teen boy in Rhode Island faced criminal charges related to a sexting case that involved dozens of girls, including some whose photos ended up on a Russian pornography website.

When you share scandalous news items, create a safe space where your child can voice questions. Pose your own questions, too, such as, "Does this surprise you? What do you think might have prompted them to make that choice? What danger signs do you think they missed?" Emphasize that some problems are best solved with adult help.

Give them a sense of purpose.

Michael Gordon knows that kids who engage in meaningful activities stay out of trouble. He asked me whether I'd ever watched the dog behaviorist Cesar Millan's TV show *Dog Whisperer,* then explained how Millan turns disobedient dogs into pack mules, dressing them in special harnesses fitted with water bottle holders. The dogs have a purpose; they're serving their owner. As soon as the harness goes on, the dogs are transformed and begin to behave.

Gordon decided to try something similar with a group of twelve students who frequently got into trouble. He created a technology squad, giving them responsibility for the school's expensive computerized lighting and sound systems. He bought them black outfits emblazoned with the words "Tech Squad" and their names spelled out in glow-in-the-dark letters. The kids had no preexisting technology skills, but they learned how to use the boards and move giant mechanical curtains.

"At my last graduation at the middle school, the tech teacher called in sick," Gordon recalled. "I called the Tech Squad, and this tiny, eleven-year-old sixth grader said, 'Don't worry about a thing, Mr. Gordon, we've got your back.'" His mother later came to the school in tears and shared that after years of hating school, he now ate, slept, and dreamed about it. None of the kids were referred to the main office after they joined the squad. Gordon told me, "Their chests got bigger and they became heroes among the kids instead of the class clowns." Find that one thing that gives your child a sense of purpose, whether it's singing, running, volunteering, peer mentoring, or creative writing. Kids who feel competent are more resistant to peer pressure.

Share your own missteps.

Parents tend to gloss over their personal and career missteps, but this isn't necessarily protective. You may prevent your child from making a similar error. You also normalize imperfection and make it safe for them to seek help. While it's helpful to confess that you ran a stoplight or planned poorly for a work deadline, it's even more powerful to share a big blunder. Perhaps you got caught shoplifting or plagiarized a paper in high school. If you think your child has the maturity to handle the information—or they've made a similar mistake—tell them what went wrong, what you learned, and how you regrouped. Maybe you succumbed to peer pressure, felt insecure, wanted instant gratification—or didn't think at all.

The reverse is true when you withhold information. Your child knows more than you think. Several years ago, a student told me that his father was cheating on his mother. He said, "I heard him talking to another woman, saying things." He hinted to his father that he had concerns, but his dad denied it. When the boy grew increasingly anxious and started to fail a few classes, he gave me permission to contact home. I met with his father, who decided to come clean. They talked openly about how poor decisions have consequences, and how hard it can be to do the right thing. The boy was still angry, but his father's admission helped him shift his focus back to school. He also resolved to approach his own future relationships differently.

Talk about the pros and cons of technology.

I spoke to Sameer Hinduja, professor of criminology at Florida Atlantic University and codirector of the school's cyberbullying research center, about kids' invincibility complex. "If they send a nude, they think everything is going to work out," he told me, adding that kids don't have the life experience to know that bad decisions can follow them for years.

Underscore that your child's public and private lives should match, and that they should be civil and ethical in both contexts—not because some secret could be exposed or dog them forever, but because there's a right and wrong way to behave. Parents get overwhelmed by all the different apps, but this is about raising decent human beings.

Kids are wired to be impulsive and may need help slowing down. Many of the mistakes they make are because they don't pause before they post. Hinduja encourages children to stop and ask themselves two questions: "Could this be screenshotted and come back to bite me?" and "Can it be forwarded?" When he speaks at schools, he shares stories of students messing up, but he also talks about kids using technology for good, whether they raise money for causes using Kickstarter or blog about an issue that matters to them. Children want to hear uplifting stories, not just get mired in negativity. Focus on the importance of leaving a positive digital footprint. We live in a world of snap judgments, and employers and admissions officers are looking at applicants' online presence.

TOP TIPS FOR PARENTS

- Remember that middle schoolers can't think like adults and need guidance.
- Encourage healthy sleep habits (and other forms of self-care).
- Teach peer negotiation strategies before they're in difficult situations, such as using a code word to contact you for help.
- Encourage them to develop critical thinking through activities such as joining a debate team or writing for their school paper.
- Teach media literacy and make distinctions between good and bad news sources.
- Model flexibility in your own thinking when discussing current events.
- Remind them they don't need to do anything or go anywhere that makes them uncomfortable.
- Expect mistakes, but maintain high expectations.
- Get them involved in activities that instill a sense of purpose.
- Share times that you succumbed to peer pressure, along with how you regrouped.
- Tell them to pause and consider possible repercussions before posting anything online.

CONVERSATION STARTERS

- "How do you know that's a reliable source?"
- "What do you think would be a reasonable consequence for breaking that rule?"
- "If you want us to rescue you from an uncomfortable situation, what's a code word you could use?"
- "What would you tell a friend who keeps pressuring you to do something you don't want to do?"

CHAPTER 3

FOSTERING HONESTY

> **KEY SKILLS**
> 2—Negotiate conflict
> 5—Consider others' perspectives
> 7—Self-regulate emotions
> 9—Make responsible, healthy,
>   and ethical choices

"Why do my parents need to know everything about everything?"

"My parents get mad when I hang out with Joe because he cuts class a lot, so I just say I'm with someone else."

"If I say that someone is being mean to me, my mother calls their mother. It's better to say nothing."

MY FRIEND JESS STOPPED IN HER TRACKS OUTSIDE HER DAUGHTER's bedroom door. Anna was on the phone telling her eighth-grade classmate Julia that she had spent the day with her boyfriend. Jess knew that Anna had been with her, sorting through outgrown clothes and watching reruns of *Modern Family*.

As she listened, she learned that Anna's "boyfriend," Evan, was a soccer goalie, attended private school in Atlanta, and was in town for a family wedding. Jess called me hoping that I could reassure her that Anna wasn't a pathological liar. "She's so convincing," Jess told me. "The details are really specific." She had no idea what to do next, and she felt that she had failed as a parent.

I suggested that Jess state what she had accidentally overheard without passing judgment. She'd get more traction if she approached Anna with an attitude of curiosity and listened for the underlying motivation. As soon as she shamed or embarrassed her, the conversation would shut down. If Anna admitted she really wanted a boyfriend, Jess could say, "That makes sense to me. If all my friends had boyfriends, I'd probably want one too." Once Anna felt heard, she'd be more open to a broader discussion about behavioral expectations and the value of honesty.

After Jess and I talked, she calmly told Anna that she heard her mention a boyfriend. "I just wanted to check in. Everything okay?" she asked. Anna shared with her mother that Julia had been taunting her about spending Saturday nights with her parents. She hadn't wanted to subject herself to more humiliation by admitting the truth.

After Anna opened up, she admitted that she hated working so hard to keep one person off her back. Jess was sympathetic and said, "I'm sure it's been hard to keep all the details of your story straight, too." As the conversation continued, Jess emphasized that while she understood Anna's feelings, she did expect honesty at all times. The following week, Anna simultaneously "broke up" with her imaginary boyfriend and pulled away from Julia. She told her mother that no friendship was worth feeling like a liar.

As kids go through elementary school and transition to sixth grade, their reasons for lying change. In early elementary school, children don't make a big distinction between truth and fiction. They're simply sharing a story. The "lie" is either a manifestation of their creativity or a vehicle for wishful thinking. If your six-year-old says she can't eat breakfast because she's playing with her imaginary friend, she's not trying to deceive you. My coworker Melanie Auerbach, the director of Student Support at Sheridan School, joked with me that her seven-year-old daughter "has been on the lying shtick since she was three." Last year, she told a physical education (PE) teacher that her mother was pregnant. In kindergarten, she told the front office staff that her grandmother had died. When condolences started rolling in, Auerbach felt a jolt of confusion and panic.

To lie, children must be able to sell a false reality and then recall the details of their lie. As Ashley Merryman, coauthor of *NurtureShock: New*

Thinking About Children, told me, "It's a really big day when children realize they can get away with it, and it changes their self-image."

By middle school, children are attuned to the subtle nuances of deception. I spoke to Mary Alice Silverman, a clinical psychologist in Washington, DC, who often has to talk parents off the ledge. "It really pushes parents' buttons when children lie," she said. Address your own anxiety first so you're able to rationally determine the reasons behind your child's dishonesty.

In contrast to very young children, middle schoolers have more-complicated reasons for lying. One of my former students told her father she'd enrolled in a cooking class to avoid revealing the truth—that she was attending Gay Straight Alliance (GSA) meetings. The lie was protective—she feared her homophobic father would punish her if he knew the truth. When the parents of an eighth-grade boy discovered porn links in his browser history, he vehemently denied that he had visited the sites. He eventually admitted he'd lied because the truth was embarrassing and he worried he'd lose his phone privileges.

Parents often ask me how to handle their child's lies. What should they do if their son claims his homework is completed when he hasn't even turned on his computer? How should they respond when their daughter falsely denies cutting math class or sending derogatory texts to a friend? Lies can range from small fibs to whoppers. Kids may say they brushed their teeth when they didn't. They may claim it's too late to hand in an assignment when the deadline hasn't passed. They may download a prohibited app in the morning, only to delete it each afternoon when they go home. Parents may discover outlawed candy hidden under their child's bed or a cigarette butt in the toilet. (The father of that child carried the additional worry that his son was "a dumb criminal.")

Sometimes, the lies are higher stakes and involve academic dishonesty or theft. A seventh-grade boy denied taking his friend's new set of mechanical pencils, then openly used them in class. A sixth-grade girl plagiarized an essay from a website when she panicked about meeting the deadline. An eighth-grade boy denied cheating even after his teacher caught him looking at notes scribbled on his arm. In our increasingly tech-focused world, the methods kids use to cheat aren't always easy to spot. According to a survey by McAfee, a computer security firm, 29 percent of students admit to using tech devices to cheat in school. This finding mirrors a Common Sense Media survey, in which researchers found that 35 percent of teens with cell phones admitted to cheating with them at least once. Half of those polled admitted to cheating using the Internet, while 38 percent had copied text from websites and turned it in as their own work. Perhaps most startlingly, many kids didn't consider this cheating at all. Meanwhile, only 3 percent of parents said they thought their own child had used their cell phone to cheat.

Elementary school students are most likely to cheat to win a competitive game, but middle schoolers cheat in response to heightened academic pressure. An Educational Testing Service survey showed that 90 percent of twelve- to fourteen-year-olds reported cheating on exams and copying homework. Regardless of the statistics, don't accept the excuse that everyone cheats. Reinforce that you're focused on them and that you're far more interested in what they learn than the grade they earn.

Everyone twists the truth at times to protect someone's feelings or to get out of an awkward social situation. "We would kill each other if we were honest all the time," Pamela Meyer, the author of *Liespotting*, told me. When your child's friend asks them what they did last night, it's okay for them to say, "Not much. I was at the mall." There's no need to say they were hanging out with a huge group of kids who didn't want to include their friend.

Meyer makes a distinction between offensive and defensive lies. Offensive lies are used to create a positive impression, control information, or obtain a reward that's otherwise not easily obtainable. Your child might cheat on a test, gossip to increase their popularity, or steal candy from the drugstore. Kids lie defensively to avoid punishment, preserve personal dignity, protect themselves from harm, maintain privacy, or keep a secret. They may say, "I never saw your text," or, "I left your birthday gift at home." Lying is not always a clear-cut matter of right and wrong, and you need to convey that complexity if you want to promote a culture of honesty. Here are several strategies to help you foster honest communication and address the root cause of your child's lies.

Help them take the long view.

Stay calm and nonreactive. "The best research about lying shows that it's not about the lying, it's how you respond to the truth," Merryman told me. Children will pull away or omit more information if they sense that telling the truth will invite drama or disappoint their parents. "Kids are testing you. If you freak out because they didn't do well on their quiz, you're never going to know why there's a dent in a car," she said. Be curious and ask questions. "Why did you lie? What was going through your mind at the time?"

Keep in mind that what appears to be a lie may not be deception at all. Your child may legitimately believe that he handed in his homework, but lost it somewhere along the way. It may be crumpled on the bottom of his backpack next to that permission slip he also thought he handed in. (Don't be surprised to find dirty gym clothes in that backpack, too!) By staying inquisitive, you'll increase the likelihood of tackling the right problem. Don't be too hard on yourself, either. The lying isn't evidence that you're a bad parent or that your child is a bad person.

Lying is often about short-term gratification, and you need to help your child understand how it hampers their longer-term goals. Maybe they want you to stop bugging them about their schoolwork, or to give them a later curfew, or to stop monitoring their texts. You can underscore that trust is the key to increased independence and privacy. For example, the parents of the child who lied about viewing porn suddenly started monitoring his texts more—an unwanted but logical consequence of breaching their trust. The mother of the boy who cheated asked his teachers to position him directly in front of them during tests—another logical, if humiliating, consequence for a fourteen-year-old.

Teens live their lives in front of an invisible audience and are hypersensitive to judgment and rejection, and you can use that to your advantage. Point out that if their friends catch on to their lie, the situation will become ten times worse. Talk about the idea of permanence, especially if your child lies using technology. Cori, an eighth grader, attended a party where kids were drinking beer, and a few of his friends were caught red-handed by the adults supervising the teens. Cori thought he'd escaped detection, and his parents believed him when he swore that he hadn't been drinking. But then they scrolled through his social media feed and came across a photograph of him holding a beer can. Cori didn't remember anyone taking his picture, but his parents told him that was the point. Anything he did could be beamed out to the world forever.

Consider the root cause.

I've explained that tweens and teens lie for a number of reasons—to avoid judgment, get attention, protect someone, experience a thrill, or cope with frustration or fear—but the vast majority are lies of omission. As Merryman told me, "A child may ask if he can go to Sue's house to study, but then not mention that there will be 100 other people there partying." If your child is lying repetitively about a specific issue, dig deeper. They may be trying to escape academic or family stress, or looking for a way to cope with insecurity about their social status. In the case of the party, your child might have been intrigued by a more precocious group of kids, or they might have known that the boy or girl they liked would be there. Ask, "Who was at the party? What did you fear would happen if you told me the truth?"

If they're skipping class, zero in on any kids who join them, and inquire about the content of the class they're missing. Ask, "Is there something about this course or this teacher that's making you check out?" Similarly, if they're cheating, try to figure out the source of their insecurity. You might say, "Why did you feel you couldn't handle this on your own? Could you have prepared differently?"

Teachers know that some parents can't imagine their child is capable of plagiarism or cheating. Others will readily accept the information, but feel intense embarrassment or rage. Many educators dread calling home to share that a student has been dishonest. Try to be open to that call, and recognize that every middle schooler is going to lie at one point or another. As Sheridan's middle school principal, Jay Briar, told me, "I cross my fingers and hope I'm dialing that super-realistic mom or dad who will understand that this is a teachable moment, not a catastrophe." Life lessons don't have to be life sentences.

— IDEA FOR EDUCATORS —
TEACH PARENTS ABOUT THE DEVELOPMENTAL PHASE

At Back to School Night, address lying, plagiarizing, and cheating directly. Warn parents that they may get a call at some point during the middle school years informing them that their child has made a mistake. Ask them to view the situation as a teachable moment and an opportunity to partner with the school, not evidence that their child lacks character or that they're bad parents.

Insecurity can be a big driver for lying in general, particularly if there's a big gap between who your child is and who they want to be. If your child is on social media at 3 a.m. every night, ask them who they're talking to and why they have such a hard time logging off. You might discover they don't want to blow it with an exciting new peer group, or that they need help disengaging, or that they're depressed and are drawn to other impaired kids online.

For kids who have a tough time with self-acceptance, lying can be a form of wishful thinking. They may want to feel like a star student, top swimmer, or social success, so they spin a story. In these cases, respond constructively. If your daughter falsely claims that she's auditioning for a movie, don't cut her down to size by overemphasizing the lie or questioning her acting chops. Instead, enroll her in a drama class.

Other kids may lie because they can't handle delayed gratification and lack impulse control. While this is common for many teens, it may be more prevalent in kids with attentional issues. If your child is lying compulsively or putting themselves at risk, consult a mental health professional. Until you start inquiring, you won't know what's going on. And if you simply address the lying, you won't be able to mount an effective response. Once you've gathered information, you'll have a sense of whether you need to talk to the school about a possible learning issue, take a closer look at their friends, consider professional help, or enroll them in activities that will boost their confidence.

Model honesty and provide a runway.

Whenever you can demonstrate that you're doing something honest, say it out loud. Share when you're tempted to take a shortcut, such as sneaking into a long line or disobeying a traffic rule when you're late. When you do make a mistake, tell your child what you should have done differently. Children take note when you lie, go back on your word, or punish them after promising not to penalize them for telling the truth. If you find yourself telling a white lie in front of your child, explain why. You can say, "I know I just lied, but I couldn't deal with talking to that telemarketer right now."

Encourage honest dialogue by acknowledging that it can be difficult to tell the truth. Give your kid a way out to tell you what's really going on so you're not just throwing it in their face, judging, or embarrassing them. Kids often feel better unburdening themselves, but choose the right time and place for the discussion. Talk to them alone, when siblings aren't in the vicinity and there are few distractions. You want them to feel comfortable saying, "I wish I hadn't said that—it was a total lie." To encourage her own fifth-grade daughter to own up to mistakes, Meyer told me she's verbal about when she screws up, feels embarrassed, or wishes she'd done something differently. When your child steps up, praise them for taking responsibility.

If you think your child will be tempted to lie, don't pose questions you can verify on your own. For example, avoid asking, "Did you turn in your homework?" Instead, say, "Let's look to see if your homework was checked in online." If honesty is a chronic issue, check in directly with teachers to monitor work completion. Sheryl, whose daughter Melly is in seventh grade, tries hard not to set her daughter up to lie. "It's exhausting trying to sort truth from fiction with her," she told me. "We have a rule that she has to put her phone 'to bed' in our electronics basket by 8:00 p.m., and she'll say it's there when it's obvious that it's not. Then she'll try to sneak it in when my back is turned."

Sheryl doesn't want to reinforce Melly's behavior, spur her to go to even greater lengths to spin tales, or add to her own aggravation, so she's stopped trusting her to provide accurate information. "I just tell her to do things instead of asking about them, and I focus on verifiable facts. I'll be matter-of-fact and say, 'Your teacher posted that it's due tomorrow, and she didn't mention any extensions, so you'll have to finish it tonight,'" she explained. When her daughter cheated on a test and earned a zero, Sheryl insisted she go back and learn the material. She doesn't want her to view cheating as an easy way out.

I spoke to Rick Wormeli, an education consultant and the author of *Fair Isn't Always Equal*, who suggests that when kids cheat or plagiarize, they should be made to write letters of apology to the class or teacher and their families. They also can do service to the school as a form of restitution, and they should repeat the whole learning and assessment process. Once kids rebuild trust, however, they should be able to put the cheating behind them. Remember, their brain isn't fully developed until about age twenty-five, and the prefrontal cortex is the part that's responsible for planning and inhibiting impulses. Reinforce that while you don't expect perfection, you do expect honesty.

Focus on values.

Move beyond simply telling kids about the personal consequences of lying. Underscore how lying impacts others around them. In the 2012 Josephson Report Card on the Ethics of American Youth, 57 percent of teens stated that successful people do what they have to do to win, even if it involves cheating. This thinking has a ripple effect and undermines the social contract we have with one another. We tell kids not to cheat because it can lead to negative consequences in their own life, but it also impacts other students. It changes the curve, gives false status, changes what's taught, and undermines the whole culture of fairness in the classroom. Explain to your child that lies strain relationships and hurt others. Watch the news together and point out that the truth has a way of coming out.

Your child may be more likely to lie if they think the odds are unfairly stacked against them. One student told me she cheated because "everyone else was cheating." She felt that she had no other option or she'd fall behind. I once observed a seventh grader make questionable line calls during a tennis match. As I watched, I realized her competitor was doing the same thing. Middle school kids may have a finely tuned sense of fairness, but that doesn't always translate into doing the right thing. You can capitalize on their quest for equity. If you're trying to create a culture of honesty at home, give all siblings the same rules and punishments, and make sure you're viewed as impartial.

Don't be afraid to have it out.

The opposite of lying is arguing, Merryman explains, and it can be a positive sign that your child respects you. When they're debating an issue, they're sharing details of their life and trying to understand your point of view. It may seem counterintuitive, but they consider it a productive exchange. "Arguing is communicative, and kids appreciate knowing what mysterious thing is going on in your head. Respect that they're putting something on the line and actually listen to them," she said.

Teens are much less likely to lie and rebel if they think you've been fair and care about their perspective. That means leaving room for negotiation and considering whether you're being unreasonable. Rules need to be modified as your children mature. It doesn't weaken your authority to make an exception if your child presents a coherent and rational argument.

Don't hesitate to address a lie. When your child claims to have forgotten to do a chore, you can say, "It would make me really happy if you'd just say you don't want to empty the dishwasher." You can then deal with the shirked responsibility and explain that everyone in the family has to do their part. Merryman tells parents to be clear about whether they're punishing the transgression or the cover-up, and to specifically address both wrongs. "Don't make them guess why you're angry, and don't collapse them into one thing."

Punishments should be logical, consistent, and fair. If your child lies about using their phone at midnight, the consequence might be loss of phone privileges. If they lie about where they are, the consequence might be increased monitoring, and you can explain that it's safety-related. My friend Rona takes that approach with her fourteen-year-old daughter, who often lies about her social plans. Whenever she attends a party, Rona calls the host's parents to make sure there's supervision. As Merryman said, "When it comes to safety, most teens think mom has a right to information, but if they have a crush on a guy, mom doesn't need to know the details." You can keep your child safe while still respecting their need for privacy.

TOP TIPS FOR PARENTS

- Be nonreactive, calm, curious, and nonjudgmental. Otherwise, your child may lie to avoid drama.
- Try to discover the root cause of the lie so you can address it effectively.
- Don't try to "catch" them in a lie. Give them a runway to tell the truth instead.
- To decrease the likelihood of cheating, tell your child you value what they learn more than the grades they earn.
- Tell them you expect honesty, but know they'll make mistakes. Remind them that life lessons don't have to be life sentences.
- Don't let them off the hook, but treat the transgression and the lie as separate issues. Use natural and logical consequences.
- Be authentic and share when you're resisting the temptation to lie.
- Help them understand that the truth has a way of coming out.

CONVERSATION STARTERS

- "I'd like to understand your perspective. Why did you feel uncomfortable telling me the truth?"
- "Tell me about the class where you were caught cheating. Is it difficult for you? Were you unprepared? Did you feel uncomfortable approaching the teacher for help?"
- "What do you think you'd do differently if you found yourself in this situation again?"

CHAPTER 4

ENCOURAGING KINDNESS AND EMPATHY

KEY SKILLS

1—Make good friend choices
2—Negotiate conflict
5—Consider others' perspectives
7—Self-regulate emotions
9—Make responsible, healthy,
    and ethical choices

"I try to avoid Mira. No matter what I say, she twists it and someone gets mad at me."

"When we play dodgeball, Sam throws the ball at my face. He thinks it's funny."

"I hate talking in class because Joe and Max pretend to stutter like me."

SEVERAL KIDS HAD BEEN TARGETING BETH FOR WEEKS. BETH was sweet, absentminded, easygoing, and resigned to being mistreated. Some of her fellow eighth-grade students were using social media to call her fat and stupid, and they'd drop dirty tissues on her head as they passed her desk. As her school counselor, I wanted to help, but Beth would never call out the bullies. She worried she'd make the situation worse, and she insisted she was fine.

Beth's classmate Jenna, however, was so disturbed by the mean behavior that she brought me a handwritten list of the perpetrators and pleaded with me to make them stop. Jenna—a confident, popular student—barely knew Beth, but she couldn't stand the cruelty. Her discomfort was the one positive in a bad situation. The Jennas are rare; I can't recall another recent situation when a student so vehemently refused to be a bystander. I knew that it would be difficult to change the kids' behavior, and that quick solutions, such as detentions and phone calls home, would only give Beth a short-term reprieve.

In the end, Beth still didn't want me to get involved, but she gave Jenna permission to confront the kids who were bothering her. Beth's instinct to resist adult intervention had been on the mark. Jenna's forceful and self-assured approach stopped the tormentors. Beth felt enormously comforted by having a supportive ally. She also shared that Jenna's rare and generous move had empowered her and made her more likely to stand up for herself and others in the future. Jenna felt good about her role, too. It was satisfying to know that she could right an injustice, and it reinforced her self-image as someone strong enough to do the right thing.

Fostering kindness and empathy in kids goes much deeper than making sure everyone has someone to sit with at lunch. There's so much evidence that kind kids lead richer lives; they tend to be happier, better-liked, mentally healthier, and more accomplished. In *Greater Good Magazine*, psychologist Sonya Lyubomirsky reflected on her research. She's discovered that students who do five acts of kindness in one day experience a boost in happiness. "I believe that when you're kind and generous to others, you start to see yourself as a generous person, so it's good for your self-perception," she explained.

In a longitudinal experiment in Vancouver, researchers found that students who performed three purposeful kind acts a week were significantly more popular. A study from Duke University and Penn State found that kindergarteners who shared and helped others were more likely to graduate from high school and have full-time jobs. And a study commissioned by Lady Gaga's Born This Way Foundation found that young people who describe their environments as kind are more likely to be mentally healthy.

On the other hand, when empathy goes down, narcissism, bullying, peer cruelty, racism, hate, violence, and mental health needs go up. I spoke to educator Michele Borba, author of *UnSelfie*, about why parents need to prioritize compassion. "Thirty-six percent of our girls are suffering by age seventeen from some kind of depression element," she said. "We're raising them from the outside in, focusing on their dress size, when we should be working from the inside out."

Kids are born hard-wired for empathy, but some need help activating it, or they may need the occasional reminder. Psychotherapist Katie Hurley, the author of *No More Mean Girls*, worked with a fourteen-year-old girl and her eleven-year-old sister. By eighth grade, the older sister had been through her share of social struggles and knew how to be an upstander when others were unkind. But when the younger sister entered sixth grade and couldn't find a peer group, her older sister wasn't sympathetic. "She had to revisit empathy and remember how it felt when you didn't know who to eat lunch with, or when someone criticized something you wore," Hurley told me.

No one sets out to raise an unkind child. But as middle schoolers try on different identities and establish their place in the social pecking order, they're going to test limits, push boundaries, and occasionally horrify their parents. They care deeply about peer approval, but they also care what *you* think. You still have the power to instill integrity, kindness, and empathy.

Don't ignore it when your child is being mean.

One of the worst parts of my job is telling parents that their kid is being mean, but it's worse to ignore it. My goal isn't to shame parents, it's to help their child, and I focus on changing specific behaviors, not fixing character deficits. It's hard for parents to hear that their kid isn't behaving kindly. They may ask me what they can do with the information. One solution is to partner with the school. Tell your child that their principal, teachers, and counselor will be working with you, acting as your eyes and ears on the ground. Let them know that if the school does call you with concerns, you'll take it seriously and hold them accountable.

When you get a report from the school, initiate a conversation with your child. Ask them why they chose to act that way, listening carefully for their motivation. Then ask, "How would you feel if someone treated you that way? How do you think that other child felt? How do you think the adults and other students perceived your behavior? Do you think you were your best self? How could you make amends?" Kids this age need to be taught that a solid apology includes admitting what they did wrong, whether they over-reacted, spilled a secret, or made a false accusation. They should reference the behavior without making justifications, then express remorse and share what they plan to do differently going forward. Psychologist Adam Grant has written that it's much more powerful to say, "I'm sorry *for*" than "I'm sorry *if*." (We'll explore this idea more in the chapters on bullying and gossip.)

This stuff matters, and parents help set the tone. If you know your child is being mean, try to identify and address any underlying insecurities. You also can try to get a handle on peer group dynamics. Anyone who has spent time in a toxic environment knows that behaviors such as gossip, jockeying for power, and negativity spread rapidly. Being in a mean climate can alter individual behavior. In one study, Harvard University researchers found that emotional states can be transferred directly from one individual to another through mimicry. Fortunately, that means that happiness also can spread through a social network.

If the issue is more with the social environment than individual be-havior, the community needs to come together as a whole to address it. To establish positive social norms, everyone needs to understand and target systemic problems, such as anxiety or powerlessness. In the school setting, educators and other staff members can identify "kindness catalysts," stu-dents who can model positive behavior and take on roles such as lunch buddies or new student welcome ambassadors.

Coaches can play a role, too, making sure that no one displays cruelty on the field. Consistency is important. A middle school football coach told me about a time an opposing team's players taunted one of his black players. Every time they piled on top of him, they called him "boy." The coach quickly intervened, but he got no support from the other team's coaches, and there were no repercussions for anyone. At a different mid-dle school, soccer players yelled "Taco Bell" at one of the opposing team's students as he scored a goal. They thought the child was Latino, but he actually was Lebanese, which added an extra layer to the players' insensi-tivity. In this case, every adult in attendance was on top of the situation and took it seriously.

Remember that apples don't fall far from trees.

Model compassion by treating friends, acquaintances, and colleagues with kindness. When you expend energy on caring, reciprocal relationships, you teach your child to prioritize friendship and positivity over popularity. Children hovering at the periphery of "alpha" groups often struggle the most. Constant maneuvering for position in the social hierarchy can lead to insecurity, envy, anxiety, or competitiveness, all of which promote meanness. Children with sensitive adult role models and gentle friends tend to behave similarly.

Be intentional with your messaging, or your child might make inaccurate assumptions about your values. When the Making Caring Common project at Harvard's Graduate School of Education surveyed 10,000 middle and high school students and asked them what mattered to them, "achieving at a high level, happiness, or caring for others," only 20 percent said that caring for others was their top priority. Eighty percent of the students said their parents "are more concerned about achievement or happiness than caring for others."

Still, be authentic or you'll damage your credibility with your child. Kindness doesn't require liking or speaking positively about everyone all of the time. Validate your child's feelings when they accurately point out that someone has been mean-spirited. Take the opportunity to talk about why a specific action was mean, and remind them that it's possible to make bad choices but still be a good person.

You don't need to pretend that your child has to be friends with everyone, but you can teach them to be respectful and polite and to avoid burning bridges. Friendships often cycle in and out as kids change and mature. Promote this social growth by praising them when they're considerate or altruistic, even as they outgrow some friendships and move on to others. Make it a habit to share when you've done something nice or when someone has been kind to you. Talk about examples of meanness, too. Express how those actions made you feel, and ask them how they think the other person may have felt. They may be surprised to realize that it feels pretty bad to hurt someone else.

That's what happened with Tim. Karl came to me to complain that every time he chose the desk next to Tim, Tim would physically recoil. He'd move his desk as far away from Karl as possible. Karl was socially awkward, but he was perceptive. He knew that Tim didn't want to be associated with him. I told Karl that he had every right to feel rejected, and that we'd make sure it didn't happen again. When I spoke to Tim, he admitted that even physical proximity felt risky. Tim had spent sixth grade feeling lonely and isolated, but he'd made some friends and felt like he had to protect his reputation. He viewed Karl as a social liability. With Tim's permission, we called his mother together. She reminded him how he had felt when he was in Karl's shoes. Tim was embarrassed. He said he'd behaved instinctively and never meant to hurt Karl. He also apologized to him. The teacher assigned seating to prevent future problems, but Tim made a point of publicly acknowledging Karl whenever their paths crossed.

In middle school, kids may intellectually know how to behave, but fail in the execution. I recently spoke to a friend, Jill, who was feeling left out at work. Her colleagues would go out to lunch together, but they wouldn't invite her. They never insulted her, but they acted like she didn't exist, and Jill felt like she was back in middle school. Jill knew that her daughter Orly wasn't welcoming to outsiders who wanted to join her clique, and she used the experience to build her empathy. She talked to Orly about how she felt at work, and they dissected why the other women might be so standoffish.

Thirteen-year-old Orly ended up giving her mother advice. "Either invite yourself or find some other friends to eat with," she told her. "I don't think they'll tell you to your face not to come, and maybe they'll realize they're being rude." For the next several weeks, Orly checked in with her mother about her lunch situation. She also started to share examples of exclusion she observed at school, and she developed a heightened sensitivity to kids who seemed lonely. Jill recalls being surprised by Orly's insight. Despite her history of excluding classmates, she clearly had the capacity to be thoughtful and compassionate.

Use these teachable moments to help your child rationally consider the consequences of their harmful actions. Dacher Keltner, a psychology professor at the University of California at Berkeley, notes that simply telling your child what is right or wrong—or reacting with strong emotions or physical punishment—produces people who are less likely to want to alleviate others' pain. You can't make a kid be kind by shaming them or screaming at them.

Consider the difference between authoritarian and authoritative parenting. The authoritarian parent expects their child to display "no-questions-asked" obedience to authority, whereas an authoritative parent will explain rather than go straight to punishment. Authoritative parents use positive discipline, inviting their child to explain why they did what they did rather than trying to bend their will. A study published in the journal *Child Development* found that this parenting style builds empathy. So coach your child. If they're mean, explain why their behavior is unacceptable. Factor in their point of view, but tell them you know they can do better. Don't browbeat them until they cry. Their behavior might improve, but they probably won't internalize your values.

Help them view a situation from multiple angles.

Help your child understand the subtle differences among emotions such as disappointed, frustrated, sad, and worried. Some middle schoolers are social chameleons and astute observers who can read cues and adapt to any audience, but most are still working on understanding themselves, let alone others. They may overshare, then feel rejected when more-reserved friends don't respond in kind. They may take a scowl personally when someone is simply hungry. Help them analyze issues from various perspectives, and encourage them to write down their emotional reactions to interpersonal experiences. As they begin to understand that feelings are complex and layered, they'll become more self-aware and perceptive.

I view this approach as a home version of Denmark's "Klassen Time," which translates to "The Class's Hour," a core part of that country's school curriculum. In The Class's Hour, teachers facilitate weekly problem-solving sessions to foster empathy. Students bring in a traditional cake and spend an hour listening carefully to one another and collaborating to solve sensitive problems, such as a conflict between friends or something a student is dealing with at home.

Your family could approximate this experience by holding a weekly family meeting. Talk about anything from chore division to sibling issues. At school, teachers could set aside time for the same purpose, tackling whatever issues arise. At Sheridan, I do this with my seventh graders during designated morning meetings. They choose the topic based on active concerns, come up with three guiding questions in advance (which they clear with me), and then lead the discussion. They might bring up that kids are riffling through one another's backpacks without permission, or that students are pressuring one another to reveal their grades.

Teaching kids to be introspective and considerate is critical. A University of Michigan study found that college students today are about 40 percent less empathetic than college students of the 1980s and 1990s. To boost your child's compassion, try sending them to fictional universes. As they read and become invested in characters' plights, they learn to put themselves in other people's shoes. In a study published in the *Journal of Applied Social Psychology*, researchers found that children and adolescents who read the *Harry Potter* stories developed a more positive attitude toward immigrants, refugees, gay people, and individuals from disadvantaged backgrounds. (We'll discuss embracing differences in the next chapter, too.)

— IDEA FOR EDUCATORS —
TRY THE "SHADOW A STUDENT" CHALLENGE

If we expect students to be empathetic and able to consider others' perspectives, educators need to be able to model that behavior. To boost empathy among staff members, try the "Shadow a Student" exercise. When we did this at Sheridan's middle school, we all spent a full day observing a student we didn't know very well. We interviewed them about what they did and didn't like about school and logged detailed notes throughout the day. Our goal was to gather information about the student we shadowed, as well as the overall school experience. It was eye-opening. For example, eighth-grade teacher Eileen Hughes was surprised to discover that a student who was convinced that everyone hated him was clearly well-liked.

Address any jealousy.

In middle school in particular, the disparities among students socially, physically, cognitively, and emotionally can breed jealousy. Britt Rathbone, an adolescent social worker, told me how this idea can play into kids' interactions. "Developmentally, they're so focused on peer approval, and the separation from home means they have to find another group to model values," he said. "Every one of these kids is insecure. I ran a group counseling session the other night where one of the kid's goals is to express vulnerability and let people get to know him. Another kid in the group said, 'Tell us something about you that you don't like.' He said, 'I really hate my body.' This is a fit kid. It just made me realize the level of self-criticism that 80 percent of adolescents are walking around with, and they're comparing themselves to others who have their own insecurities."

I spoke to consultant Jon Gordon, the author of *The Power of a Positive Team*, about how parents can help a child who has a sense of lacking. "Share the truth," he advised. "Tell them there are always going to be smarter, better looking, and more talented people, so they need to focus on what they can control and let go of the rest." He holds regular meetings with his family so everyone can express gratitude for the positives in their lives. Research shows that focusing on gratitude helps kids "want what they have" instead of fixating on what's missing.

You also can share examples from your own life that illustrate that not everything has to be a competition. Are there specific times when you helped someone else, or when someone you considered a competitor gave you an assist? To remove the shame, share your own moments of jealousy. Claire Shipman, the author of *The Confidence Code for Girls*, will say to her daughter, "There was this woman who made me feel a little jealous because she had so much energy, but this is how I got through it, and her life doesn't have any bearing on mine." My friend Alicia shared with her son that she struggled with jealousy in middle school. "If I didn't want my friend to have a boyfriend, I'd try to make him look bad so she'd lose interest, or I'd make her feel insecure about herself," she told me. "I'd say, 'Are you sure you're pretty or popular enough to go out with him?'"

When kids act mean-spirited, they may not realize that jealousy is driving their behavior. Help them identify the feeling, then work on their sense of self. I Skyped with Lea Waters, a psychology professor at the University of Melbourne and author of *The Strength Switch*, who told me that children go from "something is missing" to "I am enough" when you point out their positive traits, whether it's their knack for putting others at ease, their sense of adventure, or their ability to stay cool under pressure. Avoid comparing your child to anyone else, and encourage them to focus on achieving their personal best. Help them get in the habit of elevating others, even if that means acting "as if" until the behavior becomes ingrained. Over time, they'll discover how much better it feels to build someone up than to tear them down.

You can even come up with a funny name for the jealousy to help your child understand that it's not who they are; it's simply an uncomfortable but fleeting emotion. Waters coaches parents to say, "Oh look, Jane the Jealousy is back, but I've got my own strengths and can let her pass." She explained that the persona acts as a circuit-breaker in that micro-moment when a child is most likely to do something that could hurt their reputation or a friendship.

There's no point in trying to vanquish the emotion altogether. Psychologist Lisa Damour, author of *Untangled*, told me that scrubbing away dark feelings actually endows them with more power. You may not be able to legislate feelings, but you can draw a hard line around behavior, starting with siblings. Damour recommends saying, "I'm sure your sister makes you crazy, and you may think and feel that, but you can't hurt her." Prompt your child to look inward and ask, "What is the feeling telling me? How can I deal with it in a healthy way?" They may find it helps to confess their jealousy. Rachel Simmons, author of *Enough As She Is*, told me she encourages kids to say, "I really care about you, and I feel embarrassed about being so jealous. I feel like if I don't say something, it's not going to be good for our friendship."

Instill compassion through mindfulness and movement.

Mindfulness—the ability to acknowledge and accept your thoughts and stay rooted in the present moment—can enhance attention span and reduce stress, but researchers have found that it also can foster empathy. In a study at Northeastern University, participants took an eight-week meditation course. When they were then faced with the option of giving up their chair to a person in visible physical discomfort, they were far more likely than control group subjects to act beneficently.

When Visitacion Valley School introduced a mindfulness program for sixth, seventh, and eighth graders, they saw a 79 percent decrease in suspensions. Administrators at the school, located in one of San Francisco's poorest and most violent neighborhoods, told NBC News they believe the fifteen-minute, twice-daily meditations decrease conflict by making students more conscious of their actions, calmer, and less angry. Enroll your child in yoga, or teach them relaxation strategies such as deep breathing or meditation. (I'll offer many more mindfulness strategies in Chapter 17.)

Researcher Dacher Keltner has found that going out into nature and experiencing "feelings of awe" also appears to heighten empathy. Those feelings of awe cause people to behave less materialistically and more altruistically, too, according to Stanford researcher Melanie Rudd. Margaret Rietano has seen this phenomenon firsthand. When her four kids were young, she often took them into the woods, and she noticed there were never any other kids there. She knew how happy her children were outside, and she wanted to bring that experience to others. She founded The Elements, an outdoor enrichment program in Washington, DC.

"Especially in middle school, the stress level ramps up that much more, they're cognitively aware of the dark side of life and the world, and suddenly the news is in their back pockets," Rietano told me. "When you have something as grand and majestic and terrifying as nature, the playing field is equalized, and we're made to realize how small we are in this big world." The parents of middle schoolers enrolled in her program tell her, "My son is less anxious when he comes back," or, "He's always had low confidence, and now he feels valued."

If you don't have easy access to the outdoors, encourage your child to get in the habit of taking a walk around the block. If your school keeps students indoors every time there's bad weather, Rietano recommends advocating for change. "Schools can get shovels and have students clear their own blacktop—don't leave it to building services. They can work together and learn to become stewards of their spaces—it's so satisfying to play on the blacktop after putting in the sweat equity."

Speaking of sweat equity, don't underestimate the power of movement. Researchers at the University of Michigan studied 709 public middle school children and found that those who were more physically active (at least thirty minutes a day)—or who were involved in team sports—scored highest in leadership skills and empathy. Exercise also has a calming influence. Whether your child plays a pickup game of four square or a more organized sport, they'll learn conflict resolution strategies, flexibility, and cooperation.

Build awareness of community needs.

Meaningful volunteer engagement can widen children's worldview, teach them gratitude, and build their awareness of and sensitivity to others' struggles. Placing kids in unfamiliar settings or uncomfortable situations heightens their ability to empathize with anyone who feels like an outsider or lacks a sense of belonging. It's a powerful way for kids to see that everyone has a story. Take advantage of their natural interest in activism and service work. As University of California at Berkeley researchers wrote in the journal *PNAS*, twelve- to fourteen-year-olds show greater activation in brain regions responsible for self-perception and social cognition, which may explain why they like to be at the forefront of social change. Still, it's not always easy to get middle schoolers involved in service work.

To help your child get started, identify their interests and talk about problems they've observed. Perhaps they love soccer and could canvass businesses to raise money to provide a local school with soccer equipment. "In my community, there's a home for young adults with disabilities, and many love video games," said Sheila Sjolseth, the president of Pennies of Time, a nonprofit that supports families trying to improve their community. Kids who love gaming offer companionship and share their skills.

If your kid chooses an outlet with a personal connection, they'll feel more invested. "You have to guide your child at this age, especially if they haven't been in charge of chores or acts of kindness before," Sjolseth told me. Face-to-face contact is more likely to build empathy than impersonal activities like fund-raising. If you collect books for a high-poverty school or holiday gifts for a homeless shelter, bring your child with you when you drop off the items. To make the activity more attractive, combine efforts with another parent. Your child may be more likely to stick with a project they do with a friend. When my son Ben was in seventh grade, he wanted to volunteer for the Special Olympics, but jumping in alone felt daunting. He started volunteering with a classmate, but eventually branched out on his own. He taught tennis to a sixth-grade girl with Down syndrome, and her spunk and fearlessness left a big impression on him.

Don't give up if your child is initially negative or indifferent. Try to get them to stick with an activity long enough to make volunteering a habit. Children don't develop an empathetic mind-set from one-off acts of kindness. Over time, the "why" will become ingrained. They'll experience the boost in self-confidence that comes from seeing they can change their own or others' circumstances. And don't underestimate your child. As Washington, DC, principal Alexandra Griffin told me, we need to give middle schoolers more credit. "They're often looked upon as self-centered, which they are, and immature, which they can be. But they also can be amazingly empathetic and kind."

TOP TIPS FOR PARENTS

- When your child is mean, address it directly. You can't legislate feelings, but you can set expectations around behavior.
- Model kind behavior and surround yourself with kind friends. Don't spend time with people who mistreat you.
- Encourage your child to focus on achieving their personal best. Don't compare them to others, and discourage them from comparing themselves to peers.
- Keep it real—kids don't need to be friends with everyone, but they do need to be empathetic, respectful, and polite.
- Help your child engage in meaningful community service.
- Talk about times you were mean, or when you personally experienced unkindness. Share how it made you feel.
- Label their feelings to broaden their emotional vocabulary and ability to consider other perspectives.

CONVERSATION STARTERS

- "Do you think some kids have a harder time than others being kind? Why do you think that's the case?"
- "Is there a difference between saying something mean to someone and leaving someone out?"
- "How does it feel when you can tell you hurt someone's feelings?"

CHAPTER 5

EMBRACING DIFFERENCE IN SELF AND OTHERS

KEY SKILLS

1—Make good friend choices
5—Consider others' perspectives
9—Make responsible, healthy, and
   ethical choices

"I feel completely invisible."

"How can I not feel fat?"

"Whenever I bring curry for lunch, Darren says, 'Yuck, what's that? Diarrhea?'"

WHEN JESS WILSON'S THIRTEEN-YEAR-OLD DAUGHTER, Brooke, was younger, people would try to tamp down any behavior that made her stick out, including any noncontextual noises. "In order to be a successful autistic person, you're supposed to look neurotypical," says Wilson, the author of the *Diary of a Mom* blog. She bristles at the goal of indistinguishability, which puts the emphasis on making other people comfortable. "Brooke isn't hurting anyone, and her behavior helps her self-regulate, so let's work on society instead," she told me over the phone. "Just because *you* don't know what's funny doesn't mean you have to stop her laughter."

A behavioral analyst once discouraged Wilson from arranging play-dates with another autistic child. "She said, 'Don't do that, they act really

– 49 –

autistic together, and she's a bad influence on Brooke.' I decided I didn't want to play that game. My kid does stand out, but I want her to feel pride, not shame." There are strengths in differences—and even in disability itself. As Wilson noted, "If you're in a wheelchair, you have to get really creative about approaching things that aren't accessible. You end up taking pride in finding a workaround. The deaf community is a perfect example. They've created a culture around a community that's a source of pride."

To help build Brooke's self-concept, Wilson seeks out adults who share her profile. "We want to show her how cool this community of different people are. I have a friend who's a lesbian who grew up never knowing anyone gay, and she said, 'I can't imagine the effect it would have had on my life if I'd known even one gay couple as a kid, and seen that they're happy and well-adjusted.'" So far, the approach is working. "Brooke will say, 'Yay, I'm me! I love being autistic, it's cool.'"

Instilling a positive self-concept is easier said than done. Kids can get targeted for pretty much anything—including physical traits, clothing choices, socioeconomic status, or family structure. Carlos had to deal with questions about his immigration status throughout middle school despite the fact that he's not an immigrant. Kids teased Mark for wearing sneakers to go sledding. His parents were out of work and couldn't afford snow boots. A girl was called out for wearing "Thuggs" from Target instead of brand-name Uggs. Although middle schoolers are highly attuned to slights, that doesn't necessarily translate into sensitivity. I've often marveled at this disconnect. A bunch of eighth graders taunted my friend Brian's fourteen-year-old son, Eben, about having two dads, and Eben's coping strategy was no better. He'd lash out at unathletic boys, calling them trannies and fags. "My son has been bullied, but he's also been the bully," Brian told me. "It's his defense mechanism."

Middle schoolers can be intolerant of any differences, including their own. They're trying to get a handle on any sort of "otherness." That essential question, "Who am I?" is complicated. There are endless ways to feel like an outlier, and a corresponding need for reassurance. By explicitly requiring your child to honor everyone's humanity, you'll reinforce the message that they, too, deserve respect and inclusion. This has been a harder message to transmit in recent years, when a divisive cultural climate among adults has spilled over to schools, but that only makes your role more critical. If you teach your children now to embrace difference in its many forms, they'll benefit for the rest of their lives. They'll grow up to be decent people with a strong sense of self who can thrive in an increasingly diverse world. Here are some strategies.

Raise your child's awareness.

I met with Rodney Glasgow, the chief diversity officer and head of middle school at St. Andrew's Episcopal School, after he led a diversity training session for school counselors. "We're seeing a rise in antisemitism, sexism, and homophobia," he told me, and children can take hateful behavior to the extreme. "On the one hand, that's great because if we don't know it's there, we can't address it, but it also puts the spotlight on certain kids in a negative way." He's seen this manifest in many ways. "Black boys often feel excluded by both classmates and educators. They might say, 'I know my teachers don't like me and are afraid of me.' Students who are part of the DACA (Deferred Action for Childhood Arrivals) program are saying, 'I was part of the country, and now it's debatable whether I get to be part of the country, let alone the school.'"

Kids who express unpopular political viewpoints also may feel excluded. Be careful not to transmit the message that their voice is unwelcome. If you do, their feelings may bubble over in ways that hurt their peers. Instead, say, "I want to hear your opinion, but you can't say anything that will degrade someone else's humanity." Set that boundary and challenge them from a standpoint of morality. Pretending that something isn't divisive won't make it disappear, and most kids want a positive school culture. Glasgow told me his students are asking, "How do I support my friends of color, my gay friends, my friends who are immigrants? I don't want to make it worse for them." For starters, they shouldn't ignore their classmates' reality.

If a disturbing event is in the news, initiate a dialogue with your child. You don't need to have all the answers. Acknowledge what happened and ask, "Would you like to talk about it?" Give them a chance to respond before weighing in with your own opinion, and focus on listening, not lecturing. In that first exchange, it's okay to say, "I'm still trying to make sense of this myself, but I think it's important that we talk about it." Your job is to hold the space, not move your child from point A to point B. Raise the issue again once you've had processing time. At that point, prompt them to think about the incident more analytically. Ask them, "If that were to happen here, how do you think it would impact your community?"

It's equally important for educators to acknowledge what's going on in the world. As Lauren Mascareñaz wrote in *Teaching Tolerance* magazine, "When we ignore or dismiss an important event, we show our students that it isn't worthy of our time. Say something, and show your students the power of voice—yours and their own. Students want and need their parents and school staff to help them make sense of troubling situations."

Encourage authentic inclusion.

Laura Talmus's daughter Lily was born with Apert syndrome and cranial facial differences. Lily was always soulful and bright, but by seventh grade she stopped wanting to go to school. "When Lily started a new middle school in fifth grade, we knew it would probably get a little harder for her socially, but we didn't expect the bottom to fall out the way it did," Talmus told me. "She'd never been teased or bullied, but it was just as devastating to be socially isolated." She homeschooled her until Lily asked to try boarding school. Shortly after Lily arrived at her new school, she died in her sleep. When her mother delivered her eulogy, her former classmates were shocked to learn that she'd left middle school because she felt so left out. "I turned back to those early classmates and said, 'If you want to honor Lily, let's start a conversation about this,'" Talmus said. She cofounded the nonprofit Beyond Differences, and Lily's former classmates started giving presentations at local middle schools.

Seventeen-year-old Edyn Jensen is a member of the Beyond Differences' Teen Board and speaks at those assemblies. We talked over the phone about her memories of Lily and her commitment to teaching kids about social isolation. She advises parents to let their kids know that everyone is welcome at their house, and to encourage them to notice marginalized kids. "Let them know that if a kid comes to school with a different pair of shoes than you, they might have a different backstory, but they're not less than," she said. She shared a story about a middle school girl who used a wheelchair and ate lunch every day with an adult aide. On National No One Eats Alone Day, a Beyond Differences event designed to foster inclusion, the child suddenly was surrounded by kids who wanted to eat with her. "From that one meal, the kids learned her name and saw that she was funny and sweet," Jensen told me. "She's now sitting around other kids, not in the back with an aide." The students needed help with the introduction, but the face-to-face interaction took care of the rest.

True social engagement can't be an act of charity. Avoid saying, "You need to take care of those kids." As Wilson pointed out, "It infantilizes the other kid, and there's never going to be inclusion if we're not giving kids a chance to be a real friend." Ask yourself some tough questions. Who are my friends? Who am I showing my child that I respect and want to befriend? Some people don't fit into our worlds easily, and inclusion takes effort.

All children benefit from inclusion, whether it's social or academic. According to researchers at the Harvard Graduate School of Education, students with disabilities in inclusion classes are more engaged and develop better communication skills than students in self-contained, segregated classes, but kids without disabilities learn to more readily embrace individual differences. The Maryland Coalition for Inclusion Education released a report showing that they also experience a boost in self-esteem and gain access to instructional methods that benefit all students. It's win-win.

Inclusion is also a way to challenge kids' assumptions. For the first thirteen years of his life, Matthew Lager, who has non-verbal autism, had no way to communicate. In middle school, he learned to share his thoughts by typing one letter at a time. He now advocates passionately for other kids with autism. His mother, my friend Karen Lager, sent me a copy of the speech he delivered in Atlanta in 2017 at TASH, an organization that advocates for people with significant disabilities. Now sixteen and a sophomore in high school, Matthew shared the difficulty of living in an unreliable body, explaining, "I can easily be passed over as an obscure scientific oddity." But while much is out of his control, he told the TASH audience that he's felt joy that many believe those with his type of autism aren't able to experience.

Matthew has come a long way, and now teachers and therapists contact him for guidance. They want to know how to show students with defiant bodies the presumption of competence. Matthew tells them how to include him in classroom conversation, assist with peer interaction, and engage him by moving the curriculum along faster. His day-to-day challenges can still be exhausting, including "putting on a brave coat of armor" to brace himself for people's reactions to him. He experienced verbal and physical bullying last year that shook him. "Particularly upsetting was the notion that some thought I wasn't bothered about it because I didn't have the expected motor response and didn't defend myself," he said.

Make sure your child understands that bullying and exclusion hurt everyone, regardless of how they seem to react. Matthew made this plea: "When I make an unusual noise, look at me once rather than multiple times. It's not polite to stare at anyone, and I'm no exception. Realize I hear your snickers and see your sneers." Tell your child to talk to individuals with differences the way they'd address any other human being. That means using normal pronouns, sharing opinions, and even arguing. As Matthew pointed out, he's like every other teen; he wants to be seen as "cool, intelligent, and attractive—and sometimes to not be seen at all."

Provide windows and mirrors.

In a photograph of two-year-old Parker Curry that went viral, she's staring in complete awe at a large portrait of former First Lady Michelle Obama hanging at the National Portrait Gallery in the Smithsonian museum. Obama had hoped the portrait would elicit precisely that kind of "mirror moment." When it was unveiled, she said, "I'm thinking about all of the young people, particularly girls of color, who, in years ahead, will come to this place, and they'll look up and see an image of someone who looks like them hanging on the wall of this great American institution."

It's so important for children to see "mirrors," or images of beauty, power, and intelligence that look like them. At St. Andrew's Episcopal School, Glasgow brings in black women (and other minority) speakers. He also makes a point of stopping and talking to black girls in particular. "They feel literally invisible," he told me. "They're academically outshining males, but these are the girls who often are socially excluded or don't get asked to the dance."

Dena Simmons underscored this point when we chatted at Sheridan School after she gave a presentation on culturally responsive practices. Simmons, the assistant director at the Yale Center for Emotional Intelligence, told me about her experiences as a black girl attending a predominantly white boarding school in New England. Before then, she'd attended a diverse school in the Bronx, and the change was seismic. "I was fourteen, and it was the first time I understood visually what it felt like to be a minority—and I was constantly reminded," she said. She remembers wishing she saw more people who looked like her, "Even one faculty member who could have said it would be okay—that I was part of the family." She urges parents to work with their school to diversify the curriculum and make sure everyone sees visual representations of themselves.

Both fiction and nonfiction can provide windows and mirrors. Books help kids understand themselves and the world around them, and may even embolden them to write their own stories. Simmons likes using the writing prompt, "I wish others knew." Whether you form a parent-child book club with neighbors or read a novel with your child, choose stories that broach issues surrounding identity, inequity, privilege, and racial and cultural differences.

Last year, my then fourteen-year-old daughter, Emily, and I read Chimamanda Ngozi Adichie's *Purple Hibiscus* together. The novel follows the story of Kambili, a wealthy fifteen-year-old girl in Nigeria. Despite the gap between their experiences, Emily was surprised to realize how much she had in common with Kambili—the book provided a "window" into that experience. She related to how much pressure the character puts on herself to succeed. She also realized they both take friendship seriously and are trying to sort out who they want to be. I was struck by how she internalized their similarities far more than their differences.

— IDEA FOR EDUCATORS —
MAKE GLOBAL CONNECTIONS

Many teachers have been using telecommunications apps to help their students get out of their bubble and envision different ways of living. Pernille Rip, a seventh-grade English teacher in Wisconsin, has connected more than 2,000,000 students in sixty countries. She also reaches out to adults. A Canadian Iraqi Skyped with her class to share insights about the human side of the refugee crisis.

Ali Schilpp, a media specialist, teaches in a remote, rural public school in Maryland. She introduces her students to individuals throughout the world. "I want them to see how they can use the Internet to learn about people whose life experiences, backgrounds, and customs may be different from their own," she told me. Her students also make meaningful online connections with authors. When a student told Gennifer Choldenko, author of *Al Capone Does My Shirts: A Tale from Alcatraz*, that the character Natalie reminded him of his brother with autism, Choldenko told him the book was based on her own autistic sister.

Schilpp seeks out potential collaborators on Twitter and through a group called EduMatch. Recently, she launched a LEGO travel buddy program. Her students create LEGO mini-figures and mail them to schools in Hawaii, California, Australia, and China. Educators in those schools post pictures on Twitter of the LEGO figures accompanying students as they participate in activities, giving them a glimpse into other worlds.

Bring fear and bias to the surface.

Many schools use discussion groups or community circles to provide staff members, students, and parents with a space to talk about issues related to equity and diversity. Parents can partner with existing school programs or form their own. Either way, make sure you set ground rules around confidentiality and respectful listening. These topics can trigger painful emotions.

Incorporate conversations into daily life, too. Ask your child how it feels to spend time at someone's house who has a different racial or cultural background. Encourage them to identify similarities and differences. If your child volunteers for an organization like Special Olympics, ask them how they feel interacting with kids who have special needs. Bring any fear to the surface, and offer to answer questions. Your job isn't to shield them from discomfort; it's to help them move from awkwardness to a place of understanding.

No one is immune from bias—even educated, well-meaning people. A 2017 study in the *Journal of Experimental Psychology* found that people with higher cognitive abilities are actually more likely to learn and hold onto stereotypes. On the upside, those same individuals have an easier time shedding stereotypes when they're given information that challenges their existing beliefs. When you acknowledge that you carry unconscious attitudes and associations, you model that this work never ends.

If your child says something concerning, ask clarifying questions. Rodney Glasgow brought his own bias to a recent encounter. "I was hanging out with a white conservative student and other kids who were complaining about lunch, and they didn't like the milk," he told me. "One boy kept saying, 'I don't like this hood milk.' I'm burning inside, because I grew up as a fifth-grade boy with free lunch, and here's this white rich kid complaining about milk from the hood." Finally, Glasgow asked the student, "You keep saying 'hood' milk. Why?" The boy explained that Hood is the brand name of the milk. That one question shifted the whole conversation. "I had to figure out what he was saying and why, and then decide how to respond," he said. If your child says something at home that seems bigoted, probe further. Say, "Tell me why you think that."

Talk about the power of words.

Your child may behave in ways that seem benign, but are hurtful to peers. You can tap different resources to help them understand the power of their words and to challenge their assumptions. The *Seattle Times* created the Under Our Skin Project to encourage this kind of reflection. They invited eighteen people who represent a range of backgrounds and perspectives to talk candidly on video about concepts such as diversity and white privilege. In a series of short videos about micro-aggressions, participants talk about the impact of careless, hurtful, and ignorant comments.

One student said that when someone called her articulate, she could tell they meant "for a black girl." A Muslim woman talked about how she's sick of people asking, "Wouldn't you like to wear a bathing suit just once?" You can share personal stories with your child, too, whether they're childhood memories or more recent experiences. Wendy Kiang-Spray, forty-three, a Chinese American school counselor, tells her teen daughters about growing up in Maryland. "My mother would pack Chinese beef jerky in my lunch, and one time a girl said, 'What's *that*?'" she recalled. "When I said, 'beef jerky,' she yelled down the table, 'Wendy's eating jerky treats!'"

Kiang-Spray also has told her kids about an upsetting experience she had as a young middle school English teacher. An eighth-grade student stood at the back of the classroom mocking her appearance. "She pulled her eyes back in a way that kids used to do in my childhood. Racial slurs and gestures like this cut you to the core in a way that no other insult can. I think it's because it reduces you to something you can't help—that your degree, your authority, your respectability—cannot mitigate. I was about twenty-eight, and a thirteen-year-old did this to me."

Kiang-Spray says her daughters, who are Caucasian and Asian, more readily embrace their culture than she did growing up. She considers it a positive sign that her seventh grader proudly calls herself a "Wasian." "That term to me means she has a sense of her own identity, and also that it's okay," she said. Her daughters also call people out when they make offensive comments, yelling, "That's racist." Kiang-Spray was more inclined to let that stuff slide, noting, "I didn't have the words, sense of identity, or support to be able to defend myself." Encourage your child to tell an adult about offensive comments. When a seventh-grade boy told a biracial classmate that she looked "Tasty, like a hush puppy—dark on the outside and white on the inside," everyone within earshot reported him. Kids won't learn from their mistakes if adults don't address these situations directly.

It's not easy for adults, let alone kids, to step into someone else's shoes. You have to suspend your own reality to adopt another person's reality. The Virtual Human Interaction Lab at Stanford University has been experimenting with immersive virtual reality (IVR) goggles to build empathy. IVR lets users embody an avatar who encounters and must cope with racism. Because we aren't able to offer our kids magical empathy goggles yet, act with intentionality.

As Michele Borba noted in one of our conversations, "Tell your child you're going to watch your own language. If you say something that's not inclusive, you want them to say, 'Check that.' You might say 'all women,' or 'all blondes,' or 'all wealthy,' and those 'isms create divisions. If your husband says, 'Those homeless people need a job,' turn to him and say, 'Check that, is that true for all homeless people?'"

Beware the danger of "a single story."

Everyone has a story, but there's always a risk that the outside world will oversimplify it. In her famous TED Talk, "The Danger of a Single Story," Chimamanda Ngozie Adichie warns against the dangers of reducing someone to a stereotype. The seventh graders at my school prepare and present a mini TED Talk in which they talk about their own lives. They may say they feel defined by the fact that they're adopted, or that they have two mothers, or that they need extra time on tests. Writing a mini TED Talk can be emotional, but the process heightens students' empathy for anyone who feels defined by one strand of their narrative. When the seventh graders at Sheridan do this assignment, they first watch portions of Adichie's TED Talk and read texts that draw from this same idea, such as Monica Harwell's StoryCorps narrative about being the first woman to climb electric utility poles for ConEdison in New York.

Students then prepare and deliver three-minute talks to their peers that focus on their own experience of being stereotyped or falsely represented. After the students have delivered their speeches, they debrief as a group. You can try a home version of this same assignment. Discuss videos and narratives such as Adichie's or Harwell's, and initiate conversation about how the idea of "a single story" applies to your family, to you as an individual, and to your child. It's particularly tough for kids to own their identity when they feel judged for not conforming to someone else's stereotype. The comedian W. Kamau Bell explored this concept in a video for *The Atlantic* magazine. He reflected on his childhood as a black kid who wasn't into the "right stuff," saying, "I was the only black kid I knew who was into superheroes or martial arts." He felt like an outsider, and that sense of alienation carried over into adulthood.

School principal Alexandra Griffin also recalls being acutely aware of being different. In sixth grade, her school wanted to bus her from her majority black school to a gifted and talented program, which was housed in a school that was majority white. At first, her mother was reluctant, but then she relented. In seventh grade, Folarin, who is black, started at the new school and experienced intense culture shock. "I felt totally out of place, partly because I was black, and partly because I hadn't studied half the material the other students had," she told me. "I was smart, but behind. I was the black girl who didn't know the material. Stereotyped from the start." Folarin didn't want to reveal her struggles because she knew her mother didn't really want her at the school in the first place, so for the first four months she studied alone and tried to figure out what she didn't know. She also asked the school counselor for help. "By the end of the year, I was totally caught up, and I didn't feel like a living, breathing stereotype. I think my pride made me not tell my mother *and* it made me seek help," she said.

Doug Karr, the president and CEO of Character Dot Org, also recalls standing out, but because of his health issues. He was an athlete with asthma before inhalers were invented. "I enjoyed baseball, but I had to wear a mask to go out in the spring in pollen season. It was white with a filter, and I looked like something out of a movie. Kids would call me the boy in the bubble." As his teammates got to know him, they saw past the difference, but he still draws on that experience today. He tells his fifteen-year-old son, who's 6'8" and often gets questioned about his height, that he shouldn't let any single trait define him.

When your kid gets caught up in one piece of their identity, help them flesh out their whole story. Talk about your family's culture or the origin of their name. Highlight any meaningful rituals, whether you fast for a religious holiday or visit the same relatives every Thanksgiving. When you instill appreciation for their history and customs, kids learn to respect their own and other families' traditions, and they have an easier time remembering that everyone has a backstory.

Encourage your child to think about the cultural identifiers that impact them the most. That might be their race, ethnicity, gender, religion, sexual orientation, family structure, socioeconomic status, or ability. That's the lens through which they see the world, and it can shift depending on whether they're at home or at school. Your child might not think about class at the family dinner table, but be extremely attuned to it when they're at the mall with a friend who has her own credit card. Explain to your child that they're less likely to relate to someone else's experience if it's unfamiliar. If they're the one who has that credit card, for example, they may not realize how hard it is for a friend whose family is struggling financially. Once they tune in, they'll be able to show more sensitivity, perhaps by suggesting a sleepover rather than a shopping excursion. Adults often miss nuance, too. Take some time to think about your own skewed perspective. If you're a thin parent, for example, you may not relate to your obese child's struggle. If you were always a stellar student, you might have to work harder to understand your child's learning differences.

Sanah Jivani, now twenty, uses her personal battle with self-acceptance to help others. When she was twelve, she was diagnosed with alopecia, a condition that causes hair loss. By eighth grade, she was bald and started wearing wigs. She had low self-esteem and fought eating disorders and depression. "From remembering the pain of waking up in seventh grade with all of my hair on my pillow to thinking about the bullying, I needed some way to cope," Jivani wrote me. She took that hurt and got to work helping others discover their self-worth. At age fifteen, she shed the wig, stopped seeking validation from external sources, and founded Natural Day, an international movement to end insecurity. Jivani purposely scheduled the event for February thirteenth, the day before Valentine's Day, because she recognized that it's important to love yourself before you can love others.

It's not easy for anyone, let alone a fourteen-year-old, to embrace the very things that make them stand out. By third or fourth grade, kids are starting to feel self-conscious and want to fit in. By middle school, forget it. Any sort of weirdness is suspect, whether you've lost your hair, have a stutter, or can't sit in a regular chair without tipping over. Tell your child that every weakness comes with a strength. There are so many examples. Chris Miller, a fourteen-year-old who was taunted for being autistic, used his outside-the-box perspective to invent a superhero alter ego named Captain Spectrum. Captain Spectrum's motto is "defend and be a friend," and

Miller has brought his creativity and antibullying message to comic book conventions. Chris is making an impact because of his differences, not in spite of them. And these efforts are needed. A 2014 Interactive Autism Network survey revealed that 63 percent of children with autism spectrum disorder have been bullied at some point in their lives.

As Dave Rendall, author of *The Freak Factor*, told me, "What makes you weird makes you wonderful." He was a hyperactive kid who talked through class and was criticized endlessly, but he now gets paid to talk for a living. There are plenty of other adult examples. Retired professional baseball player David Eckstein told me he was picked on daily for his small size and called an "overachieving Smurf." "I was never the biggest person or the most talented person," he said, "but that made me learn how to embrace failure, develop coping skills, and improve my mental game." He worked hard to prove his bullies wrong, and ended up playing Major League Baseball for ten seasons. In 2006, he won the World Series Most Valuable Player award.

Ultimately, whatever makes learning or social acceptance a challenge now might be the exact qualities that bring kids success and happiness in the future. Steer your child toward appropriate outlets for their strengths and skills instead of squelching what makes them unique. And don't be afraid to model stepping outside the norm yourself.

TOP TIPS FOR PARENTS

- Don't shut down unpopular viewpoints. Engage in discussion, but set a boundary—your child can't say anything that degrades someone's humanity.
- Don't ignore disturbing events in the news involving racism, homophobia, or other forms of hate. Create a space for discussion.
- Talk about cultural identifiers and how they skew perspective.
- Monitor your own biases. Family members can say "check that" to one another when someone makes a generalization about a group.

- Encourage authentic inclusion, not just a "hi" in the hall or a one-off act of kindness.
- Think about who your child sees you befriending and treating with respect.
- Provide "windows and mirrors"—role models and images of beauty who look like them.
- Encourage them to draw from their own experiences with feeling different to help others.
- Show examples of celebrities and successful professionals who leveraged their so-called weaknesses into success.

CONVERSATION STARTERS

- "What differences and similarities have you noticed when you hang out with Michael?"
- "What do you think it's like to have to worry about that challenge?"
- "Why do you think kids find it scary to approach people who are different in some way?"
- "Did you hear that news story? If that happened here, how do you think kids at your school would react?"

SOCIAL SKILLS

"I feel judged and ignored."

MANAGING SHIFTING FRIENDSHIPS

"We used to be best friends, but now Katy is one of the mean girls. She doesn't even look at me."

"I'm so sick of Meghan. She thinks we should do everything together just because we hung out last year."

"August made the travel basketball team, so now he thinks he's better than everyone."

JOEY WAS THROWN WHEN HIS BEST FRIEND DROPPED HIM. JOEY and Charlie had spent the summer before sixth grade biking and playing video games together, but that stopped on the first day of middle school. Charlie mostly ignored him, though he'd occasionally body slam him when they passed each other in the hall. Joey not only took Charlie's abuse, he became obsessed with winning him back. He kept tabs on Charlie's new friends, whom he referred to as the "popular" group. He knew when they got busted for texting cartoons of naked girls or flinging hamburgers across the cafeteria.

Joey's mother, my friend Jen, couldn't understand their appeal. She cringed every time he set himself up for another round of rejection. She tried to challenge his thinking. "Do you think someone that obnoxious is worth your time? What do you like about Charlie and his friends anyway?" When Joey told Jen that Charlie got suspended for yanking down a boy's pants in the locker room, she reached her breaking point. "Do you really think this is going to turn out well for him?" she asked. She still got nowhere.

"Oh my god, I can't take it anymore," she told me. "Please tell me how I can get him to move on." I told her that the best antidote to craving the wrong friends is finding the right ones, but that takes time. Jen got to work. Whenever Joey connected with a new classmate or teammate, she'd help him deepen the tie. She'd offer to drive them to the movies or take them out for ice cream. She told Joey that he seemed much more relaxed when he hung out with kids who didn't humiliate him. By the time he accepted that Charlie was a lost cause, he had a small circle of new friends.

The leap from elementary to middle school is a vulnerable, tumultuous time. Kids suddenly have a larger pool of friends to choose from, more freedom, and less adult supervision. No one is assigning them a "buddy" anymore. There's a herd mentality as kids begin to care more about their social standing than their role in their family. They start to place a bigger premium on trust, and their friendships become more intense. Complicating matters, this heavier investment in friendship is often accompanied by a decrease in social stability. This combination can cause angst and insecurity. Eileen Kennedy-Moore, a psychologist and coauthor of *Growing Friendships: A Kid's Guide to Making and Keeping Friends*, told me that only 75 percent of middle schoolers' friendships last from fall to spring. The odds are pretty low that your child will maintain any of their seventh-grade friendships over the long haul. In a study published in *Psychological Science*, researchers tracked friendships formed in seventh grade and found that only 1 percent were still intact by twelfth grade.

For some kids, middle school is a chance to branch out or reinvent themselves. For others, it's an opportunity to chase status. They're operating in a world where their friendships are both intense and fragile. While girls pair off, boys move in packs and may be more likely to jockey for position. Boys tend to focus on establishing superiority over kids who are close to them in the social pecking order. I talked to Jamie Ostrov, a developmental psychologist and professor at the University at Buffalo, State

University of New York, who said, "For boys, their social goal is hierarchy and dominance." Girls are more likely to value intimacy and two-person relationships rather than group interactions.

While you might be tempted to dismiss popularity as fleeting and superficial, don't discount it entirely. Clinical psychologist Mitch Prinstein, author of *Popular: The Power of Likeability in a Status-Obsessed World*, told me he's been surprised by how enduring the effects are thirty to forty years later. Our early experiences can change the expression of our DNA, our marriages, and even our children's popularity. "We have a give and take with our environment, and if you're popular, you're given more opportunities to practice social skills or gain access to new information," he explained. Unpopular kids don't get those same advantages, and it becomes a vicious cycle. That said, all popularity isn't created equal. When it comes in the form of likeability and making others feel included, outcomes are positive. Adolescents, however, are wired to seek the more aggressive, status-seeking variety. But if they're too focused on being visible and influential, they may fail to develop more-nuanced social skills. They also may continue to trade on status as adults, and Ostrov's research has found that these tendencies can lead to depression, anxiety, relationship difficulties, or risky behavior.

While it's normal to shift friends and experiment with social power in middle school, your child may struggle to navigate the increasingly complex terrain. Kids start going in different directions, and there's no longer a teacher at the front of the room saying, "We're all friends in here." Your child may suddenly drop a close elementary school friend, and this can be hard for parents to accept, especially if the two families have bonded. Nevertheless, resist the urge to intervene. Let your child exercise their autonomy and decide for themselves where they feel a sense of belonging. View this as a time to expand your own social circle. That doesn't mean your hands are completely tied. Here are some steps you can take to help your child manage the social churn.

Acknowledge your child's desire for popularity.

If you want to help your child build social skills, develop resiliency, and prioritize meaningful friendships over popularity, you have to understand where they're coming from. FOMO—the fear of missing out—is very real. Psychologist Adam Pletter worked with one teen who was so preoccupied with what she was missing, she used Instagram Live to talk all night to friends having a sleepover. Pletter, who founded iParent 101, told me this tactic backfired because she was trying too hard. "She was targeted in subtle ways," he said. The girls would go off camera, then say her name to provoke her interest. When they had her attention, they'd talk about all the fun they were planning—without her. To combat FOMO, have an ongoing conversation with your child about their online and offline social lives, and help them stay busy doing activities they enjoy rather than obsessing over what everyone else is doing.

Make sure you're modeling that same behavior. Sue Scheff, author of *Shame Nation*, told me she has to remind parents to "Stop liking, liking, liking, and counting their likes." Prinstein's research shows that kids will take down a picture if it doesn't get 100 likes in a certain amount of time, and parents can inadvertently play into that insecurity. One mother admitted to posting photos of puppies and kittens on her daughter's Instagram account to drum up more likes. She was succumbing to cultural pressure, but that kind of "help" sent her daughter the clear message that visibility matters.

Prinstein once saw a magazine that featured an instruction manual for conquering loneliness by getting a million followers. Depending on external validation will never lead to happiness. If we focus too much on ephemeral popularity, we could end up with a generation of kids who know how to curate their image but have no idea how to form meaningful connections. As it is, most adolescent friendships are poor quality, defined not just by the presence of aggression, but by the lack of reciprocity. I spoke to Robert Faris, an associate professor at the University of California at Davis, who researches social relationships. His data and large national studies show that when kids are asked to name their five best friends, fewer than half of their nominations are reciprocated. He's also found that there's a tremendous amount of turnover in these unbalanced relationships, with kids' best friend lists changing over two-week intervals. That's a significant finding because children who maintain durable friendships are more anchored and less likely to engage in status-seeking behavior.

Encourage your child to target high-quality friends with good character and to expend effort deepening those bonds. Pose questions that help them think critically about their friendships. Ask, "Does your friend make you feel good? Is this someone you can count on in a crisis? Can you be silly when you're together?" When your child is unhappy with their place in the pecking order, offer extra love, acknowledge their feelings, and share your values. You can't convince them not to care, but you can try to figure out why this matters to them. Examine the reality of their social circle and remind them what they'd lose if they sacrificed the great qualities in their existing relationships to pursue popularity. As Faris told me, "If you're trying to move up the social ladder and the ladder is built on friendships, you're going to leave friends behind, and that's a loss. Those friends are going to feel betrayed too."

You also can point out that the most popular kids may be disliked. Your child might assume someone has it all, but they may lack trusting friendships. Help them think more expansively about their peers' lives. A thin, well-dressed girl who seems perfect might be struggling with an eating disorder. A popular athlete might have an unstable home life. Reassure your kid that they're not stuck in the same box forever, and they'll have opportunities for reinvention. They may be relieved to know that power-hungry, empathy-deficient kids can evolve, too. According to a 2016 study at the University of Texas at Austin, young adolescents cope better with exclusion and other social stressors when they understand that people can change.

Focus on what they can control.

In every community, there are things that make a child popular. It could be anything from their athletic ability to their family's wealth. You can teach skills that make a child more likeable, but helping them attain status is trickier. The good news is that if you can attribute your child's lack of conventional popularity to external factors, they'll be less likely to suffer from depression or conclude they're not worthy. Encourage them to focus on what they can control, such as being kind.

This messaging is particularly useful when kids suffer a social setback. My neighbor Andrew called me for advice about his daughter Rachel, who felt punished for being considerate. A boy named Micah had transferred to her school in the middle of seventh grade, and Rachel was the only one who befriended him. A few months after he arrived, he sent out invitations to his bar mitzvah. Rachel was stunned she didn't make the cut. She was even more upset when she heard who Micah *had* invited—a bunch of popular kids who never spoke to him.

I encouraged Andrew to focus on Rachel's warm, inclusive nature rather than Micah's insensitivity. He reassured his daughter that kindness typically does lead to real friendship, and he tried to help her regain a sense of agency. They brainstormed her options, including ending the friendship, confronting Micah, or pretending nothing had happened. Rachel decided she felt too raw to continue the one-sided relationship, but she told her dad she had no regrets about being welcoming.

There's a primal social impulse to be part of the pack, but kids thrive when they think less about themselves and more about others. If your child says that no one likes them, turn the tables. Help them focus on how they can help others, whether they sit with a new student at lunch or carry a backpack for a classmate on crutches. Engaging in something bigger than themselves will help them stop ruminating about unreturned texts, unrequited invitations, and other perceived slights.

— IDEA FOR EDUCATORS —
THINK CREATIVELY ABOUT LUNCHTIME

For many middle schoolers, the cafeteria is a stressful minefield. By periodically assigning seating, you can alleviate that angst and expand students' social networks. Mix grades so older kids have an opportunity to assist lonely younger kids. You can designate one table for students who want to play cards or board games while they eat. This will ensure that students always have somewhere safe and welcoming to sit. Lunch also is a time when counselors can facilitate friendship groups, or teachers and administrators can host kids in their classroom or office. Educators can ask kind kids with social capital to invite peers who lack a sense of belonging.

Cultivate good matches.

Middle schoolers understand that they're supposed to interact with the people closest to them in the social hierarchy. The culture may value physical attractiveness or athletic ability, but your child may thrive in a setting that values academic achievement or community service. Look for activities that play to their strengths and draw kids with similar interests. All children need to find "right fit" friends, but this is especially critical for kids who've been mistreated. (I'll revisit this idea in Chapter 7, which deals with bullying.)

If your child is having trouble finding a peer group, their teachers and counselor can suggest good friend matches, invite them to group lunches, pair them on projects, and reinforce social skills (see Ideas for Educators). Stay proactive and involved, and don't outsource everything. Talk to your child, get to know their friends, and connect with other parents. Be strategic, too. If they want to go to a high school soccer game, for example, suggest they invite one friend rather than two. Two kids might walk away together, but one friend probably won't abandon them. If your child is socially awkward, suggest structured activities that require less talking, such as movies or bowling. Seize opportunities where you can give an assist. That might mean taking your son and a couple of his teammates out to lunch after a game, or organizing a potluck dinner with families who have kids the same age.

Prinstein noted that 50 to 75 percent of kids should be able to identify a best friend, with that same person identifying them back. That friendship may get downgraded over the course of a year, but most kids need at least one good friend at any given point. Friendless children tend to have long-term difficulties, but not all kids have the skills to develop strong ties with even one peer. If your child has difficulty with social cues, focus less on deep friendship and more on helping them interact comfortably with a broad range of kids.

At the same time, help them acquire the social skills they need to be likeable, such as showing curiosity by asking questions. You want them to focus on connecting, not impressing. Eileen Kennedy-Moore uses a simple visual to teach kids how to identify common ground. She'll draw two overlapping circles, color the middle, and explain, "This is where friendship begins." If your child talks about something that pertains only to them, it won't help their cause. Tell them to look for hooks. Is a potential friend wearing a shirt from a music group they like? Did they watch the same football game? Some kids may not know how to join a conversation. Demonstrate how to slide into action without interrupting, and teach your child to match the emotional tone of the group. "If everyone is complaining about the social studies test and one girl says it was easy, it's like a sour note in the melody of the conversation," Kennedy-Moore explained. "Deceit is not a path toward friendship, but a kid can say, 'Yeah, I can't believe there were five short answers.'"

Children who know how to make others feel valued do better socially. I've written about how gratitude can combat kids' sense of lacking, but here's another twist. In the journal *Emotion*, researchers wrote that keeping a gratitude journal teaches kids how to show appreciation, a skill that facilitates the initiation of new friendships. As Prinstein pointed out, "When we look at videos of kids who end up being the most liked, they listen to others and try to build on and shape what they're doing instead of saying, 'No, that's stupid, let's do it this way.'" Whether your child's friends are devising new spike ball rules or choosing which game to play, encourage them to think about their primary goal. Ask, "What do you think the outcome will be if you insist on doing everything your way? How can you make your point without discounting others' ideas?"

Flexibility is key, a concept that military kids seem to understand more readily than others. School counselor Rebecca Best, who runs groups for military children, points out that they may move seven or eight times before they hit middle school. Other students can learn from their openness. These kids may be more likely to approach a stranger in a crowded cafeteria or to prioritize positivity over status.

If your child has been in the same school since kindergarten, they may think more rigidly about whom they hang out with and where they belong. Point out the value in bringing new people into their world, particularly if their existing friendships are unsatisfying. Boost their social receptivity by exposing them to new people and situations. That might mean attending an overnight camp or participating in a travel sport where they won't know their teammates in advance. The burden of popularity is lifted when the goal is simply to befriend nice people. As Best told me, "Military kids have figured out what works for them and are clued into their strengths. They're not trying to find a forever friend or a best friend. There's a freedom to take risks on new friendships when you live in the moment."

Kind kids with social capital can help classmates who are struggling. If your child falls into this category, give them concrete suggestions to include others, such as inviting a struggling peer to join their after-school club. School professionals can help with this. One of my students had to travel a great distance to school, and after-school playdates were logistically difficult. When the seventh graders started to have bar and bat mitzvahs, I enlisted a few caring girls to invite her to weekend sleepovers so she could attend the evening parties. As a result, she felt less isolated and more connected to classmates. The girls who helped felt better about themselves, too.

There are reserved kids who don't need much in the way of social interaction, and parents sometimes ask me whether they should be concerned. Former middle school principal Jennifer Webster (now a director in Montgomery County Public Schools in Maryland) suggests thinking more expansively. "I'd ask, how is he with the family? Does he participate when you do game night? He might not be comfortable with a big group of friends, but does he enjoy hanging out with you?"

Contact your child's teachers to assess how they're operating in more-structured settings. Look at their performance in a range of classes, from English to PE to art. How are their interactions with classmates? Are they able to work in groups? This is a better way to gauge how they're doing than taking a tally of their friends. "As a parent, I'd feel comfortable if they say he's doing what we ask in a developmentally appropriate way, and he's engaged and comfortable," Webster told me.

You can ask your child similar questions. Say, "How do you feel in Spanish class, or in English? Do you feel comfortable answering questions, or talking to the teacher?" If they say they don't want to talk to anyone in class and they don't have any friends, take a closer look at their social world. Tempting as it may be to move a lonely or awkward child to a new environment, that probably won't help if you don't address the underlying social-skill deficits. Kids take themselves wherever they go, and they're likely to find themselves in the same situation if the only thing you do is change their setting.

Give them a path forward.

Sometimes, parents know their child is acting mean but have no idea how to help them change course. Help them play out the consequences. Ask, "What does it mean if people want to be friends with you because they're scared of you, and not because they like your personality?" Challenge them when they rationalize their behavior with statements like, "But everybody hates her!"

Middle schoolers are experimenting with social power, and their empathy muscle isn't fully developed. That can lead to meanness, but you won't help them by focusing on their badness. The key is to help them get back on track to being a "good kid" as quickly as possible. Guilt can be constructive, but shame isn't helpful. Kennedy-Moore uses a three-step process. Step one involves giving your child an excuse. Say, "I get that you were trying to get some space, or make a point, or hurt someone who wounded you." Step two is the "but." This is when you try to open their eyes to the impact of their actions. "But you really betrayed her trust when you told everyone her secret." Step three is about taking action. Ask, "What can you do to help her feel better?" and, "What can you do to prevent this from happening again?" Change is more meaningful when your child comes up with solutions.

It can take time for kids to dig themselves out of a hole, especially if they're in emotional pain themselves. One of my seventh graders, Sean, was ostracized by every one of his classmates. He had to hit rock bottom before he was willing to make amends. He knew he'd made some bad choices, such as picking fights and using racist language, and he felt depressed and confused by his out-of-control behavior. He decided he wanted to apologize to his entire grade at once. I wasn't sure this was a good idea, so we discussed what that might look and sound like, from what he'd say to the time of day when he'd say it. I told him I'd moderate to ensure the tone stayed respectful, but said he might not get the desired result. He still wanted to apologize publicly.

When Sean addressed his classmates, he spoke between tears while they listened, frozen and wide-eyed. After he spoke, I held my breath, hoping they'd meet his courage with compassion. After a long pause, they took turns praising his bravery. They told him that everyone makes mistakes and deserves a second chance. A few students admitted they hadn't been so nice themselves. His teacher and I both had red eyes by the fourth or fifth kind comment. Some kids learn only from painful mistakes, but that's okay. For better and for worse, those experiences will be seared into their memory.

Raising a middle schooler can have some rough moments, and it helps to tap extra support. Julia Guillen Williams, a pupil personnel worker and former middle school counselor, tells parents to designate backup adults, such as aunts, older cousins, or close friends. They can help impart friendship advice. "I'm Colombian, and everyone is Tía or Tío something," she told me. "These are not blood relationships, but my son understands that these are people we trust." When Guillen Williams was in middle school, she dealt with abuse. "I found family in my friends' families, and I relied on other moms for mothering and resilience," she said. Your child may be more receptive to life lessons from individuals who aren't their parents, and other adults can add credibility to your messaging. These stand-ins also can offer support when you can't. Your kid may go through a phase when they don't want to confide in you, or they don't want to burden you because you're not at your peak.

Middle schoolers need all the help they can get. When they feel slighted, they can read too much into someone's behavior. When this happens, try asking a series of "maybe" questions. Maybe that friend thought you'd appreciate it; maybe it was an accident; maybe they didn't realize it was private information. There are so many possibilities, and you can help your child assume positive intent. Maybe the friend didn't include them in weekend plans, but only because they wanted one-on-one time with a new classmate. Perhaps your child wasn't tagged in a group photo, but the omission was unintentional. Encourage them to shift away from, "Why me?"

to the more solution-oriented, "What if I?" and, "How can I?" questions. When there's no denying they've been insulted, empower them to speak up for themselves. That can be as simple as saying, "That was mean," and walking away.

There is such a thing as too much melodrama. As Prinstein says, "Seventh grade is this daily conflict resolution camp." (When I shared his observation with a seventh-grade girl who was struggling socially, she said, "Well, he's totally right—other than the resolution part.") While some children are conflict-averse and will tell everyone they're upset *except* for the person who offended them, others get an adrenaline rush from playing a central role in soap operas. It can be difficult to convince these kids that disengaging is the best long-term strategy. If your child shares details about their own or someone else's friendship conflicts, help them identify and engage solely with the core players. Ask, "Is this something you need to be involved in, or are you just curious about what happened? Who do you need to talk to in order to resolve this problem?" If your child is drawn to chaos-craving friends, ask, "What's the downside of interacting with kids who like to get everyone riled up?" Some middle schoolers enjoy throwing a grenade into every conversation.

Keep in mind, however, that good friendships aren't necessarily higher in positive experiences. Kids may only be willing to have it out with close friends. You may be surprised to discover that your child has no interest in repairing a friendship. Instead, they may be looking to you for permission to move on, or for help creating a more comfortable but distant interpersonal dynamic.

If your child can't see the big picture, try visual imagery. Invite them on an imaginary hot air balloon ride. From this new vantage point above the fray, can they see the problem more clearly? Can they identify possible solutions? Even the best parents will struggle at times to keep their cool. "I teach this and I'm trained in it, but I still had to do a lot of work to come from a healthy place and avoid being reactive with my own teen daughters," Sacramento Waldorf School teacher Megan Sullivan told me. Maintain your sense of humor without dismissing their concerns. You'll fare better, too, if you can find lightness in those dark moments.

TOP TIPS FOR PARENTS

- If your child has social deficits, work on skills such as seamlessly entering a conversation or asking questions rather than trying to impress.
- Point out what they'd sacrifice if they gave up their friends to gain acceptance from a different clique.
- Don't place a premium on "likes and follows."
- Focus on what they can control, such as reaching out to someone else who is struggling.
- Give them a path forward when they hurt a friend.
- Tap backup adults to help reinforce your messages.
- Use visual imagery to help them gain some distance and perspective.

CONVERSATION STARTERS

- "Help me understand what you like about David."
- "What do you think would change if you were part of Chloe's clique?"
- "What would you give up if you dropped your friends to spend more time with Maddie and her friends?"
- "What does it mean if people want to be friends with you because they're scared of you, and not because they like your personality?"
- "Does Mark make you feel good? Is he someone you can count on in a crisis? Is he kind to others?"
- "What do you see as the ideal resolution? Do you want to repair the friendship or disengage for a while?"

CHAPTER 7

DEALING WITH BULLYING

> ## KEY SKILLS
> 1—Make good friend choices
> 2—Learn to Negotiate conflict
> 6—Self-advocate
> 7—Self-regulate emotions

"I know I'm fat. I don't need everyone to remind me every day."

"I try to avoid the second-floor bathroom. That's where Carl and Tim hang out, and they think it's funny to pants me whenever I pass them."

"Shari and Dana stuck tampons in my back pocket when I wasn't looking, then yanked them out in front of everyone."

WHENEVER JESSIE HUNG OUT WITH HER BEST FRIENDS, CHLOE and Meg, they'd whisper about another seventh grader named Kate. Jessie didn't know Kate, and it didn't sound like she was missing out. Chloe and Meg said that Kate was clingy, told boring stories, and smelled like acne wash. Whenever Jessie would ask questions about this mystery girl, her friends would giggle and shoot each other knowing glances. This went on for weeks until a boy in her class told Jessie the truth—Kate was their code name for her.

Jessie looked to other friends for support, but they started falling like dominoes. Chloe and Meg had all the social capital, and no one wanted to risk alienating them. Every night, she cried herself to sleep. Her mother, my friend Naomi, called me for advice. Her voice caught as she asked me, "How can I help her? She's in so much pain."

Naomi's own experience with bullying magnified her panic and anguish. In eighth grade, kids regularly humiliated her. They forged her signature on love letters and left them in a popular athlete's locker. They tugged on her arm hair and called her monkey, and they invited her to nonexistent parties. Naomi suffered from depression throughout high school, and she wanted a better outcome for Jessie. She knew that Jessie loved to write, so she enrolled her in a creative writing class where she could make friends and process her emotions. For one assignment, Jessie wrote about a tormented heroine who dusts herself off and helps other kids. In both her real and imaginary worlds, she was learning that she could change her narrative. It took time, but she eventually realized that the bullying was just one chapter of her story, a lesson that resonated for Naomi, too.

Bullying strips kids of their dignity and leaves scars, and emotional recovery can be complicated. Some children bounce back while others sink like a stone. There's no one-size-fits-all intervention, but here are several ways you can build children's resiliency. I'll also offer tips to help the kids who are doing the bullying.

Find alignment situations and come up with practical strategies.

When kids have been traumatized by their peers, they need a safe space to regain their footing. Parents can steer them toward activities they enjoy where they're likely to make friends. It doesn't matter whether it's organic gardening, guitar, volleyball, a book club, or fencing. When children are young, they find friends based on proximity. As they get older, they find friends based on similarity. That transition is one of the fundamental challenges of middle school, whether or not your child has been the target of bullying.

Seek out sports where your child has the highest chance of success, or art classes, or debate club, then talk to them about what they like, where they excel, and when they're happiest. You can find these opportunities through less-competitive recreational sports leagues, or at local museums or makerspaces (collaborative work spaces where kids can learn to use tools and materials, create projects, and solve problems). Some kids join religious youth groups, or take coding or cooking classes through local universities. Consider signing your child up for summer camp, and help them maintain any new friendships during the year, even if they communicate primarily through text. Having just one strong friendship is protective and will build their resiliency.

Parents are understandably worried about how their kids are faring, but don't "interview for pain." Rosalind Wiseman, author of *Owning Up* and cofounder of Cultures of Dignity, says this practice is counterproductive and will produce anxiety for your child. "Don't start off asking, 'Were the kids mean to you at school today?' If they say yes, they have to deal with your emotional response, but if they say no, they may have lost their opportunity," she explained. Instead, ask open-ended questions, such as, "How was school today?"

Children need to feel that the adults in their lives believe them and believe in them. Acknowledge that what was done to them is absolutely unacceptable, and that you know they've been wounded. Then point out their earned, deserved strengths to counterbalance all the negative messages. When kids are systematically bullied, they start to believe they're losers and can assume a victim mentality. Remind them that they should never let anyone else define them.

Work with your child to develop problem-solving skills, too. This may include brainstorming comeback lines, practicing looking unfazed, reflecting on past interactions, or looking for humor in bleak situations. You can help your child be more assertive by showing them how to use eye contact, strong posture, and firm language to establish boundaries. Figure out when they're physically or emotionally vulnerable, down to mapping hallways and avoiding hot spots. There may be one class with poor management, or your child may need to avoid sitting in the back of the bus. *UnSelfie* author Michele Borba told me that 43 percent of American kids are afraid to use school bathrooms, but added that many middle schoolers love the media center because librarians tend to be strict and watchful. Help them identify everything they can do to keep themselves safe, including limiting the frequency and duration of interactions with problematic kids. When they must engage, they should stay calm and composed.

Principals want parents to understand the definition of bullying, because parents tend to overreport it. As Borba told me, "It's cold-blooded, one-sided, intentional cruelty that's usually repeated. One kid has his head in the toilet, and the other one is holding it there." But sometimes, the problem isn't actually bullying—it's two kids who need to work out a problem, but they're on equal footing, and each can hold their own. The one commonality among targets is that they tend to stand out as different in some way. People are more likely to stick up for individuals who resemble themselves. Embracing diversity is an important message, but it flies in the face of our wiring.

It's worth taking the time to get the school's perspective. The counselor, teachers, or administrators may be able to offer some good insights or suggest good friendship matches. That friend piece is critical, especially when it's "friends" who are doing the bullying. Kids may settle for intimacy with peers who are respectful 20 percent of the time, tolerating mistreatment the rest of the time. Your child has to process the fact that a once-trusted friend has turned on them, and realize that they're sacrificing themselves. To help them get there, talk about the qualities they seek in a friend. If they don't connect the dots, they'll make the same mistakes in the future.

Power dynamics can shift frequently, so parents and educators need to carefully investigate all complaints. It's not always what you expect. In a new twist, bullied kids may be more likely to target themselves online. Cyberbullying experts Sameer Hinduja and Justin Patchin coauthored a study in the *Journal of Adolescent Health* that found that 7.1 percent of boys and 5.3 percent of girls have posted something mean about themselves, such as, "You're ugly and nobody likes you," or, "You should just kill yourself." When fourteen-year-old Hannah Smith committed suicide in England in 2013 after months of cyberbullying, investigators discovered that she had sent 98 percent of the abusive messages to herself. Parents might consider this form of self-harm bizarre, but it's a plea for help that must be addressed. In 2016, French researchers did a systematic review of sixty-four articles and concluded that 70 percent of young adults with a history of self-harming behavior attempt suicide at least once. There may be a similar link between online self-harm and suicide attempts.

Change the narrative.

Parents can help bullied kids understand that they're the main character of their story, and bullying is just one trial along the way. Matt Langdon, an Australian bullying expert and president of the Hero Construction Company, urges adults to use the hero's journey model. "Every hero story that's been written has the same steps on the path," he told me over the phone. "The hero starts out knowing the rules of the place, then they're taken to a different world with new rules, and they go on a journey and change."

Framed within that, it's better to avoid overdramatizing the bullying experience. You'll do a disservice to your child if you make that the focus. You can use a series such as Harry Potter to discuss tactics for dealing with bullying and to underscore that heroes can emerge stronger for their struggles. You also can watch the latest superhero movie or young adult romance with your child and note any parallels or lessons. Share elevating images from the real world, too. Visit websites such as DoSomething.org, or watch an uplifting video about a bullied child who's making a difference in the world. Look for articles about celebrities who talk openly about being bullied, especially ones they admire. Children are comforted when they realize they're not alone. Langdon—who offers a self-led parenting curriculum on his website, Heroconstruction.org—gets frustrated when people focus on toughening up bullying targets. "It's just so wrong-headed to ask people who've been wronged to change themselves," he told me. Instead, change the narrative.

Another way to change the story is to reframe perceived weaknesses as strengths in disguise, a technique I use with my students. When they focus on their deficits, I ask them to identify two good things about each so-called flaw. *The Freak Factor* author Dave Rendall draws on his own life to give kids hope. "I was bullied for so many things," he told me. "I was grotesquely skinny and called Twiggy, after the first skinny model. No 13-year-old boy wants to have his body compared to that. But that's why I can do Ironman Triathlons."

Convince your child that the kids tormenting them are short-sighted and off-base, and help them feel pride instead of shame. As Rendall noted, "At what point does that nerdy kid become an inventor? At what point does the kid who dresses weird get praised because he's a fashion designer?" In middle school, any kind of deviance will generate tremendous pressure to conform, and that makes it especially hard for targeted kids to envision a bright future.

I talked about middle schoolers' intense desire to fit in with parenting expert Annie Fox, a teen advice columnist and author of the Middle School Confidential series. She urges parents to emphasize that different doesn't mean broken, noting, "Middle school kids either twist themselves into a pretzel to smooth down the edges of whatever makes them different, or they wear the mask of not caring." When your child stops trying to be something they're not, they're likely to attract a different kind of friend.

Consult advisors and use mantras to limit rumination.

When kids are bullied, they often feel alone. To combat that sense of isolation, Langdon recommends that parents help their child identify a group of real and fictional advisors who can serve as companions on their journey. He frames it as King Arthur's Round Table.

"They can ask their kid to think about the different roles people can play in their story, whether it's sidekick, mentor, or cheerleader," he explained. Your child can then ask their advisory board questions. "If this kid is giving me trouble at school every day, what should I do? How can I stop thinking about what happened to me all the time?" They can have imaginary conversations with fictional, famous, and historical figures, while also talking to their real-life friends and family. Encourage them to fill their advisory board with a range of people they admire, whether it's Harriet Tubman or Selena Gomez. This exercise reinforces the importance of reaching out to others, and helps them understand that everyone hits bumps in the road.

If your child can't stop ruminating about their bullying, they may need a mantra or music lyric to help them manage intrusive thoughts. Ruminating magnifies pain and slows recovery, and it raises the risk that they'll think their tormentors are right about them. When something is happening, that song can pop into their head. Rosalind Wiseman urges kids to try this exercise as many times as it takes to make it a habit. The mantra can be any statement that affirms their right to exist in the world, such as "I don't deserve this," but let your child choose it. Tell them that although you can't magically make the bullying disappear, you'll always be there to offer strategies and support.

Here's the upside: targets of bullying tend to develop a greater capacity for empathy and derive meaning from sparing others the same type of pain. When they do help others, their confidence goes up and their stress levels go down. Michele Borba shared a story with me about a teen who immigrated from Haiti a few years ago. At first, no one would look at him or eat with him, but after he made the football team and gained acceptance, he remembered what it felt like to be excluded. He mobilized other students, including his entire football team, to sit with kids who were eating alone. Similarly, sixteen-year-old Natalie Hampton created the Sit with Us app. At her last school, she'd been completely ostracized. She remembered those feelings of shame and isolation, and she wanted to reach out to others in the same situation.

Manage your own anxiety—and know when to shift gears.

There are times when parents should change their child's school, especially if there are safety concerns. Be alert for excessive crying, changes in sleeping and eating habits, social withdrawal, school refusal, or drops in academic performance. If you notice your kid spiraling downward, take them to a therapist trained to work with bullied children.

"A girl from Texas wrote me a few years ago," Annie Fox told me. "During swim class, someone stole her bra from her locker. She's large-breasted and had to go to her next class without it." The girl was videotaped in the hall, and she was so humiliated she wanted to kill herself. Fox contacted her father, who set up a meeting with the principal, the school counselor, and the parents of the girls who stole the bra.

"When she shared in this supposedly safe place how it felt to go to her locker and then walk through the halls, the other girls' moms laughed,"

Fox said. The principal said he couldn't ensure the girl's safety, and he blew it off. She switched to another school, where she thrived.

Your child needs to feel safe in order to learn, and if the school isn't rectifying a situation, you need to be their advocate. Don't promise you won't tell, and save any evidence. You may even have to call the police.

That said, give schools time to investigate and identify the right perpetrators. Parents tend to move really fast. As Wiseman said, "If you're in a self-righteous temper tantrum kind of place, the only thing that's going to happen is you're going to make the situation worse." If your child comes home feeling wounded, it's normal to hurt for them and feel angry, but start by collecting data. Is it a passing complaint or a constant source of misery? Are they consistently targeted by the same child? Are they able to manage without your interference? Have they tried getting adult help at school, or filled out a bullying report form?

There's no need to wait before contacting a counselor or teacher for context or advice, but take that step before you storm the building demanding consequences. You might discover your child instigated the situation, or toggles between being the aggressor and the target. Keep an open mind and recognize that you may not have the full picture. You don't want the right solution for the wrong problem. Trust that educators want to nip bullying behavior, too. Most of us weren't the alpha types ourselves, and we have no interest in tolerating peer cruelty. Plus, one aggressive child can wreak havoc on the entire climate.

— IDEA FOR EDUCATORS —
BE THOUGHTFUL ABOUT CONFLICT RESOLUTION

Do some legwork before bringing an aggressor and their target together. If you force a quick truce, you might inadvertently reinforce the power of the perpetrator and retraumatize the other child. Make sure both students are ready to meet before you do anything. Talk to the aggressor to confirm they're ready to deliver a sincere apology, and make sure the other child feels comfortable with the plan. After you've dealt with the situation, continue to monitor the targeted child's well-being. The effects of bullying can linger for a long time.

Travel in time to the future.

Researchers at the University of California at Berkeley found that when people are able to imagine how they'll interpret an upsetting event in the distant future, they experience less anxiety, sadness, hurt, and anger. Ask your child, "How do you think you'll look back on this ten years from now?" Robert Sutton, a professor at Stanford University and the author of *The Asshole Survival Guide*, wrote about this kind of mental time travel in the *Wall Street Journal*. He explained that it's a variation on the aphorism, "This too shall pass." He told the story of a US Air Force Academy cadet who was hazed by upperclassmen during his freshman year. The cadet imagined it was a few years later, he was flying a plane, and the temporary torment was a small price to pay for accomplishing his goal of becoming a pilot.

Sutton also suggests creating emotional distance from the perpetrator. He wrote about a university administrator who copes with bullies by pretending to be a doctor who specializes in diagnosing rare and extreme cases of "jerkism." Instead of stewing in negative feelings, the man tells himself how lucky he is to find such a "fascinating case."

Bullies need help, too.

If your child is exhibiting bullying behaviors, it's just as important to intervene, whether it's the first or twentieth time they've hurt someone. There's good reason to sweat the small stuff. Kids who bully not only damage others, but their aggression comes at a personal cost. As researcher Robert Faris told me, "A lot of the behaviors we think of as adolescent in nature are really the products of the environment. School isn't like a workplace where people have jobs, bosses, and subordinates."

Without a status structure, kids have to work it out for themselves. Aggressive children may accrue social capital, but there are psychic costs. Faris pointed out that these individuals have higher rates of depressive symptoms in high school, and probably in middle school as well. There also are long-term negative consequences. As Prinstein notes in his book *Popular*, kids who focus more on status than likeability and kindness tend to have higher rates of addiction, hatred, and despair later in life. (I'll come back to this idea in Chapter 8.)

Nip the behavior early, don't let your child make excuses for pathological behavior, and don't make the mistake of thinking it's a phase. As Borba told me, "Each time the behavior is repeated, it starts to wreak havoc with their moral compass." They depersonalize their target, their empathy levels go down, and they start to view the bullying as acceptable. None of this will serve them well in the adult world. I exchanged emails with Kathy Noll, author of *Taking the Bully by the Horns*, who recommends asking the following questions: "What did you do? Why was that a bad thing to do? Who did you hurt? What were you trying to accomplish? Next time you have that goal, how will you meet it without hurting anybody? How will you help the person you hurt?" These questions will help them acknowledge their actions and the consequences of their behavior.

You also can gather evidence and information that points to where, when, and why your child is being cruel. Do they want social power? Are peers egging them on? Have they learned the behavior from observing it in other children or adults? Do they lack the empathy to understand the impact on others? Do they have anger or jealousy issues? What does the behavior look like? What are the coaches, counselors, teachers, and other adults in their life observing? Bullying peaks in middle school, and some children may view it as a normal way to get their needs met.

If the school contacts you about an incident or pattern of behavior, take it seriously and work together to brainstorm effective interventions. Does your child need to be separated from certain kids? Should they join a social skills group, or watch videos and read books about bullied children? Perhaps they have a poor self-concept and would benefit from engaging in meaningful service work. Ideally, any school consequences will involve making amends, because restorative justice is more impactful than suspensions. As soon as you're aware that there's a problem, start monitoring your child's progress. Ask for regular updates from the adults in their life, then hold them accountable for their actions. You can be loving and empathetic, yet still firm about your expectations.

Don't be afraid to intervene when you overhear your child talking with friends about mean behavior. And don't count out boys when it comes to relational aggression. Contrary to gender stereotypes, boys form alliances, gossip, and make derogatory comments, too. As Faris noted, "Most kids want to be kind people, but meanwhile they're waging this coordinated campaign of ostracism and harassment on social media, and they're torturing someone." Your child might believe the person did something to deserve that kind of treatment, and you need to explain that it's never acceptable or justified. Talk about what it means to be an upstander, and say, "That's not what a good person would do." There's tremendous power in the disappointment of a parent, especially if it's because of a lapse in character.

Parents may not worry about their child's behavior because they do well in school and have plenty of friends, but look deeper. What is the quality of those friends? Faris told me, "I'd be concerned if my child were super popular, because it brings a lot of risks, and parents can be complacent." For his research, he followed children from sixth through twelfth grade and found that as they got closer to the dense core of a social network, they were more likely to bully their peers to achieve status. When they reached the top, however, they no longer acted aggressively.

"This was an important finding, because it suggests it's not just sadistic behavior," Faris explained. "It's consistent with the idea that they're using aggressive behavior to climb the social ladder." When they get there, they no longer need to behave that way. He was shocked by the fact that kids are far more likely to act aggressively toward their friends than non-friends. They get the biggest status boost when their targets are high status, or aggressive themselves, or in their own friendship circle. As a result, your aggressive child probably lacks close, loyal friends. They can be popular, mean, and wildly disliked. By definition, they're occupying a position near the top and probably have more frenemies than friends.

In the same way that you'd help a bullied child branch out socially, aggressors need to expand their friend group. When kids feel rooted, they're less likely to social-climb or prioritize toxic friendships. You can emphasize that engaging in behavior for status is ephemeral, but the scars from bullying last forever. Your child is likely to encounter some meanness throughout their life, whether it's in the workplace or in their personal life. Teach them now that no one benefits from acting like a bully, and no one deserves to be bullied.

TOP TIPS FOR PARENTS

- Never promise your child you won't tell—they need you as their advocate.
- Don't interview for pain, and try to manage your own anxiety.
- Document everything and understand your school's bullying policies. There may be forms to complete. Work with the school.
- Find alignment situations that play to your child's strengths.
- Brainstorm a list of real and imaginary advisors your child can consult in difficult situations.
- Highlight celebrities who talk openly about being bullied.
- Have kids list their idiosyncrasies and the upside of each trait.
- Show how body language can establish boundaries. Identify problem spots, whether it's the cafeteria or online.
- Help them choose a song lyric or personal mantra they can repeat to avoid ruminating, such as, "I don't deserve to be treated like this."
- Don't assume your aggressive child is fine because they have lots of friends. Kids who bully pay a price, too.
- Intervene whenever you overhear kids planning to do something mean or talking negatively about a classmate.

CONVERSATION STARTERS

- "I can't ignore what's happening to you, but we can figure out together what you'd like me to say to your school."
- "When and where do you feel unsafe at school?"
- "Let's come up with some strategies for when you can't avoid that person who's giving you trouble."
- "I know you feel bad about this part of yourself, but here's why I think it's a strength in disguise."

CHAPTER 8

COPING WITH GOSSIP AND SOCIAL TURMOIL

[
KEY SKILLS
1—Make good friend choices
2—Negotiate conflict
9—Make responsible, healthy, and ethical choices
]

"This girl keeps telling everyone I stole her North Face jacket from her locker. It's such a lie!"

"I wouldn't go out with William, so now he's telling his friends I'm a lesbian."

"Everyone is saying I got arrested for shoplifting."

STEPHANIE CALLAS, A SCHOOL COUNSELOR IN TEXAS, WAS shocked by the uptick in drama when she switched her job from an elementary to a middle school. One of her new students, Gina, had been well-liked until seventh grade. That's when her classmate Caitlin accused her of hooking up with Caitlin's ex-boyfriend. It wasn't true, but it didn't matter. Caitlin and her friends started writing nasty comments about Gina on the bathroom wall. "They called her a ho and a bitch," Callas told me. "She was so upset she started to have thoughts of self-harm." The more Gina fell apart, the more attention she got.

Callas told Gina to stop feeding the negativity by dragging friends to the bathroom to look for new insults. She told the other girls to stop posting pictures of the graffiti on social media. Gina's friends kept giving her up-to-the-minute updates, which made it nearly impossible to end the cycle. "The mean girls and ringleaders would lie about doing it when I confronted them," Callas said. "I felt like I was spinning my wheels."

Middle school kids are acutely aware of the imaginary audience and believe they're being watched constantly. To them, gossip is hard evidence that they're being judged. They may feel wrongly characterized, angry, hurt, or powerless, then isolate themselves socially or refuse to go to school. Adults can feel as helpless as their child. Parents will ask me, "Should we get the school involved or would that make it worse? Should we call the other kid's parents? How can we protect our child's reputation?"

Gossip and bullying are both painful forms of relational aggression that can destroy a child's confidence and self-esteem, but gossip poses some unique challenges. There may be multiple parties involved, from the person who starts the gossip, to the object of the gossip, to the children debating whether to spread the gossip. Kids' futures and reputations are at stake when lies are spread online. When it's underhanded, a target may be completely unaware they're being trashed. Gossip gets altered and exaggerated as it spreads, and it can be used for any number of reasons. A child might resort to gossiping to fit in, impress someone, hurt a romantic rival, boost their own self-esteem, or get attention.

Containing gossip is like squeezing a tube of toothpaste, then trying to put it back inside. Or like emptying a pillowcase full of feathers on a windy day, then expecting to retrieve each one. It's impossible. But parents can help kids shake off embarrassment, compartmentalize negative social interactions, and shift to a gentler social group. Here are concrete ways to minimize drama and get them back on their feet.

Help your child regain a sense of normalcy.

It's not easy to extinguish gossip, especially when social media stokes the fire. Former middle school counselor Julia Guillen Williams shared a hypothetical situation with me, imagining herself as a middle schooler today. If she liked a boy, and she thought he liked her, too, she might send him a picture of her topless. He *might* like her too, she continued, but he's thirteen and impulsive, so he pulls out his phone to show the photograph to his friends at lunch. When they see it, they ask him to forward it to them. "Even if he's a straight-up guy, he might feel the pressure," Guillen Williams explained.

In a matter of seconds, everything changes for Julia. "I'm suddenly a whore for sending the picture, it's everywhere, and maybe it's been doctored so now I have someone's penis in my mouth. And my parents know, and everyone is gossiping about me, and that's not even the picture I sent. It's so hard because we can't get it back." Even adults may not know how to fix the mess; if they tried to collect all the kids' phones, the image could still crop back up on social media. Complicating matters further, the students may have violated statutes related to the transmission of illicit images. Most twelve-year-olds are living in the moment and have no idea about legalities.

Students in Julia's position may need help returning to school, especially if they stayed home for one or more days after the incident. Meet with your child, their school counselor, and an administrator to come up with a dry, boring statement they can repeat until everyone loses interest. "She can decide what she wants to say to the first fifteen girls who call her a slut or say they saw her photo," Guillen Williams said. "We encourage kids to say, 'That was a mistake and it's in the past,' or, 'I don't want to talk about it,' or, 'I'm not allowed to talk about it because someone will get suspended.'" When kids stay in a heightened emotional state, they keep the story alive.

Recognize how painful this is for your child, offer unconditional love and acceptance, and remind them that no one can take their dignity without their permission. Consider sharing your own traumatic experiences, too. That's what Dara did when kids spread mean gossip about her fourteen-year-old daughter, Lindsay. "These two girls knew she was recovering from bulimia, and they kept saying her hands had vomit on them," Dara told me. Lindsay retreated to her room to cry for hours at a stretch. Dara told her daughter that when she was thirteen, kids taunted her at overnight camp. At dances, her bunkmates would tell the boys that she never flushed the toilet. "I still remember the boys yelling 'Yuck' and running away from me," Dara said. "At the time, I thought I'd die, but I got through it. I told Lindsay that it hurt, but I'm okay, and I know she'll be okay too."

Children fare better when they understand that their social status isn't fixed. Emily Bazelon, author of *Sticks and Stones*, shared a personal experience with me to underscore that point. "I can joke about my friends 'firing me' in eighth grade because I'm fine. It's a painful moment, not the rest of your life. I wish I had believed that in middle school, because it would have made the whole thing a lot less loaded."

When your child comes home feeling raw, don't criticize or lob accusations. Give them a hug and listen. When they're able to engage in discussion, acknowledge their feelings. Say, "I can understand why that made you feel terrible." Then shift to problem-solving mode. Ask, "What do you want to try?" Let them take the lead, but help them generate a list of options and don't back off completely. Tell them not to engage with anyone who isn't directly involved in the drama. If they're angry, hurt, and plotting revenge, discourage retaliation. Ask, "How do you think that person will respond if you do that?" As difficult as it is to imagine in the rawness of the moment, your child might want to resume the friendship at a later date. Help them keep that door open by suggesting they "take a break" rather than write the person off forever. Then fight the urge to contact the other child's parent. You can't force another kid to be kind, and the conflict could get blown out of proportion.

Be mindful that you bring your own issues to the table. Jessica Donovan, head of Sheridan School, tells parents about the time her best friend, Jennifer Hale, dumped her in sixth grade. "Out of some miracle from heaven, the popular group decided that she could be part of their group. I wasn't invited and was devastated," Donovan told me. When she was forty, she forwarded an email to her father from a realtor coincidentally named Jennifer Hale. He wrote her back immediately. "Jennifer Hale, that bitch—we're not talking to her, are we?" She had healed, but her father still remembered her old wound. "It's important for parents to know their kids can get through these things, and we need to let them let it go," she said. Send the consistent message that time will help, and that you believe your child can and will rise above the drama.

Beyond platitudes, point out to kids that they can't control how others perceive them. Teach them to let go of the need to defend themselves or to restore their reputation. Although they can and should contradict a rumor at the outset, they can make it worse by persistently and widely denying it. Ask, "If someone accused you of being an alien from outer space, would you feel the need to contradict such an absurd statement?" Encourage them to discredit gossip by moving on to other topics of conversation. As cyberbullying expert Sameer Hinduja said to me, "Kids talk smack. How much does it really matter in the scheme of things? People are always going to hate on you." He suggests that parents use examples from pop culture, politics, and sports to illustrate that people who have tons of fans also have plenty of haters. He'll reference the singer Taylor Swift. "Look at her body of work, which is so good. If we're okay with our decisions and the difference we make, we have to let people squawk."

You also can point out that this is a struggle for adults, too. Child and adolescent psychotherapist Katie Hurley explains, "We're in murky waters, trying to cope with political turmoil and 'fake news.' We turn to magazines like *Us Weekly* and say, 'Did you hear what happened to Gwen Stefani?' We have this feeling in America that it's our right to talk about celebrities and comment on what's going on in athletes' and musicians' personal lives." If you're in the drugstore, point out inconsistencies among magazines. One might claim a celebrity is having a baby, while a second claims she's divorcing, and a third says she's struggling with infertility. As Hurley noted, "One probably isn't true, and two aren't very nice." She'll ask her daughter how that celebrity might feel if she were trying to have a baby, walked to Rite-Aid, and saw the article. Break down why it's harmful.

Don't spread the meanness.

Kids don't always know how to respond to gossip. Give them the language to leave a conversation that's making them uncomfortable. They can act dubious and poke holes in a snippet of gossip by saying, "That doesn't sound true." Or they can offer a more positive perspective. For example, if their friend says, "Gina steals makeup from Walmart," your child can say, "That doesn't sound right—Gina has always been really honest." If they ask enough questions, the gossiper eventually will lose interest, get flustered, or run out of lies. A non-assertive child can still send a powerful message by refusing to engage, even if they have to bury their nose in a book.

In reality, kids often get drawn in because it's a tantalizing story or because they don't want to be left out of the conversation—or cast aside altogether. One seventh-grade girl told Hurley that the worst part of lunch is that "the best story" wins. It might be the most hurtful story, or a self-inflating story designed to elicit sympathy or attention. For that child, lunch always ended up being an exercise in one-upmanship, so she opted out entirely. "I tell kids, 'Think of the iceberg; what you see at the top is only the part that's sticking out," Hurley said. "If you go under the water and put on that scuba suit, you can think about what's driving them." Maybe the gossiper is lonely, or not getting enough attention at home.

Once kids have heard the gossip, they may not know what to do with the information. When the gossip is about a friend, it can feel disloyal to keep them in the dark. Explain that if they don't want to spread the meanness, they have to let the rumor die with them. When kids don't know what was said about them, they can't internalize the message. Plus, what others think about them is none of their business. Eileen Kennedy-Moore told me she tells parents, "You don't want your kids devoting their life to tracking down what anybody ever said about them. Kids will say, 'But it's about me, I have to know.' No, you don't."

— IDEA FOR EDUCATORS —

FACILITATE STUDENT-LED DISCUSSIONS

Ask students to lead a discussion in homeroom or advisory about gossip. They can consider a range of questions: "What's the difference between benign and mean-spirited gossip? What can someone do to squelch gossip, or to change the tone of a conversation? How can a person disengage when they feel uncomfortable? Why do people gossip in the first place? What conclusions do you draw about classmates who regularly spread gossip? How does gossip erode the school climate for everyone?" The students also can brain-storm their own questions. Afterward, have them create and sign a social contract laying out their expectations for one another.

Protect their reputation.

When it's destructive gossip, social media can magnify a rumor and give it staying power. Use headlines to help kids understand the potential consequences. There are so many stories, including one that came out of the white supremacist rallies in Charlottesville, Virginia. Civil rights activists identified people they thought had marched, but they misidentified Kyle Quinn, a professor at the University of Arkansas. Quinn's life was totally upended. Strangers threatened him and people pressured the university to fire him. He told NPR it felt like being chased by a mob.

.If your child is portrayed online in a negative light, it can have a lasting personal and professional impact. According to a CareerBuilder survey, 70 percent of employers look at an applicant's online presence, and 37 percent look to see what others have posted about a job candidate. I spoke to *Shame Nation* author Sue Scheff about how social media has magnified shaming and gossip. She advises parents to look at the memes and comments their kids post, because everything is public, and their on-line friends reflect their character. Even if other people post crude comments on their Facebook page, they can be read. As Scheff noted, "It's hard to teach that to eleven- and twelve-year-olds." To help your child understand the line between acceptable and inappropriate, go online with them. Point out comments you think are mean, stay involved, and use any mistakes as teaching moments.

To minimize reputational damage, remind your child not to friend or follow people they don't know, or to interact with anyone who pressures them to share sexual images or disclose private information. Tell them not to respond to online comments that make them feel belittled, ashamed, or uncomfortable, and to seek adult help when they're unsure how to proceed. "I'm a big fan of blocking," Hinduja told me. "If someone is a jerk, cut them out of your life. Kids are hesitant to block or unfollow and unfriend, but they should just protect themselves. Then report. Social media companies will get the content down."

Parents and schools also can contact officials at companies such as Instagram, and they'll remove posts that violate the terms of use. Do whatever you can to help your child preserve propriety, including discouraging oversharing. Children are spontaneous, and they chase likes, comments, and laughs. Remind them that anyone could use something they say or post to harm them. You can't count on your child to initiate conversation with you when they're in over their head, so talk often and keep that door open. "Years ago, we had the sex talk, and now we have to add the text talk," Scheff told me. You don't have to monitor every single text and post (and you probably don't want to), but spot check them periodically to make sure your child is making safe and responsible choices. Ask them to teach you the latest technology as a way to encourage dialogue about their online life.

The decisions they make online can have repercussions that leak into their school life. Julia Guillen Williams recalled one student, Jon, who enjoyed gaming on a public forum with strangers. "One of the players, 'Boogie Man 5,' teased Jon about liking this girl Catherine. Boogie Man 5 wouldn't reveal his identity, and Jon had no idea who he was," she told me. Jon worried it was a classmate who'd tell everyone about his crush, and the possibility of exposure made him too anxious to focus or talk to anybody at school. In cases like this, enlist the help of counselors and administrators. Some kids worry they'll be exposed as a snitch if they seek help, but reassure them that schools can claim they obtained the information from "someone in the community."

Technology makes everything more challenging, but it's hard to rein in kids' social media consumption. According to the Pew Research Center report *Teens, Social Media & Technology 2018*, 95 percent of thirteen- to seventeen-year-olds have access to a smartphone, and 45 percent of teens say they're online "almost constantly." That's nearly double the number of kids who admitted that much use in the last Pew report. Meanwhile, the news is full of stories about pernicious gossip, Internet addiction, increased suicide risk, early exposure to porn, and wrecked reputations. It's no wonder parents are unsure what to do. They may ask whether they should instruct their child to avoid social media altogether, delay giving them a smartphone, forbid certain apps, use blocking software, or monitor everything they do online. They may not feel their child has the maturity to handle having a computer in their pocket, but worry they'll isolate them socially.

There are no easy answers. Regardless of when you give your child a phone, they'll be exposed to social media at friends' houses or at school. Every child needs to learn how to navigate sticky situations. Present your child with hypothetical scenarios before they get online. What would they do if they became embroiled in a malicious text chain, or a friend threatened self-harm, or they saw doctored photos on social media? The apps du jour will keep shifting, so teach your child how to behave across platforms. Emphasize that your family values civility and kindness in all contexts, and that there's no such thing as true privacy or secrecy online.

Some parents are mobilizing to delay smartphone use. In Westport, Connecticut, the "Wait Until 8th" pledge empowers parents to put off giving their children a smartphone until at least eighth grade. They hope that by banding together, they'll decrease the pressure felt by both kids and parents. Emily Bazelon believes we've made a mistake culturally in giving iPhones to eleven-year-olds. "The danger isn't stranger danger, it's the harm they cause people because they're not getting the empathy cues you get from face-to-face contact," she explained. "If parents can collectively delay, that's better."

Researcher Jean Twenge has studied the connection between cell phones and teen mental health. She's written that between 2010 and 2015, the number of US teens who reported that they felt joyless surged by 33 percent. Teen suicide attempts increased by 23 percent, and the number of thirteen- to eighteen-year-olds who committed suicide jumped 31 percent. She has found that the generation of teens she calls "iGen"—those born after 1995—is much more likely to experience mental health issues than millennials.

After looking at several large surveys, Twenge concluded that one possibility for the shift is teens' use of smartphones and their accompanying increase in social isolation. By 2015, 73 percent of teens had access to a smartphone, and those who spent five or more hours a day online were 71 percent more likely than those who spent only one hour a day online to have at least one suicide risk factor. These risk factors rose significantly after more than two hours of use a day, and increases were more pronounced among girls.

Among eighth graders in particular, those who spent ten or more hours a week on social media were 56 percent more likely to say they were unhappy than those who devoted less time to social media. As Twenge noted in an article in *The Atlantic*, "Have Smartphones Destroyed a Generation?," the reverse is also true. Kids who spend an above-average amount of time with peers in person are 20 percent less likely to say they're unhappy than those who hang out with friends for a below-average amount of time.

That said, Devorah Heitner, author of *Screenwise*, says that "thoughtful, sensible mentorship and staying observant about your child's mental health will lead to a better understanding than simply reading headlines and growing concerned." When Twenge discussed her study in *The Atlantic*, she "stirred something of a panic among parents," Heitner told me. "It garnered so much media attention that it seems like more than one study, but the research cited is far from conclusive. We don't know that devices and time spent on them makes kids depressed, but we do know that if kids are not getting enough sleep, it can wreck their physical and mental health."

National Institutes of Health researchers are conducting a study to collect more information, using MRI machines to scan the brains of 11,000 kids at twenty-one testing sites across the country. Early results show that more than seven hours a day of screen time changes how adolescents' brains develop, and more than two hours a day lowers their scores on language and thinking tests.

While scientists collect data, I recommend that parents limit their child's non-school-related technology use to less than two hours a day, and lay down the law when it's time to power down electronics and go to sleep. Stay present in your child's online and offline life, and be attuned to their emotional state. Make sure they're engaging with people, whether they play a sport, join a chess club, or participate in a religious youth group. If they've been the subject of mean gossip, help them reach out to old, trusted friends. And remind them that face-to-face adult support is always available. Kids who spend excessive time online may need it the most, but could be least likely to reach out in person. I've started asking all of my students to silently identify the adult they'd go to in a crisis. Many don't understand that peers are ill-equipped to handle big problems. By asking this simple question at home, you'll normalize seeking help.

The silver lining is that targets of gossip often develop skills and insights that foster resiliency. They may become more adept at choosing a supportive peer group. The experience also may heighten their empathy or hone their ability to accept criticism. They may develop a more nuanced grasp of human behavior and the role of emotions such as jealousy or insecurity. They may also begin to understand that the person spreading malicious gossip is probably trying to make themselves feel better because they either have low self-esteem or want to rise in the social hierarchy. In other words, the behavior reveals much more about the gossiper than the target.

Your child also can learn from their own mistakes. Although nothing excuses relational aggression, self-reflection is never a bad idea. Maybe they wouldn't have sent that text or used that app. Perhaps they would have enlisted an adult's help before the situation got out of control, or spotted the brewing problem earlier in the game. If they can take an objective, unflinching look at their own role, they may avoid a similar situation in the future. Debrief with them and ask, "What have you learned about yourself, or about protecting your reputation?" This might be small comfort in the moment, but they might fare better than the gossiper in the long run. As researcher Jamie Ostrov told me, "It's a little counterintuitive, but we know from longitudinal studies that relational aggression is associated with substance abuse, relationship troubles in general, eating pathology, and personality disorders."

TOP TIPS FOR PARENTS

- Help your child flesh out a dry, boring story they can repeat to decrease interest in gossip about them.
- Share personal stories that normalize their experience and show you can come out on the other side.
- If your child shares details about their own or someone else's friendship conflicts, help them identify and engage solely with the core players. Discourage retaliation.

- Consider therapy if your child refuses to attend school, can't stop ruminating, withdraws socially, cries frequently, loses interest in once-loved activities, or exhibits changes in eating or sleeping habits.
- Instruct them to let any gossip they hear die with them so they don't spread the meanness.
- Get online with them and point out comments you think are mean or gossipy. Stay involved and use any missteps as teaching moments.
- Talk about the apps they like and make social media part of your normal discussions. Limit their use of technology.
- Give them lines they can use when someone else gossips, such as, "Well, she seems to like you," or, "I wonder if that's even true."
- Remind your child not to reply to comments that make them feel belittled or ashamed.
- Instruct them to unfollow, unfriend, or block people as needed. Contact officials at social media companies if you need them to take something down that violates their terms of service.

CONVERSATION STARTERS

- "When you're ready to talk, I'm here to listen. I'm so sorry this happened."
- "I can understand why you're upset. Is there anything you'd like to try that you think might improve the situation?"
- "How would you handle a situation in which someone spread mean gossip?"
- "If someone tried to gossip with you, how could you change the topic?"

CHAPTER 9

GROWING UP SEXUALLY HEALTHY

> ## KEY SKILLS
> 1—Make good friend choices
> 6—Self-advocate
> 9—Make responsible, healthy,
>   and ethical choices

"What happens if I put the tampon in the wrong hole?"

"If I ask the same girl out, like, ten times, is that sexual harassment?"

"I hate the way I look. I don't like my hair, my skin, my body, my clothes, really pretty much anything."

"I DO KNOW HOW BABIES ARE MADE," MY THEN NINE-YEAR-OLD son, Alex, told his thirteen-year-old sister, Emily. She ignored him. "Mom, he really doesn't," she told me from the back seat of the car. "You better tell him before he goes to camp and hears it from older kids." She was right. I'd talked to him about love for years, but I must have glossed over the mechanical piece. I was late to the game. As sex educator and author Deborah Roffman told me, "If we're not deliberately reaching out to kids by third grade, almost everything they learn after that is going to be remedial." You can explain sexual intercourse in the service of reproduction to six-year-olds.

The statistics underscore the importance of talking about sexuality. According to the results of the 2009 Youth Risk Behavior Survey, up to 20 percent of sixth graders, up to 33 percent of seventh graders, and up to

42 percent of eighth graders have engaged in sexual intercourse, depending on the geographic location. For many parents, the entire topic feels overwhelming. By middle school, there are so many components to cover, including dating, sexual orientation, gender identity, consent, harassment, and pregnancy prevention. Throw in information about puberty, body image, self-care, and safety, and it's no wonder we miss a few details along the way.

Not long after I got my son up to speed, I taught middle school health and wellness for the first time. No amount of parenting readies you for a roomful of curious thirteen-year-olds in varying stages of maturity. To prepare me, my principal showed me questions kids had asked anonymously in the past. "How many times can you ask a girl out before it's considered harassment? Is it possible for a boy to put his penis in the wrong hole? What does 'giving head' mean?" Well, okay, then. I could do this. I took a deep breath and dove in.

Since then, I've come to understand that middle schoolers want to know about much more than just the mechanics of sex. They're also curious about relationship issues and body image. They've asked me questions including, "How can you convince someone to like you as more than a friend? What if my crush lives on my street and I'm too nervous to go outside?" A male student asked me if it's okay for boys to diet, and a group of girls once came to see me to make a plea: "Can you PLEASE tell the boys that it's not okay to ask girls to take off their clothes?"

Alas, unlike school counselors and sex educators, parents can't offer their child anonymity. It's not always easy for kids to ask questions and share concerns. And with so much factual ground to cover, you can get stuck in the weeds and fail to connect with them. To avoid overloading them with information, consider the broader framework. As Roffman explains to parents, kids have five core needs when it comes to sexuality. They need affirmation and unconditional love; information about healthy and unhealthy behaviors; clarity about values such as respect and integrity; appropriate boundaries and limits; and guidance about making responsible, safe choices. At an age when the body tends to mature faster than the mind, kids want to know what's normal and what's next. It can take some courage to tell them.

Admit discomfort, stay calm, and fill in gaps.

Start by acknowledging your discomfort, then tell your child you're going to talk about it anyway. You'll normalize the dialogue and create a safe space for them to ask questions. If they say something that shocks you, give yourself time to process. That may mean talking to a friend or partner first, or coming up with an excuse to leave the room and collect yourself. Be authentic and tell them if you need time to reflect. Do your best to stay nonjudgmental.

The payoff is that your child will turn to you when they need you most. One of my former students, Nicole, grew up openly discussing sex and other sensitive topics with her parents. One afternoon in eighth grade, she engaged in a sexually provocative online conversation with someone who claimed to be a local teen boy. She told him personal details, including where she lived. When he asked her to meet him at the mall, Nicole decided to go, but she told her parents she was meeting a girlfriend. At the last minute, Nicole got cold feet and confessed her plan. Her mother called the police, but they never figured out whether the person was a fourteen-year-old boy or a fifty-year-old man.

Nicole's mother didn't overreact, but she explained to Nicole that she could have put herself in grave danger. She alerted the school to be on the safe side, and she talked to her daughter about exchanging personal information and sexual innuendo with a complete stranger. Nicole cried because she was scared and embarrassed, but she was receptive to the advice.

While some kids are open books, others are intensely private. They bring their own issues to the table, whether they're uncomfortable with their developing sexuality or have secret fears. One of my students, Carla, believed she'd get a disease every single time she had sexual intercourse, so she planned to stay celibate forever. Her parents tried to talk to her about her worries, but Carla shut them down. When that happens, don't force the issue. Give your child space and say, "I can see you're really uneasy, and that's okay. We don't need to talk right now, but let's figure out the best way to get you the information you need."

In Carla's case, her parents gave her developmentally appropriate, factually accurate books about sex, gender, and reproduction to read on her own time. It's a method I've used as both a parent and an educator. I keep several books on sex and puberty visible on my counseling office bookshelves. On more than one occasion, I've returned to find giggly kids racing out. When that happens, I know I'm going to find several books scattered across my floor. Provide online resources, too, such as the website AMAZE (amaze.org), which is geared toward ten- to fourteen-year-olds and features animated videos about sexual development.

Don't make assumptions about what your child knows. Kids can make incredible leaps in logic and come to outlandish conclusions. One of my friend's daughters believed that horseback riding and bicycling would endanger her fertility. A sixth-grade student worried that tampons could travel up through her body. One morning at work, I found three eleven-year-old girls waiting for me. They wanted to discuss their fears about getting their period, so we set up a time to talk. They returned with six more friends. All nine girls crammed into my small office and started rattling off questions. I really felt for them. They worried that others would know when they got their period for the first time, and that they wouldn't know how to find tampons or pads if it happened at school. They wondered what they should do if they got their period during a sleepover, or while wearing white pants. One girl asked, "Exactly how much blood and pain are we talking about here?" Only two had discussed menstruation with their parents.

This is a conversation you want to have long before your daughter turns eleven. You can allay her anxiety by talking through different scenarios. For many girls, it's reassuring to know they can keep a pad in their backpack just in case.

Boys also need you to debunk myths and misconceptions. Some are concerning. A sex educator told me he taught a boy who believed that if he cleaned his genitals with a medical disinfectant after sex, he wouldn't get a sexually transmitted disease. A father once told me his eighth-grade son was using a stain remover stick to masturbate. "Doesn't he realize that stuff is full of chemicals?" he asked me. "I'd never think to spell that out for him, but seriously? Anything else in his bathroom would have been a better choice."

Parents often incorrectly assume their child will make logical inferences. One mother gave her son detailed information about intercourse, but later discovered he had no idea what he was supposed to do with the condom *after* sex. "It didn't occur to him that he should take it off before it leaks," she said. She realized she needed to break down sex the same way his teachers broke down big assignments.

Talk about your family's values.

When Roffman talks to parents, she asks them to list at least five values they want their children to bring to every sexual situation they encounter over the course of their lives. Help your child internalize the importance of compassion, integrity, and respect. Talk about the concept of personal space and what it means to respect your own and others' boundaries. Emphasize self-determination, safety, and honesty, too, because these are the kinds of values that are violated in a sexual assault. If you don't share your values with your children, they'll draw their own conclusions. It's a developmental imperative. As Roffman says, "Adolescence is a time of pushing and pulling against parents, so you have to know what your parents believe. If you don't, you'll make it up."

As with any topic, you can share your own experiences with your child, but think deeply about why you're doing it. Will the anecdote teach them how to assess a situation or make smart decisions? Don't hesitate to draw a line if your child asks you intrusive questions. You'll be modeling that it's important to be judicious with self-disclosure. You want your child to recognize the risks of oversharing. If they spell out every detail of their first heartbreak in a group text, for example, they might end up feeling exposed.

Consider your child's developmental readiness, too. For example, it would be inappropriate to share your past drug use with an eleven-year-old who can't contextualize the information. That doesn't mean you can't talk about how drinking beer or using marijuana could adversely impact their ability to make good decisions. Similarly, you can emphasize that sexual situations should feel comfortable and unpressured without having to discuss your own sex life.

Take steps to prevent sexual harassment.

When Roffman's eighth graders wanted to teach fifth graders about consent, they showed them an image of the prince kissing Sleeping Beauty. They also showed them nonsexual examples of consent. By the end of the presentation, the students understood why Sleeping Beauty was incapable of agreeing to the kiss. Roffman often will weave in metaphors to make a point. She likes to walk around her classroom, take valuable objects from kids' desks, then walk out of the room with them. When she returns, she'll ask, "How was I supposed to know that I shouldn't take it?" Her students learn that it's not about the absence of no, it's about the presence of yes.

The news is full of adult examples of sexual harassment, but middle schoolers aren't immune. A 2014 University of Florida survey of 1,300 middle school students found that 25 percent had experienced verbal and physical sexual harassment. The statistics don't improve as they enter their later teens. As part of the Making Caring Common project, Harvard Graduate School of Education researchers interviewed more than 3,000 young adults and high school students nationally and found that 87 percent of the female respondents reported experiencing some form of sexual harassment, but 76 percent of survey respondents had never had a talk with their parents about how to avoid sexually harassing others.

As a school counselor, I often see kids test out inappropriate behavior. A few male students once invented "Hump Tag," a game that's exactly what it sounds like. They only got to play that game once. Students also will make comments about one another's bodies. One boy kept referring to a classmate's breasts as "double eggs." (He didn't quite have the terminology down.)

Every few years, girls will complain to me about boys snapping their bras. The first time this came up, I had a middle school flashback. In seventh grade, "Darren" demanded to know my cup size. We were at a pool party and I was wearing a bathing suit, which only added to my discomfort. At school, he'd snap my bra, using a ruler for extra leverage. I'd spin around and slug him, but it never occurred to me to tell an adult. In contrast, my twenty-first century students are much more sophisticated. A few of my female eighth-grade students invented a prototype for a "Shock Bra" designed to electrically stun anyone who touched them against their will. They were surprised to discover that a twenty-four-year-old female aeronautical engineer in India had already invented this product in 2014. Manisha Mohan, the creator, called it "SHE," an acronym for Society Harnessing Equipment.

Social media is creating new avenues for harassment. Girls Leadership founder Rachel Simmons wrote in *HuffPost* about a fourteen-year-old girl who pulled out her phone in class to find a Snapchat from a boy asking if she wanted to measure the size of his penis. And a therapist in Toronto told Simmons that a male student texted her fourteen-year-old client during class to ask her to perform oral sex on him in the bathroom. These types of incidents are not rare. A seventh grader once told me that a male classmate couldn't understand why she wouldn't take off her clothes if he was willing to do the same thing. "How many times do I need to tell him no? Can you tell him I don't even *want* to see him naked?" she asked me. (I worked with an administrator to put an end to that.)

When I teach students about consent, they often get bogged down in legalities. They'll ask, "Will you get arrested if you're the one sending the photo of yourself?" Or, "If you date someone a lot younger, can you go to jail?" I could spend hours answering these kinds of questions, but it's more preventive to teach kids how to step into someone else's shoes. Jelena Kecmanovic, a psychologist in Arlington, Virginia, who writes about consent, explained to me that perspective-taking and increasing empathy are the best safeguards against sexual harassment. Ask your child, "How would you feel if someone treated you like that? How do you think your friend would feel? Or your sister?" Point out the distinction between emotions, which can't be controlled, and behaviors, which can be. No matter how they feel, they can choose to behave respectfully.

As you discuss sexual harassment and consent with your child, don't neglect to discuss pornography, which can contribute to unhealthy attitudes and beliefs about sex, even among middle schoolers. Parents often tell me there's no way their child has seen porn, but statistics suggest they may be naive. In one study, researchers at the University of New Hampshire found that 42 percent of a sample of 1,500 Internet users ages ten to seventeen had seen porn in the prior year, with two-thirds reporting only unwanted exposure. According to the organization Break the Cycle, the average age of first exposure to pornography is now around eleven. I shared this number while at dinner with a friend whose son is eleven, and she was dubious. The next day, however, she sent me this text: "So, you were 1000 percent correct. A. admitted that he's seen pornography! Now what am I supposed to do?!"

In a 2018 *New York Times Magazine* article, writer Maggie Jones reported that increasing numbers of teens are using porn as a "how-to" guide. As a result, teen boys in particular are confused and asking, "Do girls really like rough or violent sex, or does porn misrepresent their desires? How could their own performance possibly measure up to what they're seeing online?" One teen boy told Jones that he wonders whether girls will like him if he doesn't do it like the guys in porn. Several of my male students were exposed to porn in elementary school when a classmate shared a link to an X-rated website. Those boys are all in middle school now, but they were nine at the time. One of them told me, "I really wish I hadn't seen it then. I didn't understand what I was seeing, and it really upset me."

After the *New York Times* article was published, I was deluged with calls from parents. A few knew their kids were frequenting porn sites, and others just wanted to be proactive, but they all had the same question as my friend: "How should we address this issue?" I facilitated a group conversation with interested parents, and one mentioned that she had set up a firewall to block access to sites. "When can I stop policing him?" she wanted to know. "When will he just *know* not to do that? I know I won't be able to prevent his access forever."

I had to break it to her that she couldn't prevent his access even then. No firewall will protect against friends with phones or older siblings. Never underestimate a thirteen-year-old's curiosity. And that makes education and modeling that much more important. Focus on teaching critical thinking skills rather than steering behavior, and help your child think through their choices and the potential outcome of their actions.

That means talking openly with them about the differences between healthy, unhealthy, and abusive behaviors in relationships. (We'll return to this idea in Chapter 10.) Initiate a two-way conversation about porn that doesn't involve judgment or blame, especially if you know they've already viewed it. Acknowledge that it's a difficult but important topic. Use these conversations to emphasize that both partners should agree beforehand to any sexual activity, and that manipulation and coercion are never okay. Share how pornography perpetuates misconceptions about sexual intercourse. Though it seems obvious to us as adults, kids need us to point out things like, "It's not realistic that the moment a woman and man meet they can immediately have penetrative sex for thirty minutes." Author and sex educator Yuri Ohlrichs, who teaches at Rutgers Netherlands, told me he also urges parents to point out that porn tends to portray a one-sided, stereotypical, heteronormative picture of sex.

As parents, we simply can't afford to ignore the topic. As Break the Cycle reports on its website, "Both violent and nonviolent pornography can make users more likely to support violence against women and to believe that women enjoy being raped. Worse yet, studies show these beliefs are predictive of a person being sexually aggressive in real life."

Address stereotypes and gender differences.

Try to maintain a positive approach to both male and female sexuality. While it's necessary to cover issues such as unwanted pregnancy, disease, and sexual harassment, that's not the whole story. You also want to address stereotypes and emphasize that sex should be pleasurable. As Ohlrichs told me, "Not all boys or men are going out there to have sex as much as they can. We have to make sure that boys understand that you're just as much a man if you're not experienced sexually as if you are."

Boys may struggle to admit they're not an expert, or that they feel pressured to achieve a certain body ideal. When we think of body image, we tend to think about girls, but researchers reported in the *Journal of Early Adolescence* that middle school boys are suffering just as much—and the more time they spend on social media apps, the worse they feel about their appearance. As one seventh-grade boy told me, "The stuff I see on social media makes it seem like I should be able to get abs in five minutes, but it's not so easy." Tell your son that taking a break from social media can preserve his confidence. If you provide openings to talk about his insecurities, you may even prevent problems from ballooning. As researchers reported in the journal JAMA *Pediatrics*, parents who neglect these kinds of concerns raise boys who are more likely to engage in high-risk behavior.

Address stereotypes about female sexuality, too. Girls throughout the world internalize the conservative idea that they need to protect their reputation, conceal excitement, and avoid taking initiative. The Making Caring Common survey supports this idea. The report revealed that 32 percent of male and 22 percent of female respondents think that men should be dominant in romantic relationships, whereas only 14 percent of males and 10 percent of females think that women should be dominant. Underscore that in the healthiest relationships, partners treat each other as equals.

Although there are no hard-and-fast distinctions, males and females might approach sexual scenarios differently. "Boys don't always understand that a girl might stop kissing because she's focused on what's going on around them. They might be all green lights and responsive to visual stimulants, but if a girl hears someone in the house or the boy says something that reminds her of a negative experience, it's over," Ohlrichs explained. Tell your child that in cases like this, the couple needs to work together to make it comfortable. You also can explain that if someone is giggling or nervous, it might not be a positive situation for them.

Girls may put someone else's needs in front of their own, have trouble expressing their limits, or second-guess themselves, *Girls & Sex* author Peggy Orenstein told me. They may think, "I don't want to be here, this is bad, but maybe it's not as bad as I think." Prompt your child to think about the signals that indicate someone isn't into the behavior. Orenstein often shares sexuality educator Al Vernacchio's pizza metaphor. "Sex is like pizza—you want the other person to like it; it's a shared experience; and you negotiate your toppings. If you don't negotiate your toppings, you'll end up with green pepper, and no one wants green pepper."

It's not enough to give girls a sense of agency; boys also must learn their part. Parents need to tell their sons that it's not okay to pressure girls for any reason, including to solicit nude digital photographs. One analysis found that more than two-thirds of girls had been pressured to send explicit images. As psychologist Lisa Damour wrote in a *New York Times* column, "That our focus has been so preponderantly on the sending, not requesting, of sexts underscores the exact problem we need to address. We accept and perpetuate the boys-play-offense and girls-play-defense framework because it is so atmospheric as to be invisible." If we don't talk about mutuality and reciprocity, and not just consent, then we're abdicating that responsibility to the media and the Internet.

As we share those messages, be aware that boys are grappling with the idea that they could be viewed as sexual harassers. They're asking how they can avoid crossing the line, and wondering whether it's just what they say and do, or if it's possible to simply look at someone the wrong way. When a boy at middle school head Rodney Glasgow's school announced, "I can look as much as I want," a girl called him "a future harasser." Another girl said, "Well, it depends on what you're looking at, and in what way." As Glasgow told me, "There's no space for them to process what it feels like to live on high alert, to be held accountable in a way that they've never been held accountable."

Make a point of having a serious conversation with your child about what constitutes sexual harassment. Ask them what they know about cat-calling and related behaviors. Let them know that both girls and boys can commit an offense, and that even comments intended as jokes can offend or scare someone. Role-play scenarios, such as how to get help if they're being harassed or see someone else getting targeted.

Even if you're thoughtful at home, schools may reinforce gender stereotypes. In 2017, a father in New South Wales was outraged when sixth-grade girls at his daughter's school were sent to get their hair done while their male classmates visited a hardware store and went out for a barbecue lunch. His letter to the principal made international news. He wrote, "When Ruby left for school yesterday, it was 2017, but when she returned home in the afternoon it was from 1968. Are you able to search the school buildings for a rip in the space-time continuum?" He wondered if there was perhaps a "faulty Flux Capacitor" hidden in the bathroom, adding, "I look forward to the school being returned to this millennium where school activities are not divided sharply along gender lines."

Then there's the issue of dress codes, which can be lopsided. When sex educator and writer Karen Rayne's daughter was in eighth grade, one teacher repeatedly tried to dress-code her because her straps were too narrow. "The epitome of creepy is a male middle school teacher telling a middle school student that her clothing is sexy," she told me, adding that blaming girls for their male classmates' inability to pay attention is equally offensive to boys. "We send the message that boys can't control themselves, so girls have to restrict their identity and movement in ways that are counter to their identities. Often what they're wearing isn't sexual to them—it's the school seeing it as sexual."

In an indirect way, Catherine Pearlman's thirteen-year-old daughter, Casey, an eighth grader in Southern California, changed her entire district's dress code policy. Pearlman, founder of The Family Coach and author of *Ignore It*, said the school dress-coded Casey two days in a row because her fingers didn't reach the end of her shorts. Casey had to change into boys' mesh basketball shorts before returning to class totally humiliated. "If she wasn't a distraction before, she definitely was now. Everyone was saying, 'Oooh, Casey was dress-coded.'" Pearlman already was annoyed by the double standard. A gym teacher had told the parents at Back to School Night that girls couldn't wear yoga pants to PE because "The boys could get turned on and get erections, and that would embarrass them."

Casey wrote to the principal, arguing that it was an unfair policy that disproportionately affected girls, but the principal responded that she had to adhere to district rules. Pearlman then wrote the principal a tongue-in-cheek letter inviting her to take her daughter shopping so she could experience the challenge of her "ridiculously long arms." She posted the letter on *The Today Show* website for parents, and it went viral. "Fifty percent thanked me, and 50 percent shamed me as a mother, saying I was raising a 12-year-old skank, or that a better mother would sew her daughter appropriate clothes," she told me, adding that not long after that, the district changed the policy. "They can no longer bring attention to girls' bodies in ways that make them uncomfortable. Before, they'd have the girls kneel and call them distracting."

Suspend judgment when it comes to gender or sexual identity.

In the past several years, my students have become more comfortable identifying as LGBTQ+, and more likely to use the expanded vocabulary available to them. Fewer middle schoolers are telling me, "I think

I might be gay." More often, they'll tell me they're pansexual, bisexual, or bi-curious. The New Oxford American Dictionary describes pansexual as "not limited in sexual choice with regard to biological sex, gender, or gender identity," meaning a pansexual just sees the person as a whole. Bisexual means they're attracted to both boys and girls, and bi-curious means they're interested in having a sexual experience with a person of the same sex. My friend Kerri, the mother of an eighth-grade girl, tells me her daughter is constantly scolding her for using the wrong terminology. She admitted, "It's so hard for us parents to keep up."

But even seemingly sophisticated kids who talk fluidly about gender and sexuality can be impressionable. A bunch of sixth-grade girls once stopped by my office to tell me they were lesbians. "You're all lesbians?" I asked. One of the girls nodded solemnly. "Yes. We took an online quiz." This was a new one. "What were the questions on the quiz?" I asked. There were only a few, including, "What's your favorite color?" and, "Do you smile when you see a pretty girl?" I told them that no quiz could determine their sexuality. That seemed to satisfy them and they headed to class. One girl, however, lingered behind. "What if I really am a lesbian?" Kate asked me. "Like, what if I want to kiss girls?" I asked Kate if she'd shared this information with her parents, and she said she was thinking about it.

The next morning, Kate stopped by my office. "I told my mom, and she didn't freak out at all," she said. I wasn't surprised, but I also knew she was lucky. Some parents may be shocked and struggle to remain calm, or they may insist their middle schooler is too young to know their sexual orientation. Try to imagine how you'd react if your child made this kind of disclosure. You want to be able to respond constructively in the moment. As Alisa Bowman, coauthor of *Raising the Transgender Child* and the parent of a thirteen-year-old transgender boy, told me, "Parents may think that if they make their child's life miserable, they'll somehow turn their child into something they're not, but that backfires in so many ways." If kids don't have their parents' acceptance, their self-confidence erodes and they can become easy targets.

One of Bowman's son's seventh-grade friends doesn't fit into traditional masculine ideals, and he shared with her that other students had been telling him to kill himself. "I said, 'That's completely unacceptable.

If I were your mom, I'd be in that school and talking to your teachers and those other students' parents.'" The boy was surprised by her reaction. He hadn't even told his parents about the mistreatment because he knew they'd be dismissive. As Bowman said, "As soon as you think who you are is wrong, you think, 'Wow, maybe I deserve to be bullied.'"

At the other end of the spectrum, I've had some parents tell me they're sure their kid is gay and wonder when they'll figure it out. Alex Myers, the first openly transgender student at both Phillips Exeter Academy and Harvard University, met with me in my office at Sheridan School after he presented to our parent community. He suggests that parents open the door but don't push them through it. "Don't tell your kid they're transgender or that they might be gay—let them come to that." He does recommend providing an opening. You can say something like, "I heard from the middle school that a sixth grader came out as transgender. What do you think about that?" Give them the language, and show them you're open and positive. Even supportive parents will make mistakes. It's important to do some self-reflection and information-gathering to get to an accepting place. You can't expect your child to help you work through it, so join a PFLAG support group or share your feelings with a friend.

Seek support from the school, too. Your child can connect with an understanding teacher or counselor or join a GSA (see Idea for Educators). GSAs provide kids with a safe space to explore their identity. According to a GLSEN school climate survey, in middle schools with GSAs, students hear 20 percent fewer homophobic remarks, feel 29 percent safer, and are 48 percent less likely to fall victim to bullying. GSAs also improve school culture by fostering inclusion and acceptance for everyone, not just those who identify as LGBTQ+.

Unfortunately, GSAs are still somewhat uncommon in middle schools. When my former principal, Chris Nardi, and I helped students start one in 2015 at Pyle Middle School in Montgomery County, Maryland, we were told that only one other middle school in the large district had one. I recently reconnected with teacher David Peake, the club's first faculty advisor. He said, "The chemistry reminded me of the most successful high school lacrosse team that I coached. It's a feeling of total trust, shared purpose, and togetherness." (I'll share the student founder's perspective in Chapter 16.)

Last year, Sheridan's middle school principal, Jay Briar, and I realized that we needed to supplement our school's GSA with an affinity group. Several students, including a few who were questioning their sexual identity, had been asking both of us for a way to connect with other "non-straight" kids. Briar brought the entire middle school together for a morning meeting, then sat on a stool at the front of the room. "I've only half-planned what I want to say," he told them, "but I realized it's been a while since I told my personal story. Most of you know I'm gay—after all, I'm married to a male teacher in this school. But I want to share a personal story that might help some of you."

Briar told them he met his spouse at an organized get-together for gay men in their twenties. "By that point, I'd been out for ten years and was old enough to have some confidence, but I was still so anxious," he said. When he arrived at the church where the meeting was held, he asked a stranger to pretend they were friends so he wouldn't have to walk in alone. The point of his story was clear—he understood how scary it could feel to show up for an LGBTQ+ affinity meeting. He reassured the students that he wouldn't need to ask for parent permission. He also said he'd do his best to be discreet about meeting times, "Not because it's a bad thing, but because it's a private thing. There will be no announcement saying, 'Hey everyone, the gay affinity group will be meeting at noon at table 10 for gay cupcakes.'" Four students approached him right after the meeting to ask if they could join the group "if I think I *might* be gay." As I watched the scene unfold, I was once again reminded of the importance of mirrors and windows (see page 54).

— IDEA FOR EDUCATORS —
FORM A GENDER AND SEXUALITY ALLIANCE

If your school doesn't already have one, form a GSA. Keep in mind that when straight allies participate, clubs may spend more time on advocacy than on supporting one another. To address this gap, consider offering LGBTQ+ students a designated meeting every month to talk about more intimate, personal concerns. Alternatively, create two separate clubs: a GSA and an LGBTQ+ affinity group. Make sure there are multiple avenues for sustained support, including the ability to refer to outside groups, in-school counselors, and other educators who can sensitively address these issues.

Weave the topic into regular conversations.

Even if you find the whole topic of sexuality awkward, the good news is that so much in life can be connected to human sexuality. You can find natural segues in everything from music to sports to romantic comedies, or draw inspiration from websites with adult-moderated dialogue boards for teens. At the dinner table, you don't have to say, "Sit down, I'm going to teach you about birth control tonight." You can get to the same place by discussing health-care policy, contraception co-pays, or news stories about the changing hookup culture. You also can use the news to pose indirect questions. If there's a story about inappropriate locker-room talk, you can ask, "Why do you think the men were talking this way?" Know that your son or daughter may be worrying about anything from their physical appearance to whether their fantasies are normal.

As you lean into the discussion, remember that different ages pose different challenges. As Deborah Roffman pointed out, "Parents will say, 'My child used to talk to me all the time and now they've stopped, what am I doing wrong?'" In her experience, more often than not the child in question is an eleven-year-old girl. "Girls that age can be self-conscious about their changing or not-changing bodies and pull in. They're not adults. They need us, but they're also looking for increasing independence." To earn that privilege, parents can explain to kids that they need to be willing to engage in conversation when they start new behaviors, such as dating.

Just because your child possesses factual data doesn't mean they comprehend it. When they pull information off the Internet, they may think they're experts. But even if they've spent hours on sites reading about gender identity or sexuality, they're still processing like middle schoolers. They don't know what they don't know. Use clear terminology and recognize that they're just as interested in the social piece. They may want to know the normal frequency for masturbation or sex, but they also want to explore their emotions and insecurities. Your most important task is to stay present, unfazed, and open to discussion.

TOP TIPS FOR PARENTS

- Make sure your child has accurate information. Debunk myths, whether they relate to sexual experience, consent, or ideas about what constitutes "normal." Get a sense of their current knowledge base.
- Talk about your core family values, such as responsibility, respecting personal boundaries, honor, courage, safety, or kindness.
- If your child says something shocking, take a moment to process with a partner or friend before reacting. It's okay to admit your discomfort.
- Have a conversation about pornography, which most kids will have purposely or inadvertently seen by age eleven.
- Recognize that you may misinterpret your child's comments. Stay calm and ask for clarification.
- Suspend judgment when your child talks about issues related to gender and sexual identity.
- Find ways to raise issues in a way that creates some personal distance.

CONVERSATION STARTERS

- "What are some stereotypes about girls and boys when it comes to sex and dating? Are there any that bug you? Are there ones that you agree with?"
- "Does your school teach you about sexuality? Do they give kids a chance to ask questions? Have any of the other students' questions really surprised you?"
- "Do you think I have a good sense of what you know about sex?"
- "If someone touched you inappropriately or commented on your body parts, how would you feel? What could you do? If someone did that to someone else, how do you think that person would feel?"

CHAPTER 10

PREPARING FOR LOVE

[
KEY SKILLS
1—Make good friend choices
2—Negotiate conflict
7—Self-regulate emotions
9—Make responsible, healthy,
and ethical choices
]

*"I think Ari is going to break up with me. Should I
dump him first?"*

*"If my parents were just going to fight all the time, why
did they bother getting married?"*

*"My best friend's bat mitzvah and my boyfriend's bar
mitzvah are on the same day. I've been crying all day
because I don't know which one I should attend."*

MELISSA, FOURTEEN, HAD JUST BROKEN UP WITH HER BOY-
friend, and she couldn't understand why he had lost interest. I was
her school counselor at the time, and she tearfully asked me what she had
done wrong. Had she texted him too much? Did she embarrass him when
she decorated his locker?

Whether my middle school students have a crush or need help coping with their parents' divorce, they often ask relationship questions.
"How do you know whether someone likes you? Is it possible to escape the
'friend zone' and convince someone to date you?" I grew up on romantic
comedies like *Sixteen Candles*, in which a love-struck girl rides off into

the sunset with a handsome older boy (who barely knows her name). I absorbed a skewed version of romance rooted in the idea that lasting love is nearly instantaneous. I had no idea that love can stealthily grow out of friendship.

The media influences may be different today, but the results are similar. If we don't teach our children about love, the outside world will do it for us. As child psychologist Richard Weissbourd told me, "We spend an enormous amount of time preparing people for work, but do nothing to prepare them for love. We've created this vacuum that TV, film, and video have filled, and there are a lot of immature ideas about love."

When kids learn to have healthy relationships, the impact is far-reaching. Kids who can navigate interpersonal minefields are more engaged and productive in school and life. There's no blueprint for this difficult, amorphous topic, but the answer isn't to avoid it altogether. According to Harvard's Making Caring Common project, 70 percent of teens want more information from their parents about the emotional aspects of romantic relationships, and 65 percent want more information from their schools. As one student in the report noted, "I think lots of middle schoolers and high schoolers experience trauma at their first and failed attempts at relationships, and this needs to be a focus."

In our culture, we have only one word, love, to describe a continuum of emotional states and experiences, and we're equally likely to apply that word to a middle schooler's first heartbreak or a couple's fiftieth anniversary. Weissbourd told me he thinks that's confusing and limiting. "When I said, 'I love you' to my wife on my wedding day, it meant something different than it does now. I may not be vibrantly excited about her every single day, but it's dazzling in a quiet way." If we want our kids to enjoy the full extent of that gift, we need to teach them how to take those first giddy, tentative steps toward love. Here are several ways to get the conversation started.

Give them what you've got.

Many parents have wisdom about love but feel insecure about their ability to advise their child. It's easiest to model a healthy relationship when you're in one, but you can draw on what you've learned from good and bad experiences. Whether you're divorced, married your first love, or have a history of choosing the wrong partners, you bring a valuable perspective to the table. Families and relationships take many forms, and everyone's journey will be different. This isn't about how happily coupled people can teach their children about love. Think about your relationships that floundered. Were there warning signs? What distinguished the ones that made you feel hopeful and happy? Share these observations with your child so they can begin to understand that meaningful relationships require empathy, focus, and mutual respect.

As you start to have these conversations, reflect on your middle school self. What did it feel like to have a crush? Do you recall being shy? Excited? Embarrassed? I shared my middle school "dating" memories with my then fourteen-year-old son and thirteen-year-old daughter, and they were appalled. When a seventh-grade classmate invited me to see a movie, I was taken off guard. I awkwardly answered the phone, told him I had seen the movie already, and hung up. The following year, a boy asked me to the eighth-grade dance, and I didn't do much better. I initially was okay with the idea, but then I panicked. When he called to arrange a time to pick me up, I bailed. My behavior reflected my immaturity, not any intent to be mean. I clearly wasn't ready to date anyone. (By today's standards, I was unusual. According to an RTI International study, 75 percent of middle schoolers say they've had or currently have a boyfriend or girlfriend.)

Whether or not your child is interested in dating, double down on teaching friendship skills. Like love, friendship requires kindness, tenderness, and considering someone else's perspective. To negotiate friendship, you need to be able to communicate effectively, regulate your emotions, resolve conflict, and recognize someone's strengths and weaknesses. It's great practice for future relationships. Help them identify the traits that make someone an attractive or unappealing friend. Ask, "How does it make you feel when your friend doesn't want you to hang out with anyone else?" Or, "I can tell you really like spending time with her. Why do you think you feel so at ease when you're together?" From there, pose questions that address kids' ethical obligations to one another. "What would you do if your best friend was cheating on her boyfriend? Do you think it's kind to break up with someone over text?"

You might be surprised by what you learn. An eighth-grade girl, Cora, once came to see me about a boy who kept trying to get her alone. She knew he wanted to kiss her, and she did not want to kiss him. She told me her solution was to carry an apple in her pocket at all times. Every time he leaned toward her, she took a bite and started chewing. He must have thought she really liked apples! Cora was proud of her ingenuity and pleased she didn't have to hurt his feelings. I was a bit alarmed that she didn't realize it was okay to just be honest. Role-play scenarios so your child can practice potential responses in advance.

Talk about online manipulation.

Emphasize that you expect your child to behave ethically online and off-line with romantic interests. "Kids are falling into relationships way too young and may practice emotional manipulation in the way they post, share, or invade digital privacy," cyberbullying expert Sameer Hinduja told me. "Even among twelve- to seventeen-year-olds, there's digital dating abuse and extortion. Someone can get something compromising from your phone and use it against you, whether they want more sexual content or money." A study published in the journal *Computers in Human Behavior* found that nearly a third of middle schoolers reported being a victim of electronic dating aggression, and nearly one-fifth reported being a perpetrator. The study also found a positive correlation between electronic dating aggression and physical dating violence.

Explain to your child that love shouldn't involve shaming, controlling, humiliating, or embarrassing anyone. Make sure they understand that online manipulation can take many forms. It might involve uploading sexual images of a partner, checking their text messages without permission, texting multiple times an hour to keep tabs on them, or putting them down online. Someone might demand that they "unfriend" former boyfriends or girlfriends, pressure them over social media to engage in undesired sexual acts, or leave threatening cell phone messages. Urge your child to seek adult help if they're victimized in any of these ways. If they're drawn to someone who mistreats them, help them talk through any confusing or intense feelings. Most middle schoolers don't yet have the tools to tell the difference between healthy and unhealthy relationships.

At the same time, give them information in a way that honors their intelligence. They're making the shift from thinking concretely to thinking abstractly, and lecturing won't work. When you engage them in dialogue instead of talking "at" them, they'll own their conclusions and be less likely to rebel against the content. Tell them how you fell in love with your partner. What were the qualities that you admired? Then ask your child what love means to them. Thomas Lickona, a developmental psychologist and professor emeritus at State University of New York College at Cortland, told me he recommends using relationship advice columns to spur conversation. Read the question together, but ask your child to share the advice they'd give before either of you looks at the answer. Don't be afraid to debate them, but don't dismiss their ideas as wrong.

Don't ignore outside influences.

The media can be detrimental, but parents can use it to their advantage. If you watch romantic comedies with your child, you can broach relationship issues without delving into the deeply personal. A misogynistic song or a young adult novel can prompt a discussion about love and respect. (If you're looking for suggestions, the Dibble Institute, which helps teens learn healthy relationship skills, provides parents with guided questions to encourage critical thinking about a number of popular teen movies; you can find them online at dibbleinstitute.org/movie-guides.)

Media literacy is an important skill. Lickona knows one teacher who had students watch a sitcom and log the number of insults. Afterward, the kids discussed how the interactions might impact the characters' relationships. I often use this strategy at home. My teens love the dating show *The Bachelor*, but the whole premise bothers me. A single man starts out with a pool of about twenty-five beautiful women, sleeps with an assortment of them, then eliminates contestants in each episode. At the end of the season, he picks a bride and proposes marriage. When my kids watch *The Bachelor*, I yell judgmental comments at the TV. My son will tease me and say, "But Mom, it's true love!" As much as I'd like to ban shows like this forever, I won't. They kick off too many productive conversations.

Schools can support parents' efforts by looking for natural segues in the curriculum to introduce the idea of healthy relationships (see Idea for Educators). Educators don't have to wade into controversial territory by dictating what students should value or by divulging details about their personal lives. They do need to build their empathy and their comfort with the topic. I spoke to Julie Frugo, head of Premier Charter School in St. Louis, about how important it is for teachers to understand what's going on cognitively, socially, and emotionally with kids this age. As she explained, "Yes, they may be twelve-year-olds breaking up with their boyfriends, but it's real, in-the-moment heartbreak for them."

Frugo's school offers elective courses that dive deeper into relationships than traditional health and wellness or sex education courses. Students break down common issues in relationships, such as how to handle a controlling boyfriend who constantly demands to see them. Teachers can use games to teach these concepts. Alexander Chan, a 4-H educator in Maryland, has kids play red flag, white flag. He told NPR that he'll describe a romantic scenario to the students, then ask them to hold up a red flag if they think the partners should break up, and a white flag if they think the situation can be remedied. Teaching these skills may even lead to calmer classrooms. As Lickona noted, "Ask any teacher—the disruptions in the class are never related to the lesson plan. If we can help young people navigate the minefields of relationships, their engagement and productivity in school and as adults will be better."

— IDEA FOR EDUCATORS —
LOOK FOR TIE-INS IN ALL SUBJECTS

Assign work that encourages critical thinking about healthy relationships. Don't limit the topic to health and wellness or sex education classes. In English class, students could act out a scene from a play like *Romeo and Juliet* and talk about where things went awry, or rewrite a scene to produce a happier ending, or discuss how the romance might have played out differently in contemporary times. In history class, students could analyze the role of relationships in a conflict they're studying. In science, they could talk about brain chemicals, hormones, and impulsivity. (As for math, I'm stumped. If any readers have ideas, please share them with me!)

The sex talk is important, but it's not everything.

The last chapter focused on teaching kids about sexuality, but parents need to prepare kids for the emotional risks, too. Tell your child that heartbreak is painful, but failed relationships serve a purpose. They can help them identify what they need from a partner and what they offer a partner. They'll also discover that powerful chemistry doesn't necessarily translate into good relationships. As Ginsburg says: "Lovemaking might include sex and heighten the experience, but healthy sexuality begins with simply caring about someone." When you talk about love this way, you give your child permission to feel sexual a very long time before they consider actually having sex. "They can feel as if they're growing up just by holding hands or noticing someone across the room," he explained.

TOP TIPS FOR PARENTS

- Tell your child that you love them and they deserve to be in a mutually supportive relationship.
- If you have a partner, model mutual respect, kindness, integrity, and generosity at home.
- Role-play tricky or ethically murky scenarios.
- Use teen or adult dating advice columns, movies, music, and shows to trigger conversation.
- Share your good and bad relationship experiences, highlighting what you learned.
- Explain that heartbreak is a possibility and relationships require emotional vulnerability.
- Remind them not to tease or gossip about a friend who discloses a crush.
- Talk about the importance of basic friendship skills such as reciprocity, reflective listening, turn-taking, and sharing.

CONVERSATION STARTERS

- "If your boyfriend wants to hang out, but you're busy doing something else, how could you respond?"
- "What would you do if your best friend was cheating on their boyfriend?"
- "Is it appropriate for an eighth grader to date a sixth grader?"
- "Is it ever acceptable to lie to a partner?"
- "How could you help a friend whose boyfriend or girlfriend is mistreating them?"
- "If you ask a girl out and she says no, is it okay to keep asking?"
- "What's the difference between physical attraction, a crush, and love?"
- "Why might someone be interested in someone who plays hard to get?"
- "What are your friends' relationships like?"
- "What do you like and respect about yourself? How can you respect yourself in a relationship?"

LEARNING

"Everyone is getting A's except for me."

CHAPTER 11

ENCOURAGING BALANCE AND SETTING REASONABLE EXPECTATIONS

> ## KEY SKILLS
> 2—Negotiate conflict
> 3—Manage a student-teacher mismatch
> 4—Create homework and organization systems
> 6—Self-advocate
> 7—Self-regulate emotions
> 8—Cultivate passions and recognize limitations

"If I don't get all A's, I'll go to a shi**y college, get a shi**y job, and have a shi**y life."

"My parents are constantly on me to do this, do that. They want me to be like Matt or Beckett, but they're total geniuses."

"I don't mind getting an A-minus sometimes, but a B-plus would kill me. I'm not kidding."

REBECCA WAS DIFFERENT FROM HER SIXTH-GRADE FRIENDS. She didn't care about social status or social media or fashion. She cared about grades, and she cared about them a lot. By the end of the first semester, she'd become so obsessed that her mother contacted me, her school counselor. "She can't sleep, can't think about anything else," she told me. "Every night, she sleeps on our floor drowning in tears. There's no way she can sustain this stress." Her mother tried to shift her daughter's focus away from grades, but the anxiety only intensified.

When I met with Rebecca, she was adamant that everyone got straight A's, and that she would, too. She'd come to my office crying on the rare occasions when she earned a B-plus. This was middle school, and I worried that the higher stakes in high school would send her into a tailspin. Rebecca's parents and I wanted her to keep an even keel, but they lacked a framework for talking about grades at home. They felt disingenuous denying that grades carried significance, but they also didn't want to pile on the pressure.

Fortunately, Rebecca had time on her side. Using approaches like the ones I'll discuss in this chapter, her parents, the school staff, and I helped her recognize when she was off-kilter and needed to utilize coping strategies. She now devotes more time to sports, downtime, and spending time with friends and family. Grades no longer keep her awake at night, and she knows she can survive the disappointment of earning an imperfect grade. Although she lives in a community that overwhelmingly emphasizes achievement, she's determined to maintain her equilibrium.

Alan Goodwin, who recently retired as principal of Walt Whitman High School in Bethesda, Maryland, is familiar with students like Rebecca. He also has seen other iterations, including kids who struggle academically and parents who worry disproportionately about their kids' school performance. Many students start feeling the pressure in middle school, so he'd always meet with ninth-grade parents right away to encourage perspective. "Usually, this is the group that's most concerned about report cards," Goodwin told me in his office at the school. He'd tell parents it can be an adjustment when their child earns their first B, particularly when peer pressure is involved. Even when parents try to back off, kids may compare grades, test scores, and numbers of AP classes.

To encourage balance, Goodwin also would try to debunk the myth that perfect grades are common. At graduation, he'd ask groups of students to stand, honoring everyone from athletes to musicians. He'd deliberately save the straight-A students for last. "In twelve graduations, I never had more than a handful, maybe five students stand up," he told me. Despite this message, some kids still worried excessively about grades, and he'd try to mitigate their stress. Between final exams, they could play dodge ball, practice mindfulness or yoga, engage in art activities, or snuggle with borrowed puppies. But even if your principal isn't like Goodwin, you as a parent can help your child gain the right perspective about grades, and it's critical to set the stage for an easy high school transition when your child is still in middle school.

Here's the reality: not everyone is getting straight A's. Even those who do won't necessarily end up at Harvard; there are too many other factors. As the college admissions process has grown more competitive, parents have become increasingly concerned about academic performance. Even in middle school, I've observed more parents pushing for higher grades when their child earns less than a B. They may be worried they'll fall off an advanced course trajectory, or that they'll grow accustomed to earning low marks. But grades are subjective, and they can be deceptive. Teachers may inflate grades. A student who takes an easy course load may get higher scores than a student taking advanced classes. Some teachers may be exceptionally harsh graders. By acknowledging these inconsistencies and limitations, you can help your child focus on more important goals, such as accruing knowledge, determining strengths and interests, and developing a love of learning.

In fact, hundreds of middle schools are doing away with grades altogether. Instead, students are encouraged to focus on learning the material, master a set of grade-level skills, and work at their own pace. Along the way, they receive regular feedback on their progress. The approach has its detractors, but the *New York Times* reported that increasing numbers of schools are implementing pilot programs.

Even college admissions committees are making it clear they're interested in more than grades. Richard Weissbourd, a faculty member at Harvard's Graduate School of Education, issued a report that calls on colleges to change their admissions criteria to emphasize caring for others and meaningful ethical engagement over laundry lists of accomplishments. More than fifty admissions deans have endorsed his report, including the entire Ivy League. Schools still want to see academic rigor, but not at the expense of students leading balanced lives. We want kids to work hard, do their best, and learn without buckling under the pressure. It's tough to strike that balance. The following strategies will help your child set realistic expectations and resist perfectionist tendencies.

Foster autonomy and ease performance pressure.

Encourage independence and let your child fight their own battles. Give them autonomy and the freedom to experiment, problem-solve, self-advocate, and make mistakes.

Hovering over your kid might help them do better in middle and even high school, but college could end up being a disaster. They may have difficulty talking to professors or handling disappointment. Jessica Lahey, who taught middle school before writing *The Gift of Failure*, says that it's a vital time to begin allowing kids to make mistakes if you haven't already started doing so. "They should be starting to take the reins on communicating with adults about their questions and concerns, advocating for their rights and their needs, and letting their peers and the adults around them know what they need in order to be successful, happy, and safe," she told me.

At a time when kids are hitting more difficult material and more challenging social situations, they need opportunities to safely stumble, knowing their parents will help them do better the next time. "When kids know mistakes will result in ridicule, unreasonable punishment, or censure, they'll be much less likely to talk to the adults in their lives about those mistakes," Lahey added. They'll hide them, deny them, or blame them on someone else. A study published in the *Merrill-Palmer Quarterly* supports this theory—the investigators found that controlling parents create self-doubting children who hold themselves back.

"What we're seeing is the same kids who are getting these perfect grades through school are the ones who are getting undone by anxiety," said Ned Johnson, the president of Prep Matters and coauthor of *The Self-Driven Child*. He notes that when we tell kids they have to be in the top 10 percent, we're basically terrorizing everybody. "Ninety percent can't be the top 10 percent, and the top 10 percent will be insanely driven and afraid of making mistakes. Or kids might say, 'I'm already a C student and have screwed up my life, so why even bother?'"

If it helps, I've never seen a student do better on a test because they were told the stakes were high. Praise your child for creatively solving a problem, not for getting a 97 on a math exam. Tell them you're proud of how well they collaborated on a group project instead of focusing on the end result. Pose open-ended questions about their learning process, such as, "What are you talking about in history?" Or, "Has it gotten easier to share your ideas in front of the class?" If school is a struggle, point out their strengths and urge them to look beyond academics for a sense of accomplishment. Maybe they find science difficult, but they're unusually compassionate or resilient. Denise Pope, a senior lecturer at Stanford University and founder of Challenge Success, has written, "We short-change these components of a successful life when we overemphasize grades, test scores, and rote answers. Success is measured over the course of a lifetime, not at the end of a semester."

If school is causing extreme frustration, you may need to intervene, which I'll cover in more depth in Chapter 13. If there's no underlying issue, however, figure out what your child can comfortably handle. Resist the urge to compare them to their friends, classmates, siblings, or even yourself. One mother pushed her sixth-grade son to take advanced math against the school's recommendation. His older sister had followed that pathway, but she was a stronger math student. As a result, her son devoted excessive time to staying afloat in that one class, and the ability mismatch led to constant stress.

Former middle school principal Sally Selby advises parents to "grow the tree you've got. Be willing for your child to not be in the most advanced classes in every subject. Show excitement about B's, not just A's. Don't get caught up in that drive to be top-notch. It's damaging and driven by fear, and kids catch that anxiety." It's not easy to go against the grain, especially in achievement-oriented communities.

Wendy Kiang-Spray understands that tension. She feels strongly as both a mother and school counselor that an overbearing parenting style backfires, but even she questioned her relaxed approach when she worked in a high-pressure school. "When parents knew about the paper due next week, they'd push and push their kids," she told me. "I was like, 'Wait a minute, maybe my kids are going to be mediocre unless I push them.'" She eventually regained perspective, but that kind of systemic pressure can be tough for everyone.

Like-minded adults can band together. Psychologist Mary Alvord, the author fo *Conquer Negative Thinking*, recalls relying on fellow parents who shared her philosophy. "My son was a competitive diver and made the Junior Olympics," she told me. "The coaches wanted him to practice three hours a day, five days a week. I said, 'That's insanity. He wants to play lacrosse and do other things.'" She leaned on the parents of other divers for support. "We had similar philosophies, so we could reinforce the importance of balance with each other's children."

She recognizes that it's a delicate dance. Everyone wants their child to do well, but the resilience literature shows that relationships are the most important aspect of life. Make a point of telling your child that academic brilliance alone won't lead to happiness, and be mindful of the messages you send about your priorities. According to a study in the *Journal of Youth and Adolescence*, kids who place too high a premium on academic success may end up feeling disengaged from school, which makes them more vulnerable to stress. (I'll address mental health in Chapter 17.)

Middle schoolers need to refuel as much as you do. Help your child recognize the signs that their plate is full. Are they irritable or getting headaches? Do they have time to spend with friends and family, and maybe take the occasional nap? Help them understand that there's always fallout when someone devotes excessive time to any one area. Maybe that kid with the straight A's worries about disappointing his parents, or had to give up sports to achieve at that level. Your child needs downtime and tools to relax, and that gets harder in middle school. (Suddenly, there are new extracurriculars to try, homework goes up, and recess often becomes a thing of the past.)

Give your child some leeway. They may have played soccer for seven years, but let them drop it if it's making them miserable. Ask questions that gauge their level of interest and commitment. You can encourage them to finish the season before switching gears, but middle school is the perfect time to explore. You can step in and help them make adjustments if they're overscheduled, and remind them that their lives are more than doing homework.

— Idea for Educators —
Celebrate "Failure Week"

Ivanhoe Girls' Grammar School in Melbourne, Australia, has an annual tradition: "Failure Week." The teachers all write down their biggest blunders, such as failing a course in their teaching program. At the start of the week, the school projects the teachers' failures onto a screen in every classroom. The school spends the rest of the week teaching students new skills, including juggling, painting, dancing, and reciting medieval poetry. Then it's the kids' turn to risk looking foolish. The students perform their newly acquired skills in front of hundreds of classmates in a packed auditorium. Making mistakes gets normalized, and the kids grow more comfortable with failing publicly. Schools can try this exercise, or simply devote a few minutes of class time each week to share and celebrate one another's failures.

Combat perfectionist tendencies.

Even if parents are low-key and encourage balance, some kids pile the pressure on themselves. Mira, one of my former eighth-grade students, fell into this category. Even though she was one of the strongest writers in her English class, she couldn't get started on the simplest in-class assignments. When I spoke to her, she told me she was worried she'd get it wrong or disappoint everyone. Not surprisingly, this was playing out at home, too. Her mother, Maggie, contacted me because they were battling it out daily. Mira would erase her work until she left holes in her papers. She wouldn't power down her computer until after midnight. As a result, she was chronically tired and irritable, and Maggie was desperate.

To discourage perfectionism, tell your child you love them for who they are, not for anything they do. De-emphasize performance and achievement and focus on them as an individual. Be careful about the language you use. Are you overly self-critical? When you model self-acceptance, they'll be more likely to forgive their own failures. Don't be subtle about it. If you forget to fax your boss a document, miss a meeting, or screw up a sales call, tell them. They need to know you're a fallible human being and can recover from setbacks. Say, "I made a mistake, but I'll do it differently next time," or, "I totally lost my place during my presentation, but that happens."

"I always tell kids to ask parents to tell them their biggest failures," child and adolescent psychotherapist Katie Hurley told me. "Tell them when you got in trouble, when you were most disappointed, about your worst grade. Hiding that stuff is a big mistake. My kids know my first book was rejected by thirteen publishers and never got published." It's not always easy for parents to practice what they preach. A few years ago, a father asked to meet with me. He was alarmed because his eighth-grade son was waking up at 4 a.m. regularly to do homework. The father, a reporter, confessed that he often worked in the middle of the night, too. When he connected the dots, he realized they both needed a reboot and resolved to set a healthier example. As Jessica Lahey points out, "Parents must model the same intellectual and emotional bravery they expect of kids."

At its core, perfectionism is about fear. It's hard for perfectionist kids to approach scary tasks with excitement rather than anxiety, so start with baby steps. Learn a new skill together, such as yoga, and react with humor if either of you tips over. Have your child purposely misspell a word, then sit with the discomfort. Small exposures build their tolerance. Your child also can read biographies about their heroes. They'll discover that everyone hits bumps in the road before achieving success. Combat the notion that anyone's life is perfect, and emphasize that they need to be tolerant of their own humanity.

Perfectionist kids need help setting attainable standards. Ask your child what they'd like to achieve and discuss whether it's realistic. They may be so busy shooting for the moon that they don't give themselves credit for smaller triumphs. Model that good can be good enough. You can say, "There's no way I can finish all my work tonight, but that's okay, I can review it tomorrow." If your child can't disengage, dictate a homework cutoff time that gives them time to wind down. Expect resistance and be patient. Perfectionist behaviors are tough to change because they're protective. They help kids cope with uncertainty and give them a sense of control. It's easier to hide behind perfectionism than to admit weakness.

If your child catastrophizes, don't tell them to stop thinking about it. That can make it worse. Instead, bring their fears to the surface. Have them close their eyes and visualize studying hard and still getting a C on a science test. Ask them what it feels like, what they think will happen, and encourage them to replace negative thoughts with a more helpful perspective, such as, "No one gets everything right all of the time." They may believe perfectionism is the only way to achieve a goal, or that their teacher will think less of them if they hand in one imperfect assignment. Ask, "What's the evidence to support your belief? How would you advise a friend who felt the same way?" Build their awareness of when they're thinking in extremes so they can pull their thoughts back to the middle.

Mary Alvord has kids shoot arrows at a dartboard to demonstrate the concept. She tells them it's okay to miss the bull's eye, but they don't want to be off the board entirely. If your kid can't stop perseverating, try setting aside a specific "worry time," such as ten minutes twice a week after dinner. Consider short-term cognitive-behavioral therapy, too. A therapist can teach your child skills and help them make connections between their thoughts, emotions, behavior, and physiological feelings.

TOP TIPS FOR PARENTS

- Challenge perfectionist tendencies, and don't compare your child to their peers, siblings, or even yourself.
- Don't just celebrate their A's; emphasize that no one is a perfect student.
- Band together with other parents who share your philosophy, and reinforce the importance of balance and relationships when talking to one another's kids.
- Model practicing good self-care, and help your child recognize the signs that they're out of whack.
- Tell your child when you screw up (or about past failures).
- Give them small exposures to failure, whether they purposely misspell a word or leave a typo in a paper.
- Demonstrate that there's humor in imperfection by laughing when you tip over in yoga class or show up for the wrong work meeting.

CONVERSATION STARTERS

- "Do you feel like you have enough downtime to see your friends and have fun?"
- "Close your eyes and visualize studying hard for a math test and still getting a C. How does that feel? What do you think might happen?"
- "What's the worst that could happen if you hand in an imperfect assignment? What's your evidence that that would happen?"

TACKLING HOMEWORK

"I do my homework; I just forget to hand it in."

"I know I should see my teacher for help at lunch, but I just want ten minutes with my friends."

"I can't memorize anything. It's like there's a hole in my brain where everything falls out."

MY FRIEND NIKKI WAS FRUSTRATED. HER DAUGHTER KIRSTEN, a rising eighth grader, had just finished her summer reading requirement. She needed to summarize the novel, and Nikki urged her to write the paper while the details were still fresh. "It's June, Mom," Kirsten said. "School starts after Labor Day. I can get to it later." Nikki wondered whether she should push the issue. "I want her to develop good study habits, but she's so lazy," she told me.

Peg Dawson, a psychologist and author of *Smart but Scattered*, told me she often has to reassure parents that it's way too early to worry about their child's work ethic. "Task initiation is the hardest skill to master, and future orientation doesn't kick in until tenth or eleventh grade," she explained.

"For parents, it seems simple, but a thirteen-year-old brain is thinking, 'I don't have to do it now, so why should I?'" Children deal in the now.

Nikki and Kirsten agreed to conduct an experiment instead of battling it out. On a scrap of paper, Nikki scribbled what she thought would happen if Kirsten waited until August to write her essay. She predicted that Kirsten's work quality would be low, that she'd struggle to recall the novel, and that she'd wish she'd done the work earlier. Her predictions weren't that far off. Kirsten admitted she was foggy on the plot, but said she felt okay handing in imperfect work. "I had a good summer with my friends, and I didn't spend it obsessing over some dumb paper." Parents may have an agenda, but middle schoolers do, too. As Dawson told me, "They're navigating a much more complicated social world, and from a human development perspective, that's probably as important as any academic task."

Beyond the social piece, there can be any number of reasons that kids are homework avoidant. They may shut down because they're discouraged, fail to see the relevance to their life, feel paralyzed by pressure, or prefer gaming or texting. Some kids may struggle with comprehension, reading, organization, or motivation. Others may be trying to get attention from busy parents, or are tired because they're on social media when they should be sleeping. All of this can lead to epic battles at home, complete with screaming and slamming doors.

One parent told me her sixth-grade son prefers the "duck and hide method." When she asks him to do his homework, he slides under the couch. "It's his go-to response," she said. "It's his way of asserting, 'I don't hear you or see you, so this isn't happening.' When he does that, I know it's going to be a rough night."

Homework is about control. As education consultant Rick Wormeli told me, "Kids this age want a voice, and many would rather have the reputation of being forgetful or irresponsible than actually admit they don't know what they're doing. It's a form of self-preservation in terms of ego, dignity, and energy." It's not easy to foster kids' autonomy and lower their frustration while preserving the parent-child relationship. You need to be patient and willing to experiment. While there's no one-size-fits-all solution, here are several strategies you can test.

Give kids a sense of agency, but help them set routines.

You won't win if you engage in power struggles, but that doesn't mean you should back off entirely. You can give your child choices, encourage self-advocacy, and set expectations. Options can be simple. Allow them to choose whether they want to work before or after dinner, or if they prefer to contact a teacher through email or meet in person. Kim Campbell, an eighth-grade global studies teacher and educational consultant for the Association of Middle Level Educators, told me she urges parents to "inspect what you expect." If your child promises to connect with a teacher on their own, they need to know what will happen if they don't follow through. You can say, "I'm going to contact the teacher if you don't go in for extra help by the end of the week."

If you do nothing else, try to prevent the formation of bad habits. Kids may not do homework at all, inefficiently bounce between social media and studying, or start their work at midnight. This might mean working together to devise an after-school homework schedule with built-in breaks, prohibiting them from keeping their cell phone in the bedroom, or ensuring they get adequate rest. Developmentally, middle schoolers need help with planning, organization, and time management. While each child is unique, most can't break down complex multistep homework assignments or anticipate how today's work product will impact long-term goals.

The transition to high school can be a little smoother than the transition to middle school, because your child has started to figure out how they work best. At eleven, it's all new and they may not know how to handle the academic demands. That said, every middle schooler is different. One child might need to complete their homework in the kitchen with a parent nearby, while another can work independently in her bedroom. Some kids can remember tasks such as packing a lunch or bringing in gym clothes, while others need to consult checklists. One kid might have a squeaky-clean backpack, while another needs help purging old papers and last week's lunch bag.

Despite their differences, all kids thrive on routine. "I tell parents that the perfect intervention is something that only takes five minutes a day, but you're willing to do it every day," Dawson told me. "With my kid, I'd

say, 'You have ten algebra questions, how long do you think it will take?'"
Over time, her son learned to independently run through a daily mental
checklist.

Learning how to get help from a teacher is a process. Some kids are
comfortable popping in for help during homeroom or homework club,
while others need their parent to send a note to teachers requesting a
check-in. Some kids will independently send an email asking for clarification, while others need help with the task. You can help your child develop
self-advocacy skills by modeling how to do it, then incrementally pulling
away support.

If you need to send the email yourself, have your child sit with you and
watch you write it. A sixth grader may need help with email etiquette. If
they're used to texting with friends, they may not see the value in saying
"thank you" or including a salutation. By eighth grade, children should be
able to send a respectful note on their own. To facilitate that progression,
don't go to bat for them unless there's no other option. Let them take ownership of problem-solving, whether they need extra time on an assignment
or help preparing for a test. As your child takes on more responsibility, back
away. You boost their confidence by communicating, "I believe you can do
this on your own."

While they're working on building independence, monitor their technology use. Remove their phone while they study, whether you have them
check it into a basket, seal it in an envelope, or place it on a high shelf.
Research supports this approach. A study in the journal *Social Psychology*
showed that when people had their phones in view, they made more errors
on two demanding tests of attention and cognition than subjects whose
phones were not in view, even when they were turned off. Another study
in *Applied Cognitive Psychology* found that students who didn't bring phones
to class scored a full letter grade higher than those who had phones on
hand. The students scored equally poorly whether or not they actually used
their phones.

In 2010, researchers examined the effect of interrupting students while
they studied. They sent one group of students a series of instant messages
while they read a chapter and prepared for an exam. Those students not
only took longer to complete the reading, but they also experienced more

stress. As the researchers reported in the journal *Computers and Education*, "Students who are managing busy lives may think they're accomplishing more by multitasking, but our findings suggest they'll actually need more time to achieve the same level of performance on an academic task."

Technology does offer some advantages, and there may be times it makes sense to connect the phone to learning, such as when they want to study with friends online. They can use apps to make flash cards, break up units into simpler exercises, brainstorm ideas for essays and stories, practice math problems, design planners, or learn languages.

Spruce up the study experience.

Kids see studying as dull, but parents can enhance the experience. Let your child pick out their own colorful notebooks and decorate them. Ana Jovanovic, a psychologist and coach at Nobel Coaching, an online tutoring service, told me she has kids name their planner to make it harder to reject. It also injects a little fun and silliness into the process. They'll say, "What do I have to do today? I should ask Jake." Keep the study space well-equipped, but make sure it isn't visually distracting.

Your child might want to choose special study attire to set the mood for studying, such as a "learning hat" or a pair of glasses. Have them wear the designated item for homework, but remove it when they take a break. Researchers at Northwestern University found this technique works for adults, too. When subjects in white lab coats were told they were wearing doctors' coats, they were more focused than those who were told they were wearing painters' coats. Similarly, in a study published in the journal *Child Development*, researchers found that young children persevered longer at a task when they pretended to be a superhero.

Rewards incentivize many kids, but middle schoolers work best when they're immediate. "You earn them when you do your homework for a week, not a quarter," Kim Campbell said. "Some parents say you have to get all As for the semester, but long-term goals don't work." The payoff can take many forms, from point systems to stickers to going out for ice cream. Kids should choose something small and meaningful. Even adults like to work on a reward system. I spoke to Jennifer Goodstein, a sixth-grade teacher and executive functioning coach, who said, "At Weight Watchers, if you go to eleven out of thirteen meetings, they give you a sticker and an extra charm. If adults are still being incentivized by stickers and charms, you can do it with an eleven-year-old."

One parent asked me if it was appropriate to offer $500 for straight A's. I discourage the practice. This may lead to a small initial surge in performance, but it's not a good long-term strategy. Your child won't feel responsible for their own learning, will likely lose enthusiasm for academics, and may start to expect regular payouts. And, as we discussed in Chapter 11, straight A's aren't always an ideal or healthy goal in their own right. Instead, focus on their perseverance and good habits.

Let school be the bad guy.

When homework becomes adversarial, parents may need to walk away and contact the child's teacher, counselor, or another trusted adult in the school. Goodstein told me she tells parents that if their child is melting down, they should stop immediately and write her an email. "We can be the bad guys and say, 'Okay, Brendan, you were fighting with your mother, so you're going to do the work here at school.'" She'll create a schedule so the child can get help from teachers.

Many middle schools also offer after-school homework support, which can be a good option if things get toxic. If your child resists homework club, you can use it as a negotiating tool and say, "Fine, if you complete 85 percent of your homework without a fight, then you can study at home again." There's a fine line between supporting kids and hindering their autonomy. Goodstein faces this challenge with her eleven-year-old son, Justin, who's easily frustrated. "I'll quiz him or help him understand directions," she said. If he doesn't understand a concept, however, she'll tell his teacher he needs more examples. She doesn't micromanage the quality of his work. "If he writes two sentences when I think he should write five, and he says that's all the teacher wants, that's her job to pull that from him."

Remember that teachers know what's typical output for a middle schooler. You may think your child's book report is superficial or too short, but it may be completely age-appropriate. Let the school deal with quality control and accountability. I get that this can be tough. It's challenging to keep the big picture in mind, but at some point, your child will need to know how to follow through, manage their time, take ownership of their work, and clarify expectations. These skills are as important as any grade they'll earn.

— IDEA FOR EDUCATORS —
HOLD A TEAM MEETING

When a student isn't coming to class prepared, convene a meeting with their teachers and parents. You may discover that one teacher is taking a different, more effective approach, or that issues at home are impeding concentration. I once learned at a team meeting that a child lived with a parrot that talked nonstop while he tried to work. Brainstorm solutions as a group. For example, teachers may need to check the student's planner at the end of each class, or parents may need to find the child a quieter place to study. If there's a high level of conflict over homework at home, teachers can take the lead. Put systems in place, such as setting up regular times when the child meets with all of their teachers. The team also might decide to mandate homework club or a supervised study hall.

Evaluate and modify homework.

When a student expresses disdain for homework, it may not be appropriate, interesting, or sufficiently complex. If it covers material that wasn't covered in class or doesn't further understanding, parents may need to touch base with the teacher. "My older son was assigned a diorama, and he wasn't good with fine motor skills, so we battled," Rick Wormeli recalled. He realized the assignment had more to do with suspending things from the ceiling of a shoebox than science, so he contacted the school. "Parents have every right to say to a teacher, I'm not seeing the connection between practice and subsequent understanding," he told me.

Children won't engage or improve when homework is drudgery. Wormeli tells parents, "Trust that your child wants to find purpose, meaning, and connection. When all three of those are happening, homework isn't a big deal. Ninety-five percent of all the input that goes into the young adult brain goes to emotional response centers first, not cognitive storage." To increase relevance, you can modify homework, often with a teacher's blessing. You can say to the teacher, "I took the math assignment and related it to baseball statistics, or election debates," or anything else that resonates for your child. Kids are interest-based learners, so help them make connections by going on field trips, visiting museums, watching documentaries, or doing related experiments.

You also may need to ask the teacher to break down the homework into smaller pieces, or chunk it yourself. If your child struggles with directions, try building their confidence by letting them take the lead on fun online projects with multistep instructions. Then, when they complain that homework is too hard, you can remind them that they were able to build a robot or fold an origami giraffe. If they still hit a wall, it's time to get up and move. When Campbell sees that kids are falling asleep in class, she'll have them do twenty jumping jacks or pretend they're in the ocean and need to swim away from sharks as fast as they can.

Movement also is valuable before starting homework, whether your child attends sports practice or goes on a bike ride. If they need a mental break while working, try a simple mindfulness activity, such as blowing bubbles using controlled breathing. Whatever you do, don't do the work for them. Teachers know when parents have taken over. Plus, as Wormeli says, "What's the greater gift we can give our kids, that they learn it and it goes into long-term memory, or that they get a false sense of competency?"

Name the negative voices and make it safe to stumble.

Your child might feel incompetent in one area and successful in another. Train them to notice and name any defeatist voices. For example, if they feel confident about their athleticism but insecure about their math abilities, have them name the negative and positive voices. Maybe they become Mike and Jon. Ana Jovanovic tells parents to then say, "It's not you, it's Mike causing you problems." Ask them a series of questions: "What does Mike need to feel more comfortable? How would Jon advise

Mike? Can you bring Jon the next time Mike is having trouble with homework?"

By depersonalizing the struggle, your child can focus on solutions. They might realize that Mike needs to see a teacher after school. Role models can perform a similar function. Have your child list several people they relate to and admire, whether it's a professional athlete, musician, or inspirational fictional character. Later, when the child is having trouble, you can ask, "What do you think LeBron James would do?"

Don't let your child off the hook too easily. Make it safe to stumble, but challenge them if they say they can't do something before they've even tried. Say, "Convince me that you can't do it. Give me two examples where you failed at this. What would have to be different for you to be able to do the task?" If your child truly is struggling, say, "So what?" and talk about the value of learning through trial and error. You can use movies to make this point. In *Meet the Robinsons*, one character is brilliant but feels stuck in failure. By the end, he realizes that every mistake he's made has led him to the life he wants to live. The movie *Inside Out* talks about the importance of appreciating negative emotions. For example, sadness might motivate a child to reach out for help.

When parents teach kids to manage uncomfortable emotions, it helps them develop grit, a character trait they need to stick with difficult tasks. Grit also can help your child maintain a growth mind-set, Stanford psychologist Carol Dweck's idea that intelligence isn't fixed and people aren't born "smart or dumb." Kids with a growth mind-set believe they can learn more or become smarter if they work hard. To foster that attitude, focus on effort more than results.

It's hard for kids to work through obstacles such as bombing a test, not clicking with a teacher, or deciphering a difficult assignment. Look for telltale signs of dejection. A teacher may say they filled in a worksheet with gibberish, or your child may tell you her homework is stupid, or that the teacher never shares her projects because "Everyone else is so much smarter." Children have many different ways of expressing, "This is hard. I feel like giving up." It can feel safer and even sensible to goof off or check out. When your child hits a low, take a break, lighten the mood, and remind them that they simply haven't mastered something *yet*.

TOP TIPS FOR PARENTS

- Try to figure out what's at the root of the homework problem. Does it feel irrelevant? Is your child disorganized? A perfectionist? Do they struggle with task initiation? Spend too much time online?
- Figure out where they're most efficient. For some kids, that will be by your side at the kitchen table, while others can disappear to their room.
- Spruce up the study experience. Have them wear "learning attire" that sets the mood, and ask them to name and decorate their planner. Clear the study space of distractions.
- Build in breaks, whether they do a mindfulness exercise or go for a bike ride.
- If homework time is high-conflict, let the school intervene.
- Teach your child to self-advocate by providing scaffolding.
- Small, meaningful rewards are okay, but don't pay kids for earning good grades.
- Choose one five-minute ritual you can do consistently to reinforce good habits.
- Instill a growth mind-set by reminding them that they simply haven't mastered a skill *yet*.

CONVERSATION STARTERS

- "You seem stuck. How can I help?"
- "Let's figure out a homework schedule. What do you think would work best for you?"
- "I can see you're frustrated. Why don't you plan to ask your teacher for help. Do you want to email her or go in to see her tomorrow morning?"
- "You're too upset to concentrate at the moment. Do you want to take a break?"

CHAPTER 13

INTERVENING WHEN SCHOOL IS A STRUGGLE

> **KEY SKILLS**
>
> 2—Negotiate conflict
> 4—Create homework and organization
> systems
> 6—Self-advocate
> 8—Cultivate passions and recognize
> limitations

*"My teacher says I ask too many questions, but I have
no idea what she wants us to do."*

"Math tests make me freak out and forget everything."

*"I've tried chewing gum, playing with mind putty, and
doodling, but nothing works. I just can't sit still."*

B RIAN AND DANIEL RACED DOWN THE SIXTH-GRADE HALLWAY
scribbling on anyone they could ambush with Sharpies. By the time
they got hauled into the main office, they were covered in ink. The
principal let them have it, then paused to answer his phone. That was
when Brian noticed the stamp. By the time the call was over, Brian had
branded Daniel's forehead with the words, "From the Desk of Principal
Brent."

Brian had been impulsive in elementary school, but sixth grade
brought bigger challenges. He buckled under the pressure of multiple classes,
increased homework, and no recess. Within months, a school psychologist

diagnosed him with attention deficit disorder, and the special education team gave him a Section 504 Plan (a civil rights statute) to help him meet academic and behavioral expectations. His formal accommodations mandated that teachers break down his assignments, check his planner, and build in movement breaks. Brian's parents, who called their son "a ping pong ball on nitroglycerine," were relieved to have a plan. That was several years ago. Brian is now in college, and there's little evidence of the twelve-year-old boy who ambushed classmates with pens and left his homework in the freezer. He's figured out how to address his weaknesses, from setting calendar reminders to using checklists.

Parents often meet with me when their child is struggling academically, behaviorally, or emotionally. They have questions that range from the logistical to the personal. "Should they consult with a professional or give it time? How can they know if their expectations are realistic? Would a diagnosis kill their child's self-esteem?"

Trust your instincts and intervene when your child's grades decline, they resist going to school, their eating or sleeping patterns change, or their friends ditch them. Don't wait for problems to balloon. Research shows that identifying learning, attention, or emotional issues early can improve a child's outcome, says Dr. Howard Bennett, a pediatrician in Washington, DC, and the author of *The Fantastic Body*. That said, children grow and develop at different rates, and there's no one right time to intervene. There may be no set rules, but there's an art to supporting your kid sensitively and partnering productively with their school. As you embark on the journey to identify and address issues, here's how you can support and empower your child.

Treat your child as the expert, but interview others.

"Most questions delivered to kids are really accusations with a question mark at the end," educator Ned Johnson told me. It's more effective to act like a calm, curious observer than to ask, "Why did you do that?" Say, "Do you think this is harder for you than other students? Are you the last one done on a test?" Debrief at the end of each day, and ask what went well and what went poorly with a specific class or assignment.

Keep a log so you can identify patterns, and speak to more than one person at the school, such as a counselor and a teacher. Coaches, neighbors, and partners also can help you determine how concerned you should be. Parents might discover that symptoms or behaviors change depending on the classroom setup, the skills required in a specific class, or the teacher's behavior management skills. Melanie Auerbach, director of Student Support at Sheridan School, points out that the teacher-child relationship also can play a big role. "If the teacher is highly distractible and the student likes to rap his desk with his knuckles, that's not going to be a good combination. Testing makes sense when there's been a persistent and chronic issue across settings, as opposed to situational behavior."

Partner with the school, and be as specific as possible so the team can do a thorough and accurate record review. Amanda Morin, author of *The Everything Parent's Guide to Special Education*, recommends saying, "My child isn't reading at grade level, he's struggling to assimilate information, and English causes more outbursts than math." Provide work samples, any diagnostic information, and relevant historical data.

Parents can play the role of facilitator. Morin's son got an IEP (individualized education plan) for self-regulation issues when he was nine, but his struggles escalated when he hit middle school. "He had difficulty with different teacher personalities," she told me. She shared insights about her son with the school, then helped her son understand his teachers' expectations. A parent may need to explain, "Mrs. Smith isn't mad *at* you, she's mad *near* you." The teacher might be upset about the overall classroom dynamic, but a sensitive child might assume that the teacher doesn't like *them*.

Building empathy and understanding is more productive than firing off accusations or making demands. Ann Dolin, founder of Educational Connections Tutoring, suggests that parents use "I" messages, such as saying, "I've noticed that even with my help, Jimmy is spending four hours on homework," rather than, "You're giving Jimmy assignments that are too hard." ("I've noticed" is a particularly helpful phrase.)

Be deliberate in how you communicate. Middle school principal Chris Nardi tells parents and educators to pick up the phone or meet in person whenever an email exceeds a paragraph. He recently emailed his son's teacher with a concern. When her response was terse, he knew there was a disconnect. "I said, 'Can we go offline and talk, because I think we're misinterpreting our tones?'"

"Everyone wants to do what's best for your child, so just call a teacher or counselor and share your concerns," he told me. "Ask, 'Can you help me understand? This is what my child told me; is it accurate? Should he be spending three hours on homework?'" He gives the same advice to staff. "I had a teacher once hand me a six-paragraph email he planned to send to a parent. I told him, 'This is a great guide for you to use during your phone call.'"

Go to any meeting with an open mind. Educators see hundreds of kids, so they have a different perspective about what may or may not be problematic. Always schedule a follow-up to the initial conversation to assess your child's progress. At every step of the way, make sure you understand the special education process and your rights. Section 504 and IEPs are legally binding, and parents are equal participants on the team by law. The forms are living, breathing documents that need to be reassessed and updated regularly. Parents who feel overwhelmed or alone can find resources and an online community at www.understood.org. Parent Center Hub (www.parentcenterhub.org) will connect parents with local, in-person support groups.

Informed, proactive parents can make all the difference. One in five children has a learning or attention issue, but only a small subset receives specialized instruction or accommodations. This may reflect educators' uncertainty about the identification process. Understood, a nonprofit initiative dedicated to supporting parents of kids with learning and attention issues, commissioned a poll of classroom teachers in 2014. The organization found that 61 percent were somewhat or not very confident recommending that a child be evaluated for special education for learning issues.

— IDEA FOR EDUCATORS —

BE DELIBERATE WHEN IT COMES TO ACCOMMODATIONS

When an educational team writes a 504 Plan or IEP, or implements informal accommodations, team members need to regularly assess whether the supports are working. They need to spend an equal amount of time determining whether the supports are overkill. As students make progress, tweak the accommodations to bolster their emerging independence. For example, if a student with test-taking anxiety starts out taking exams in a separate room, the long-term goal should be that they take tests in class with their peers. Consider incremental steps, such as having them take the test in the same room, but positioned in a way that makes them less aware of other kids flipping pages. Slowly expose them to the stressor and build their sense of competency. There's no need to wait for an annual review—educational plans are living documents that can be updated at any time.

Identify the right issues.

Kids with specific learning disabilities can have attention issues, and children with attention issues can have anxiety. Issues can overlap and co-occur, and answers aren't always obvious. Parents might think their child is anxious because math is a struggle, but math might be hard because of their anxiety. Ella Tager, a seventh grader who was diagnosed with dyslexia in first grade, notes that she has symptoms that are typical of someone with attention deficit disorder. "Sometimes I need to move to process the frustration of not knowing what's going on," she told me. "It gives me time to get unstuck." The right strategies and interventions will vary by child and change over time.

Children with learning issues may struggle with peers. "If your child has poor impulse control and says whatever is on his mind, it doesn't take much to imagine the social implications," says Bob Cunningham, head of Robert Louis Stevenson School in Manhattan. If he's late or disruptive, a teacher may punish the entire class. If he doesn't pull his weight on a group project, his social standing will take a hit. You can role-play scenarios at home, such as forgetting to meet a friend. "Help her say, 'Jenny, I know that was a problem for you when I was late. I didn't mean to be disrespectful to you—that's something I'm struggling with and working on,'" Cunningham told me, adding, "A fourteen-year-old girl is going to accept that explanation and think better of your child."

Professionals often emphasize the importance of having one or two close friends, but that may be a mistake for kids with social difficulties. Deep friendship can be hard for the target friend. As Cunningham noted, "Kids with social anxiety, social reciprocity, or social awareness issues will have significantly improved lives if the goal is more comfortable interactions with a broader range of classmates or teammates."

Address the needs of gifted and twice-exceptional learners.

If you suspect your child is gifted or twice-exceptional—a student who is gifted and also has a learning or attention issue—get them assessed. Investigate whether your school has an appropriate educational program. You may need to tap outside resources to meet their needs, such as the National Association for Gifted Children or Supporting the Emotional Needs of the Gifted. Be your child's advocate and meet with their teachers. This may be an uphill battle. Researchers have found that current practices mirror where we were twenty years ago, and one study found that more than 40 percent of middle schools do not use any particular approach supported in the gifted education literature.

Susan Rakow, a counselor at a K–8 school in Cleveland for gifted students, wrote in *AMLE Magazine* that "Once advanced students meet the minimum standards of their grade level, it's easy for teachers to ignore them and focus on 'the bubble kids' and others who are not achieving where others believe they could or should be." Part of the challenge is that their asynchronicity can make them hard to teach. As educator Laurel Blackmon, the founder of LCB Consulting and the mother of a twice-exceptional son, told me, "You'll have a student reading a college calculus textbook who can't write a paragraph. There's an intensity; it's not just being smart, it's taking in the world at an incredible pace." Blackmon recalls someone telling her to focus on her child's strengths 80 percent of the time. "It was excellent advice. Otherwise, he'll say, 'Why bother?' In the real world, you're going to choose to spend most of your day on your strengths and work in an area where you can excel."

Change what you do first.

Start by looking at what you can change to make things better. If your child isn't able to get ready for school on time and you turn it into a daily battle, you'll damage the relationship without fixing the problem. Consider getting up earlier, or monitor your child more carefully. You may need to confirm that they're actually getting dressed before you head downstairs. It's not about lowering expectations, it's about recognizing that your child may need more support than kids without learning or attention issues.

Don't try to address everything at once. Test one new approach at a time and stick with it for three weeks to see if it gets traction. Maybe your child has a separate alarm that reminds them it's time to pack up, or uses lists to help them prioritize their "must do's," "should do's," and "could do's." The lab due tomorrow is a must do. The teacher's recommended reading is a should do.

Make sure teachers know where your child excels, too. If a child is strong socially but has weak reading and writing skills, teachers can set them up for success by assigning collaborative work. Teachers also can give kids leadership roles that highlight their skills, build their confidence, and influence the way adults and other students view them. Cunningham tells teachers, "Think of the thing that's most challenging for you, and now think about doing that seven hours all day every day in front of the people whose opinion you care about most."

Children's specific challenges often come with built-in strengths. When Blackmon's son was diagnosed with a learning disability, she told him that kids with dyslexia can have special abilities, such as making connections across big ideas. Children with ADHD often bring energy and dynamism to a classroom, and when teachers draw on their strengths and interests, they build their capacity to sustain attention. So if your child loves astronomy, start a dialogue with the teacher about designing an assignment around space exploration.

When you stick up for your child, you model how they can help themselves. Miriam Tager, Ella's mother and an assistant professor of early childhood education at Westfield State University, told me her daughter knew how to ask teachers if they had read her IEP by the time she was in fifth grade. "We were always advocating for her, so she learned from us," Tager said. Ella added, "I figured out young how to talk to teachers respectfully and sensibly. I used teacherly language, because I found that teachers take you more seriously when they see that you understand and want to learn."

For Ella, sixth grade was a turning point. "The school gave me headphones so I could listen to stories and stay along with the class, and my science teacher gave the whole class a sheet asking us how we learn," she told me. She felt comfortable telling him when she needed something read out loud or wanted to demonstrate her knowledge orally. She also started implementing her own strategies. "I used my study hall to watch a video on evolution and cells, and when they came up in the text, the visual popped into my head and I was able to get through the lesson." There are so many things you can try in a school, Tager noted. "Ella is allowed to doodle. Some people don't like this, but it helps her process the information. She does well with assisted technology and lots of visuals and movement. Every year, we found something else that would help her."

Supports should be removed as kids learn skills. As Donna Volpitta, founder of the Center for Resilient Leadership, told me, "Is your goal to make sure they're getting everything right, or is your goal to teach them how to do it independently next time?" Take an "I do, we do, you do" approach. You can contact the school for your child, then guide them as they write their teacher an email, then step back when they can do it on their own. Don't overcompensate, especially if the struggle is unrelated to the disability. "I know I'm doing too much when I'm making three trips to the school to bring sneakers and a textbook, and it's interfering with the rest of the family's functioning," Morin said.

If you do the work for them, they also won't develop confidence in their skills, says Scott Murphy, a director in Montgomery County Public Schools. "When I was a middle school principal, I experienced that something happens between grades six and eight. Students start deciding for themselves what they're good at and what they're not, and sometimes what they decide they're not good at is untrue," he told me. "We need to make sure we don't reinforce that or shut anything down, that we continue the mathematical mind-set and stem exposures and allow that productive struggle."

Be direct but sensitive.

When school is a struggle, it can take a toll on kids' self-esteem, but withholding information about how they learn isn't the answer. "If you've been sick for two weeks and someone says you have a sinus infection, now you can address it," Ann Dolin explained. "My experience is when you tell a child they meet the criteria for dysgraphia, they're like, 'Oh, this is why it's been so hard for so long, this makes sense.'" Psychiatrist Edward Hallowell tells kids with ADHD, "You have a Ferrari engine for a brain, but you've got bicycle breaks. If you don't strengthen your brakes, you're going to spin out and crash." He advises parents and educators to emphasize kids' strengths—and to moderate the fender benders.

Ella told me she had a mix of emotions when she first got the diagnosis, but she felt better when she understood why she wasn't learning the same way as other students. A professional can debrief with your child in a nonjudgmental, developmentally appropriate way. "A psychologist is different than a teacher or a parent who carries value to a child," Melanie Auerbach explained. "They can say, 'This is how your brain works. Know why it's so easy for you to memorize those math facts? Because you have really good long-term memory. But you know how you have a hard time remembering six plus seven when you're solving a word problem? That's because your working memory is not as strong.'"

As you share information and strategies, remember that your child is looking to you for reassurance. If you find you're unable to accept your child's limitations or you're overly invested in their success, you may need counseling to work out your own issues. Your child is incredibly sensitive to your reaction, and it's crucial that you can remain calm and empathetic. My friend Mary, whose seventh grader, Zoe, has attention deficit disorder, sought therapy when she couldn't deal with her daughter's impulsivity. Mary's psychologist helped her come to terms with the fact that kids with ADHD are consistently inconsistent. "Zoe is like a nine-year-old who doesn't recognize the boundaries of privacy—she'll ask people intrusive questions about their sex lives," Mary told me, adding that she found it liberating to let go of expectations that were setting them both up for failure.

The good news is that children who face challenges tend to be resilient, know their limits, are good with people, and can advocate for themselves. With the right supports, even the most impulsive, struggling child can explode in development. It may not always be easy to take the long view, but Ella hopes parents will embrace her attitude. "Disability stands for something you can't do," she told me. "I can read and learn, just differently. When I grow up, I plan to be a rocket scientist or an astrophysicist."

TOP TIPS FOR PARENTS

- Listen to your instincts.
- Keep a log and talk to teachers, counselors, and other adults who know your child to identify patterns.
- Share your child's strengths, interests, and history with the school.
- Revisit 504 Plans or IEPs regularly.
- Help your child understand why they're struggling.
- If your child is twice-exceptional, you may need to tap outside resources.
- Remove supports as they acquire skills.
- Role-play potentially difficult social scenarios.
- Seek support for yourself when needed.
- Know at least as much as your child about their specific challenges.
- Be curious, not accusatory. Don't lead with, "Why did you do that?"

CONVERSATION STARTERS

- "Do you think this is harder for you than other students?"
- "Were you the last one done on the math test?"
- "What went well in English today?"
- "What made the history assignment so challenging?"

- "What would you like your teacher to know about how you learn?"
- "What do you think your teacher would say is hardest for you?"
- "When do you feel most confident at school?"
- "Do you find that your challenges get in the way of your friendships?"

EMPOWERMENT AND RESILIENCE

"There are all sorts of people in the world,
and we'll all find our place."

CHAPTER 14

CONNECTING WITH BOYS AND HELPING THEM CONNECT WITH OTHERS

KEY SKILLS

1—Make good friend choices
2—Negotiate conflict
5—Consider others' perspectives
7—Self-regulate emotions
9—Make responsible, healthy, and
   ethical choices

"My mom keeps asking me the same question 1,000 different ways. I just need time to think."

"It's not that I don't care, I just don't want to get into it."

"If I was like, 'Hey, can I tell you about something you did that really bothered me,' my friends would be like, 'Huh?' We mostly just joke around."

My friend Liz was worried that her fourteen-year-old son, Andy, was traumatized. While on a ski trip, he'd seen a child fall off the chairlift. Andy was sitting in close range, and he saw the paramedics airlift the boy to a hospital. Liz tried to process the accident with Andy, but he wouldn't show any reaction. She made a few more attempts at conversation before letting it go.

Although this book includes separate chapters for boys and girls, I recognize that doesn't capture the full spectrum of gender identity. For more information on raising children who identify as transgender, gender fluid, bigender, or agender, here are some additional resources:

GLSEN (www.glsen.org)
PFLAG (www.pflag.org)
GLAAD (www.glaad.org)
National Center for Transgender Equality (transequality.org)
GENDERSPECTRUM (www.genderspectrum.org)
The annual Gender Odyssey conference
Books: Jennifer Boylan's *She's Not There*
Diane Ehrensaft's *The Gender Creative Child*
Arin Andrew's memoir, *Some Assembly Required: The Not-So-Secret Life of a Transgender Teen*

The following weekend, Andy, an avid skier, refused to return to the mountain. Liz quickly connected the dots. She called me and asked me to put on my school counselor hat. How could she know whether he needed support, she wondered, if she couldn't get him to talk about it? I reassured her that her instinct to hang back and give him space was fine. Liz and her husband made sure they had unstructured time together, and they told him they were available whenever he wanted to talk.

When that led nowhere, they tried a different approach. About a month after the ski-lift accident, they persuaded Andy to give skiing another try. The drive to the mountain was tense. When they arrived, Andy's father wordlessly coaxed him onto the chairlift, and they went through the motions together. His dad's calm, quiet presence gave him courage. On the drive home, Andy finally shared his sadness and asked about the injured boy. Liz told me the experience has changed how they communicate. She no longer pushes Andy to talk, keenly aware that he's most expressive when she leaves room for silence.

Teen boys have powerful feelings, but parents often mistakenly assume their silence means they prefer to be disengaged. "That's the mythology we have to fight against," adolescent developmental pediatrician Kenneth Ginsburg told me. "Don't assume silence is absence of thought. Boys sometimes feign being deaf or exhausted to create a space they can retreat into, but it's anything but an empty space. Boys have rich inner lives, and they care deeply about loyalty, friendship, and protecting the people they love." Boys can buy into the mythology as much as their parents. As a result, they may suppress emotions with both parents and peers.

Niobe Way, professor of developmental psychology at New York University, is trying to change that paradigm. I spoke to her about her work as principal investigator of The Listening Project, which teaches boys interviewing and listening skills to help them build their capacity for relationships. She shared that when she spoke to seventh-grade boys at George Jackson Academy in New York City about a teen who loved his best friend "beyond words," they all snickered. When she asked them what was so funny, a student said, "The dude sounds gay."

Way was ready to challenge that stereotype. "What would you say if I told you that approximately 85 percent of boys feel this way about a friend during their teen years?" she asked them. One boy said, "For real?" She said, "Yes, for real, boys want close friendships where they can share their secrets." Within ten seconds, two boys shared that they had "broken up" after a fight. "They talked about it in front of the class," Way told me. "All I did was give them permission. They didn't know it was normal."

Boys this age are starting to get pummeled with masculine expectations. Seventh grader Khalab told me he finds the messages confusing. He's been a calm, mature contributor to the middle school boys' group I cofacilitate with a male teacher, and he's been clear from the start that he has little use for stereotypes. "They're limiting who we can be as we grow up, and it's hard to be something you can't see," he explained. He plans to chart a different path— one that's consistent with his desire to rely on and support his friends. "If an unathletic boy doesn't want to play a game, I'll tell him he doesn't have to. If another boy wants to share his feelings, I'll tell him I'm there for him."

Andrew Reiner, a teacher and writer who researches teen boys and vulnerability, came to observe my boys' group several times, and afterward we'd talk about how we're living in a hinge era. "First and foremost, middle school boys want the approval and acceptance of other guys; that's paramount," Reiner told me. "But there are boys who are ahead of the curve, boys who've been raised to be more self-possessed, more self-aware at a younger age, and they want that connection. There's a growing minority of kids in this generation who get frustrated and scared by the bullying treatment of other boys who won't allow this and feel threatened by this kind of self-awareness."

I spoke to Swarthmore College assistant professor Joseph Derrick Nelson, who researches how gender stereotypes influence boys' identity development. He urges parents to teach their sons how to express feelings beyond anger, frustration, and empathy when they're young. If boys don't learn how to attain emotional intimacy, he told me, "We may be setting them up for relationship difficulties, addiction, violence, or risky behavior down the road."

You can take steps to prevent that outcome, starting with your own relationship with your son. Preserving and strengthening that bond in the tween and teen years is more about embracing a philosophy than completing a checklist, Ginsburg explained. "If you stay present, really believe in the kid, treat him like the expert in his life, and talk at the pace he's able to listen, then the details will work themselves out." Some boys do become more silent as they enter adolescence, but that just means that you need to communicate with them differently. Here are several ways you can continue to connect with your middle school son, while also helping him connect intimately with others.

Focus on loving, high-yield interactions.

If you consistently show that your love is constant and your presence is unconditional, you'll create a safe space for boys to share feelings. When my son, Ben, was in middle school, he'd want to unload immediately if he thought he bombed a test. He'd open the car door when I picked him up from school, then blurt out the news before his body was fully in the seat. "There's no way I passed the math test; I couldn't answer half the questions," he'd tell me. He knew how I'd react, but he still needed to hear it. I'd say, "That's annoying, I know you studied a lot. But it's going to be okay, and it's a history test now. Anything else happen at school?"

I could have taken a different tack and suggested that he swap study methods or seek extra help, but that would have backfired. I'd have sent the message that I was disappointed in him and cared more about his grades than his feelings. In that moment, he already felt defeated and simply wanted reassurance. Besides, we had better things to talk about. Ben always shared great stories during those rides home from school, and his anecdotes revealed what he found funny, irritating, or inspiring. Those were the high-yield conversations—not the ones about his grades.

The relationship will take a hit if you fixate on deficits instead of celebrating your son's strengths. Figure out what drives him, and find ways to acknowledge his special talents and interests. I know one father who makes a point of commenting on the elaborate mazes his son enjoys creating. Praise him for making an incredible omelet, or for being known as "Switzerland" at school because he's a natural mediator. Adopting a strengths-based approach is especially important in middle school, when most kids are full of self-doubt.

I've witnessed this in action. Cameron, an introverted, sensitive eighth grader, had a combative relationship with his father, Todd. They couldn't have been more different. Cameron sketched cartoons from the time he woke until he went to sleep. He'd come to my office to recharge, often using his math protractor to carve a ball of clay into a flower or a dog. Cameron's idea of hell was the school's annual 5K run, and he hated lacrosse even more.

Todd, on the other hand, was a former Division 1 lacrosse player with a blunt personality. He not only insisted that Cameron play lacrosse, but also coached his team. He'd force Cameron to do extra drills at home, then ride him for not working hard enough. In his quest to mold Cameron into an elite athlete, he was wrecking their relationship. He also was failing to appreciate his son's many other gifts. The dynamic created a paradox. Cameron felt both attacked and invisible, and he took no pride in his impressive artistic creations.

As Ginsburg often reminds parents, "The themes of adolescence include: are my parents proud of me, do I fit in with my peers, am I capable at school, do I have any idea what I can do with my life, am I comfortable with my developing sexuality, and, most basically, am I good enough? If you put all of those questions together, you can begin to see why it matters so much that a parent loves a child for who they are." That's the foundation that offers the security for a middle school boy to answer all of those pro-foundly challenging questions.

Show interest in his life and create shared experiences.

When you demonstrate genuine curiosity about your son's passions, you're more likely to establish a strong connection. Attend his class play or soccer game, and know what he's studying in school. The more you know about his life, the more topics you'll have to discuss. Find activities that are nat-ural extensions of his interests, whether it's a sports event, movie, or mu-seum. Know the kids he hangs out with and how he likes to unwind. This doesn't mean overstepping boundaries. You can show authentic interest without violating your son's need for privacy and autonomy.

Try creating shared experiences you'd both enjoy. If that seems com-plicated, try this exercise. Take out two scraps of paper. First, write down three activities your child would love and you'd be willing to do. Then give a piece of paper to your son and ask him to write down three things he'd like to do—and that he knows you'd be willing to do. You'll end up with six potential bonding activities.

Once you're alone together, facilitate dialogue by asking concrete questions. "Ask them the best or worst thing that happened in school, or whether things went better with the math teacher," says Michael Thompson, a clinical psychologist and the author of *Raising Cain: Pro-tecting the Emotional Life of Boys*. Otherwise, "They're thinking, 'Where is this leading, and why does my mom need to know this?'" You may find it difficult to tolerate your son's long stretches of silence, but don't push too hard. If you stay patient, present, and involved, he'll start to share more about his life.

That said, you may need to get creative. Writing notes back and forth can be a less intrusive way to communicate. Buy a notebook for the kitchen or front hall table, leave your son notes, and invite him to respond. You can start with simple questions, such as, "How was your day?" Even if the exchanges are initially superficial, he may gather the courage to share that he's anxious about fitting in, or that he's more upset than you realized about getting cut from the soccer team.

The car also is a natural place to connect with your son. Eye contact is optional, and boys may find talking less intimidating in that setting. A car ride can be a prime time to talk about uncomfortable topics, but be willing to initiate those conversations. Whether you're discussing sex or another difficult topic, be careful not to overreact to a comment when your son wades into sensitive territory. You may be misinterpreting what he said, and the conversation is more likely to continue if you stay neutral. If the talk does devolve into an argument, don't halt the conversation. As I explained in the chapter on lying, kids consider arguing a productive exchange and a way to better understand your perspective. Fighting is a good sign that they respect your opinion.

Video games, like cars, provide a way to connect without eye contact. Aziz Abdur-Ra'oof, a former professional football player and educational consultant who mentors teen boys, suggests that parents ask their son to teach them how to play a game they like. He also recommends establishing a consistent time when your son expects to talk, then provide conversation starters and be really present. "That means the TV is off," Abdur-Ra'oof told me. "If you take a phone call mid-conversation with them, they'll think you don't care."

To enhance the time you spend together, limit your child's distractions, too. Create a contract with rules regarding technology. Within that, for example, you might specify that the family will have device-free dinners together three nights a week. You can do the same when technology is impeding your son's time with peers during sleepovers, hangouts, carpools, and other social scenarios. It's never too late to set clear expectations.

As baffling as it may seem, boys can feel intimately connected to people they only know from gaming and chat rooms. They may not recognize that they're missing out on more authentic face-to-face time. Online interactions do hit on some basic friendship-building skills, but at the expense of others. As psychologist Adam Pletter told me, "They're sharing, compromising, negotiating, and feeling connected and validated, but eye contact and body language are completely eliminated when you're typing." If you try all of these strategies and continue to hit a brick wall, cut yourself some slack. As Michael Thompson told me, there's no magic parent who holds the secret to getting a middle school boy to open up.

Tackle stereotypes about masculinity.

When Ben was fourteen, I started getting all of his texts on my iPad. It was a glitch, and I came clean right away, expecting him to be freaked out. "It's fine," he told me. "Whatever." I paused. The texts were popping up rapid-fire as I tried to work, and some were pretty graphic. I was certain his friends would not appreciate my reading them and suggested he fix the problem, but he insisted it was no big deal. His openness ran counter to common wisdom about teen boys, who tend to be portrayed as intensely private. And that's the point. Stereotypes won't tell you anything about your own son.

That doesn't mean that stereotypes about what it means to be a man aren't impacting him, or that you shouldn't address them. Fathers, especially, need to model how to deal constructively with difficult emotions. Do you call a friend when you're stressed, or do you suppress your feelings? Make sure your son observes you utilizing healthy coping strategies. This isn't to discount the importance of mothers or other women in boys' lives. As Khalab told me, "My dad tells me I can be whatever I want without any backlash, but I mostly talk to my mom." He debriefs with her every night at 9 p.m., just before bed. "Even though she's a woman, she offers insight into how I should interact with the opposite gender, and she assures me that I should feel comfortable talking to her even when I make mistakes," he said.

Talk about what it means to be a boy. As Joseph Nelson says, "They're getting the message, 'Stand up for yourself, be tough, don't let anyone disrespect you, don't act like a girl, don't pick a girlfriend over your friends, don't show sadness. Particularly for low-income black and Latino boys, so much of their physical safety is dependent on whether they're perceived as weak. I've spoken to black fathers who tell their boys, 'It's okay for you to cry at home, but not at the park. At home, you're loved, you're safe.'" Make a point of telling your son, "You may be getting different messages on the outside, but it's okay to be upset."

You may need to examine your own beliefs, especially if you're clinging to gender stereotypes, such as "all girls are dramatic" or "all boys don't talk." As psychotherapist Katie Hurley told me, "Boys can cook, girls can do kickboxing. Let's open the box and let them be who they want to be." At the same time, acknowledge that it can be hard to push back against masculine expectations.

Many of my students, like Khalab, *do* want to push back. In one session of my boys' group, I asked them to fill a "man box" with words that reflect cultural ideas about masculinity. Competitive, aggressive, tough, and sporty all went into the box. Then I asked them to characterize themselves. The boys determined that many of the words and phrases they used to describe themselves—including thoughtful, self-aware, smart, and likes to read and write—couldn't go into the man box. Another time, I read them a list of words including suffering, tenderness, shyness, shame, trust, joy, excitement, insecurity, sadness, and anger. They decided that a few of the words were neutral, but only anger truly belonged in the "man box." I was taken aback and asked if they could recall a time when they didn't think twice about showing pure joy. They said it was probably back in second or third grade.

"You're not supposed to care about grades or whether you can be yourself with friends," one boy told the group. "I think we all feel those things are important, but no one wants to risk getting a bad reaction." Another student added, "I couldn't just walk up to my friend and say, 'Hey, Joe, do you have the same complicated emotions that I have?' The most I'll say outside the boys' group to someone who upsets me is, 'I didn't appreciate that,' instead of saying, 'That got me down and kind of ruined my day.'"

When Reiner interviewed a few of my students for an article he wrote about the boys' group for the *New York Times*, seventh grader Harrison Goodweather told him, "This is the one place where I feel safe. I leave the group feeling better about being in school because I know that I'm not so alone about the things that bother me." Harrison and the other boys have resolved to mentor younger boys in the school, and to set a positive, "preventive" example.

Fortunately, more male adults are challenging some of these cultural norms, too—including professional athletes. NBA player Kevin Love wrote in *The Players Tribune* that growing up, he followed the "be a man" playbook. He handled tough experiences on his own so he wouldn't appear weak. At age twenty-nine, however, he started having panic attacks and realized that he needed help. He now talks publicly about the need for boys to show vulnerability, noting, "We're all carrying around things that hurt—and they can hurt us if we keep them buried inside."

Fathers can help by bucking norms themselves. This may be especially important for kids who don't identify with the sex they were assigned at birth. Alexis Lewis, an eighteen-year-old college student, didn't come out as transgender until she was fifteen. "I didn't know that I didn't have to be overly masculine," she told me. "I needed to hear that from my dad, and I needed him to act as a role model." She also believes that parents shouldn't force their sons to play a sport they hate, particularly if they'll have to engage with "toxically masculine" boys.

On the flip side, Alisa Bowman thinks her thirteen-year-old transgender son had a fairly easy time coming out in fifth grade because he fit so many masculine stereotypes. "There are some boys who are really feminine and they're not necessarily gay, and that's something to be celebrated too," she said. "They don't have a place to call home because society doesn't consider that okay yet."

Parents also can defy gender expectations by demonstrating the power of touch. William Parker, the executive director of the Oklahoma Middle Level Association, told me he makes a point of being physically demonstrative. "I hug my twelve-year-old son, Jack, just like I hug my girls, but I also show him that it's okay to put your arm around someone. I hug the guys I know; it's cultural where I live in Oklahoma. I want my son to grow up knowing that you can have deep affectionate friendships that don't have to be about romance."

— IDEA FOR EDUCATORS —
DO THE "MAN BOX" ACTIVITY

Do the Man Box activity to get boys thinking about masculine norms. First, ask them to independently come up with words they believe describe a "real man." Then have them share their list with the group. You also can talk about the derogatory names boys are called when they don't conform to societal expectations. After that exercise, ask the boys to work alone again to list words that describe themselves. Have them write their answers anonymously on sticky notes, then collect the notes and read off each descriptor. For each one, ask the group whether they think it belongs in the Man Box. The students will discover that every boy has interests and character traits that don't meet the "manly ideal."

Normalize emotional intimacy by drawing parallels.

Many moments of intimacy are accepted in the sports context, and these examples can be good teaching moments if your son is interested in sports. When boys watch a football game, Joseph Nelson pointed out, "There's lots of sideways hugging and sitting close, but it's not seen as inappropriate." The same is true for athletes. "When someone tells his teammate, 'That was a really great catch,' it's an expression of vulnerability, but I don't think boys know it," Abdur-Ra'oof said. "They just do it because they've dropped or caught a pass and know what that's like." He tells parents to say, "When your teammate didn't perform well during the basketball game, it was great how you went up to him and helped him." He told me that parents can generalize the concept by saying, "Jon, remember how you didn't like James when you first played basketball together, but then you realized he was a good guy and supportive teammate? When you approach people at school, think about that experience and how it can take time to get to know someone."

Teach them how to repair rifts, too. Boys are more likely than girls to walk away when there's a hiccup in a friendship, and that can leak to their romantic life later. "Their girlfriend may do something, and the only solution they can think of is to leave," Niobe Way explained. Parents can model that rectifying situations takes work and vulnerability. A father might say, "I was really angry with my friend and had to take time to think about my part. Once I calmed down, I called him to apologize for my behavior."

You also can work to prevent conflicts, particularly physical ones. "All the norms around masculinity for boys are about physical toughness," Nelson said. "You're not going to disrespect me; I'm going to shove you to show you that you can't do that again." If an altercation escalates, debrief after the incident. Ask your son to explain the sequence of events. What did the other student do and how did he respond? Then help him address the "why." You can say, "You pushed him and he fell—what was that about?" To create some distance, Way will discuss her daughter's or her own friendship struggles in her son's presence and ask for his advice. "It's too touchy feely for him to have these conversations about his own friendships."

Heighten your son's sensitivity by talking about his friends' boundaries. "Boys love banter and trash talking, and this is really the root of a lot of boy issues, because there are different tolerance levels for sarcasm," middle school counselor Ricky Stakem told me. "If a boy sees someone with a black eye and says, 'Your face is messed up,' that kid's feelings might get hurt even if the first kid isn't trying to be mean." Explain that if a friend looks wounded or stops engaging, it's time to back down.

Boys can have wildly varying limits. Jeff, a physical education teacher and soccer coach, told me that his middle school athletes send each other Snapchats of their private parts in a completely nonsexual way for shock value. One boy sent a photo of his penis to his best friend, and the other one sent one back to be goofy. He added that boys can take these pranks too far. "Some boys are almost desensitized, but others take it personally. And parents don't get it at all. When that kid's mom saw his friend's penis on his camera roll, she was like, 'What is this?' I have to have a lot of conversations with my team about dialing it back," he said.

Physical interactions can be off-putting to many boys, but it's hard to avoid them. Middle school boys are constantly jumping on one another's backs, and boys who don't like roughhousing might internalize their discomfort. Encourage sensitivity by asking your son if he'd like it if his friends tied his shoelaces together on the bus, or yanked on his backpack until he fell over. Middle school educators can help by facilitating interactive schoolwide advisory lessons on respecting classmates' boundaries, running structured groups for boys, and closely monitoring hallway interactions. Coaches can be influential, too, by modeling open communication, transparency, and healthy competition. In boys' contact sports, coaches may even become surrogate fathers. Reiner noted that they may be more respected than other men in a boy's life because they represent that masculine ideal.

Nurture the art of curiosity and bolster boys' emotional vocabulary.

If we want kids to have trusting, meaningful relationships, we need to give them practical skills. Way asks The Listening Project participants to reflect on what's happening in their own friendships, then pick someone to interview whom they love but don't know much about. Interestingly, she told me, almost all the boys pick their mothers. The boys become the people exploring friendships, asking questions such as, "Who do you trust the most and why?" They learn how to be good listeners and follow up with deeper questions. People place a premium on empathy, but curiosity is just as important in a friendship, and parents can nurture that trait. With her own children, Way will say, "I'm doing a project that asks people what they fear the most. What would you say?"

To further boost your son's emotional vocabulary, help him describe his relationships. Ask, "What do you like the most or least about your friendship with Nate?" Point out how a good friend treats him. Maybe he's willing to lend him his favorite video game, or he calls to check up on him when he's home sick for a few days. To tap into his emotions, your son may need to work backwards. If he seems upset, ask, "What's the physical symptom in your body? Where are you experiencing it?" Teach him that sensations can provide clues to his emotional state. By the time boys reach middle school, they're accustomed to ignoring deeper feelings. "All the messages they get from TV, social media, and pop culture are about being badass and hardcore," Reiner told me. "Action heroes are not guys who ask for help or show hesitation or self-doubt."

The ultimate clue, of course, is crying. A parent once asked Reiner whether she should be concerned that her son cries frequently. "I said, 'Crying is a window into us at our most vulnerable, and one of the few times you can sit down without pumping him full of questions about what he's feeling. He's clearly feeling sadness.'" Capitalize on those moments and say, "You're clearly feeling a strong emotion right now. What's beneath the tears? If you're ready to talk, I'm here." At the very least, you'll bear witness and let your son know that he's not alone.

TOP TIPS FOR PARENTS

- Love and honor your son for who he is, and focus on his strengths.
- Prioritize "high-yield conversations," not ones about grades or controlling behavior.
- Be strategic about when and how you connect.
- Don't assume his silence means he wants to be disengaged.
- Place a notepad on the kitchen or front hall table and leave each other notes.
- Cut yourself some slack—no parent has all the answers to communicating with a twelve- or thirteen-year-old boy.
- Address stereotypes and model healthy coping strategies.
- Don't ask leading questions—be concrete or he'll wonder where the conversation is headed.
- Hug your son and show him physical affection.
- Point out when a friend is treating him well or clearly trusts him, and remind him that it takes time to get to know someone.

CONVERSATION STARTERS

- "Who do you trust the most and why?"
- "What do you fear most?"
- "What do you like about your friendship with Nate?"
- "Do you think the main character in the movie is a good friend? Would you choose to act differently?"
- "I can see you're upset. If you want to talk, I'm here."
- "What do you think people tend to misunderstand about boys?"

CHAPTER 15

RAISING STRONG, EMPOWERED GIRLS

KEY SKILLS

2—Negotiate conflict

5—Consider others' perspectives

6—Self-advocate

7—Self-regulate emotions

8—Cultivate passions and recognize limitations

9—Make responsible, healthy, and ethical choices

"I hate playing goalie. Every time the other team scores, it's my fault."

"The teacher forgot it was my turn to lead advisory, but it's not worth making it into a big deal."

"My skin has totally broken out, so there's no way I'm going to the dance."

At age fourteen, I waited tables at Brigham's, an ice cream and sandwich shop. The manager threw me in with no training and it showed. I'd remember the hamburger but not the ketchup, or the ice cream but not the spoon. By the third day, I started to get the hang of it, but that wasn't fast enough for the manager. He pulled me aside at the end of the week. "You're not going to come back, are you?" he snapped at me. "Because you're really, really bad at this. I had no idea anyone could be this slow." I looked at my feet nervously and apologized. I also didn't return—not even to collect my paycheck. Despite the fact that I had spent the week mopping floors, serving endless grilled cheese sandwiches, and scooping ice cream, I didn't think I deserved to be paid. As an adult, I shake my head at my meekness. I may have been an imperfect waitress, but I had worked hard and earned that money.

When my girlfriends and I share stories about our first jobs as teens and young adults, timidity is a common theme. Susan worked in Paris after her college graduation, and she can still vividly recall her boss. "She'd fly off the handle at the smallest things, screaming, 'Vous êtes nul!'—you're nothing!" Susan would retreat to the bathroom to cry. "I didn't have the confidence to fix it or leave," she told me. My friend Shari felt that paralysis when she was working at a magazine in New York and forgot to fax her editorial director a document. "He waited until everyone left, then locked the door and told me he was deeply disappointed in me," she recalled. She didn't know how to handle his overreaction, explaining that it felt complicated to stick up for herself when she knew she had made a mistake.

Susan and Shari wish they'd learned to self-advocate and respond to feedback before they started working, when the stakes were much lower. They want their own teen daughters to have an easier time, but they're unsure how to impart such complex lessons. If anything, it seems as though their middle school daughters have suddenly become more apprehensive about taking risks or making waves.

Research bears this theory out. In a Ypulse study, researchers found that girls' confidence levels drop by 30 percent between ages eight and fourteen, and they're also 18 percent less likely than boys to describe themselves as confident. In addition, more than half of the girls reported feeling the pressure to be perfect. Nearly 80 percent of them said they want to feel more confident. All of these data points make middle school the ideal time to double down on giving your daughter the skills and courage to navigate tough situations. Here are several ways you can help her keep her confidence at a time when she feels most vulnerable. If you're successful, she'll be much more likely to develop and retain the skills she'll need for the workplace and relationships.

Don't breed the expectation of perfection.

As we seek to empower girls, we need to be careful not to layer on a new set of unattainable expectations. "I worry we almost box girls in," says author Peggy Orenstein. "Now, not only do they have to be friendly and nice and thin and pretty, but they also have to be brave and empowered and smart." Her fourteen-year-old daughter will say, "If one more person tells me girls need to be brave, I'm just going to go off on them." She'll mock it after a while, roll her eyes, and say, "Enough!" "We want girls to be resilient in the world, but we almost over-freight the idea of empowered so it becomes a source of anxiety for them," Orenstein added.

Girls' desire to please can magnify anxiety and backfire. Rachel Simmons, cofounder of the organization Girls Leadership, explains that when girls focus on winning approval, they shy away from risks. "If you're a quintessential good girl, you experience failing as letting someone down. Instead of saying, 'I missed that goal in the soccer game,' it's that everyone will hate me." She urges parents to help girls focus on how they performed rather than how they're perceived, and to help them avoid ruminating, which amplifies the impact of the setback.

Girls also may be more likely to attribute failure to their own lack of ability, while research shows that boys tend to blame external factors, such as not studying. Parents can counteract this mind-set by focusing more on progress than results. Girls also may be more prone to self-doubt than boys. "If you ask a child after each question on a test, 'How confident are you that you got that right?' boys do better and girls do worse," says psychotherapist Amy Morin, author of *13 Things Mentally Strong Women Don't Do*. "They change their answer because they doubt themselves. Confidence is key, so teach girls to take note of what they're thinking and how those thoughts affect their behavior."

For Claire Shipman, coauthor of *The Confidence Code for Girls* and the mother of an eleven-year-old girl, understanding that failure helps kids develop resilience was liberating. "Instead of obsessing, I'm able to quickly say, 'Okay, life lesson,' and focus on helping her move forward." Recently, her daughter didn't make a soccer team, and Shipman worried she'd drop the sport. "I told her there were other tryouts, and another team ended up really wanting her. It was a hellish twenty-four hours, but I was so glad she decided to keep trying."

To help girls maintain reasonable expectations, challenge unattainable ideals. Find and share realistic images so your daughter isn't just seeing images of women that have been Photoshopped and filtered. Shipman and her coauthor, Katty Kay, launched the #CaptureConfidence campaign to give girls a way to show that imperfection and confidence are not mutually exclusive. Girls are using the hashtag to do everything from challenge stereotypes about dancers' bodies to help black girls feel proud of their natural hair.

Teach your daughter to critique the culture as a whole, too. When Orenstein's daughter was twelve, they passed a line of Supergirl and Batgirl dolls in Target. She asked what her daughter thought of the dolls, and was proud to hear her repeating one of Orenstein's common critiques—that the dolls' eyes were bigger than their wrists. Her daughter, who is biracial (Asian and white), also will comment on how the cosmetic industry doesn't acknowledge that people come in a vast variety of skin tones. "She'll say that when they do, it tends to be black and white," Orenstein told me, adding that this can affect a girl's self-image.

Be mindful of your messaging.

Stray comments can leave deep wounds. If you want your daughter to be self-accepting, you may need to check yourself. One seventh-grade girl told me she didn't ask the boy she liked to a dance because she was "too fat." She said she first became self-conscious about her weight when her father off-handedly suggested she skip the mashed potatoes at dinner. He hadn't meant to hurt her, but the comment had stuck. She'd been upset and obsessing about her weight for months. An eighth-grade girl shared a similar story. While eating brunch at a local pancake house, she poured syrup on her waffles. When she reached for the butter, her mother grabbed her wrist. "Don't use syrup *and* butter!" she said. "That's how you get a belly."

"It can be excruciatingly difficult to keep your mouth closed when you're watching your child do something you think is self-destructive— especially if you have your own baggage about weight," Simmons told me.

Parents need to understand that criticism intended to be helpful is rarely heard by a child that way. "Girls are famously prone to hearing a critical voice as yelling, and that same sensitivity kicks in when it comes to their bodies," she said. "At some point, feedback goes from being constructive to corrosive. 'Are you really going to eat that?' means, 'You can't afford to eat that much and still look good.'" Instead, focus on what your daughter's body needs to be strong and healthy. Simmons urges parents to ask themselves, "Have I said this before? Am I saying it to help my child, or to release myself from my own anxiety? If so, is there a better way to manage my own emotions?"

It's hard to show restraint when you think you're helping your daughter. Sue Ashford, a professor at the University of Michigan's Ross School of Business who studies feedback, recalls falling into that trap when her daughter was in middle school. "I study feedback-seeking for a reason—I tend to be overly cognizant of it," she told me. "I wish I'd criticized my daughter less, had just supported her and told her, 'You're great,' but I didn't always do that because I worried about what others thought, about whether she'd have friends and fit in."

When Orenstein knows her personal baggage will get in the way, she puts her husband in charge. "I had to fake the whole idea of modeling less negative body image, and he doesn't have those issues. Let the person who has normality around food get in there. He's able to give her something that I can't." People tend to think about mothers when it comes to raising strong daughters, but fathers might be better-positioned to teach some skills. We often short-shrift them, and fathers tend to pull back when girls hit puberty. This approach is misguided. Daughters need their fathers just as much, if not more, when they hit middle school. Linda Nielsen, who teaches a course at Wake Forest University on strengthening father-daughter relationships, has found that when fathers maintain healthy relationships with their middle school–aged daughters, the girls tend to be more self-reliant, self-confident, and successful, and less likely to develop eating disorders.

While parents need to be careful about what they say to their daughters, they also need to be mindful of their unspoken messages. When certified financial planner Nancy Anderson was twelve, she desperately hoped she'd receive 200 shares of stock, the same gift her brother got when he turned twelve the year before. "I was so excited, I spent that whole year wondering what kind of stock they'd give me," she wrote in an email. "I wondered, would it be the same company or a different one? Would my name be on the certificate?" Then her birthday rolled around and she didn't get any shares. "The underlying message I learned at that young age was, 'investing is for boys.'"

To send your daughter a different message about her capacity for business, help her develop negotiation skills. "Teach her in a low-stress environment, such as hitting a yard sale or flea market," Anderson suggests. "Tell her to start by asking for more than she wants so she can come down in price. Pick something that's not important to her that she can then give to charity. This way, it's a fun game, and she can enjoy asking and deal-making." Similarly, Simmons told me she plans to encourage her daughter to negotiate her babysitting fees. "I think that learning to negotiate your salary is important, and a lot of young women don't have that skill."

Janine Shelffo, the mother of a fourteen-year-old girl and cohead of technology, media, and telecommunications at UBS Investment Bank, frequently tells stories from her work to illustrate basic financial concepts for her daughter, such as the relationship between risk and reward, the time value of money, and the pitfalls of excessive leverage. She hopes this understanding will provide a strong foundation for making good decisions down the road about saving for the future and investing wisely.

Help her build comfort with the word "leader."

We need to do a better job valuing leadership skills in girls. Ashford's research shows that women tend to avoid leading because they worry, "What if I step on someone's toes or damage a friendship?" She's found that those who do lead feel comfortable with the word "leader." Parents and educators need to work together to help girls self-identify as leaders, and that may mean examining their own attitudes. "When school systems see leadership skills in girls, they give negative feedback subtly and directly both to girls and their parents, in the hopes that parents will stamp it out," she explained.

Children internalize these messages. As researchers from the Making Caring Common project found in a survey of nearly 20,000 students, many teen boys and girls—along with their parents—are biased against female leaders, whether they're kids or adults. The school environment makes a difference. When Ashford's daughter was entering sixth grade, she transferred to a new school. She'd been labeled as strong-willed in elementary school, so Ashford decided to meet with the counselor ahead of time to ease the transition.

"The counselor said to me, 'What's your daughter like?' I said, she's always enthusiastic and trying to help, but she sometimes rubs people the wrong way.' The counselor said, 'What I'd like is for you to send her to us exactly as she is, and I'll prepare the school to receive her and accept her as she is.'"

Ashford cried for five minutes because it was the first time someone said to her, "Have you considered that those others have been wrong, and that she's fine as she is?"

The school recognized and encouraged her daughter's natural leadership qualities. She acted in the play, was elected a class officer, and was a finalist for her school's Contribution to the Culture Award as a senior. When she went to college, she had the skills to lead a major organization within her large university.

Be careful not to define leadership too narrowly or to discount quieter girls. When my daughter Emily was eleven, she attended a question-and-answer session with Hillary Clinton, who had recently ended her tenure as secretary of state. Emily isn't shy, but she's on the introverted side, and she used to wonder whether she was capable of being a leader. After Clinton spoke, Emily raised her hand. "Do you have to be in a position of leadership to make a positive change in the world?" she asked. Clinton didn't hesitate. "Not at all—teachers are leaders, nurses are leaders," she told her. "You don't have to be an elected official or the president of a corporation to make a difference. In fact, some people who hold positions of power don't use their influence to help others."

It's a message I wish I'd heard in junior high. I was too shy to speak in eighth-grade social studies, but I loved history. That was the year I first heard Sting's song "Russians" and started reading about Mutual Assured Destruction, a doctrine that terrified me. Without telling anyone, I wrote an op-ed about my view on nuclear buildup and mailed it to the *Boston*

Globe. I still remember my father's—and my teacher's—shock when my article ran in the paper a few months later. It never occurred to me then that writing and sharing ideas could be a form of leadership. To my fourteen-year-old self, the "real" leaders were the soccer team captains and student council presidents.

When I talk to quieter girls now, I try to cultivate their interests and help them think beyond conventional leadership roles. As Susan Cain, the author of *Quiet: The Power of Introverts in a World That Can't Stop Talking,* and founder of Quiet Revolution, told me, "A lot of the places students' talents take them naturally are not considered 'leadership' in the constricted sense, but leadership is when you're making an impact and taking action that shapes the lives of other people in a positive way."

Cain shared a story with me about a middle school girl who faked extroversion and "twisted herself into a pretzel" so she'd be picked to be a peer mentor. She excelled, but was kicked out by an extroverted teacher who felt she wasn't outgoing enough for the role. "She was absolutely devastated, but then she realized that what she really liked was science, not being a mentor," Cain said. The girl started working after school with her biology teacher, who appreciated her strengths, and she ended up publishing her first scientific paper at age seventeen.

Instead of giving girls the message to go out and take the world by storm, we should be telling them to go out, be themselves, and dream big. As Cain noted, "We need to make sure the role models we give our girls don't all look like Sheryl Sandberg, who I love, and who's an amazing role model for a certain type of girl. We also need to showcase girls and women who have a more understated style, so they understand there are a lot of ways to be successful, happy, and contributing to the world."

Identify mentors and role models.

Encourage your daughter to get in the habit of connecting with mentors she respects, whether they're teachers, coaches, or supervisors at an after-school job. This is a deceptively simple task that requires judgment, and it will be a critical skill in the workplace. Mentors also can provide a space where girls feel heard and validated. Girls often are unable to be authentic with peers because they worry they'll be judged or criticized. Mentors can help by encouraging girls to embrace their differences as strengths instead of failures. This isn't about forcing an inorganic relationship, but rather teaching kids to notice when they connect with a kindred spirit.

"When I was in seventh grade, I had a teacher, Mr. Ruud, who told me that I was a leader and I should take his leadership class," Sheridan School head Jessica Donovan told me as we chatted in her office. "One time we were on the bus on a field trip, and he told me my thoughts were important and I should keep a journal," she said. "He was the first person to make me feel important, and it really struck me. I became a middle school teacher because Mr. Ruud was one, and I became a leader because he told me that I was one."

Shelffo says she benefited from role models early in her career who had the confidence to embrace their own idiosyncrasies. They reinforced for her that there was no single blueprint for career success. Mentors don't have to be the same gender, she noted, adding that men with daughters have been some of her most impactful mentors. They often have greater appreciation for the subtle obstacles to female success in the workplace.

Just as with boys, girls can't be what they can't see. "Girls can do just as much as anyone else, and we need to give them role models of the same gender and ethnicity," says Alexis Lewis, now eighteen, who started winning invention contests in middle school. Books such as Rachel Ignotofsky's *Women in Science: 50 Fearless Pioneers Who Changed the World* offer a glimpse into the lives of women ranging from primatologist Jane Goodall to Katherine Johnson, the African American physicist and mathematician who calculated the trajectory of the 1969 Apollo 11 mission to the moon. Whenever you can, introduce your daughter to real women working in fields where they're the minority, such as STEM (science, technology, engineering, and mathematics) or investment banking.

Donna Orender—the author of *Wowsdom: The Girl's Guide to the Positive and the Possible*; the former president of the Women's National Basketball Association; and a retired professional basketball player—regularly organizes formal mentor walks for middle school girls. The girls wear a specific color to indicate the field they're interested in, such as medicine or technology, then pair off with women working in that field (who wear the same color). They walk along a nature path and share their hopes and dreams.

One time, Orender paired all the girls with women who were sixty-five and older. After the walk, the older women read "letters to my younger self," and the girls read "letters to my older self." "It was such a powerful way to show the girls that they're not alone, and that intergenerational connection is a two-way street," she told me. At the end of every walk, she reminds the girls that their mentor will always take their calls, and she urges them to continue to reach out for help.

— IDEA FOR EDUCATORS —
BRING IN WOMEN TO SPEAK AT CAREER LUNCHES

Start a practice of holding regular career lunches, and bring in women who work in a variety of professions, including those in which women are underrepresented. The women could be mothers of students in the school or visitors from the greater community. Encourage the speakers to share both the victories and challenges they've encountered on their journeys. They can underscore that girls shouldn't let setbacks deter them from pursuing their goals. If they're willing, they could adopt a mentor role and maintain ongoing relationships with interested girls.

Own her success.

It's important that parents encourage girls to take credit for their work. Girls are more likely than boys to be self-deprecating or to attribute their success to luck or other people. Shipman noted that girls worry about coming across as arrogant or boastful and just want to fit in, but the problem is that they start to believe their own rhetoric and experience self-doubt. "When I was a foreign correspondent in Moscow, people would ask me how I ended up there, and I'd feel kind of embarrassed and say I didn't know," she told me. She went on to cover the White House, a transition that terrified her. "It would have been a useful and powerful message to say to myself, 'Look at what I accomplished in Moscow,' rather than believing I just fell into it."

You can reassure your daughter that it's not immodest to have confidence and to know your own worth. Convey that nice, kind girls also can be competitive, ambitious, and goal-oriented. When she lacks confidence, teach her to "act as if," and remind her that everyone feels like an impostor at times.

It might help to teach your daughter how to use expansive body language. Social psychologist Amy Cuddy, the author of *Presence: Bringing Your Boldest Self to Your Biggest Challenges*, told me that when girls are young, they stand with their feet apart and their chest out, but by the time they hit middle school, they start to display shrinking behavior. "If anything, boys start to take up more space and girls pull long sleeves over their hands, wrap themselves up, slouch more, and want to make themselves small," she said. Tell your daughter that she deserves to take up space, and that poor posture will affect her mood and sense of self-efficacy. Ask, "How do you feel when you're sitting like that?" Cuddy explains, "Feeling powerful activates what we call the behavioral approach system and makes us more optimistic, generally happier, and more confident and willing to take risks."

Teach girls to invest in one another's success.

Encourage your daughter to celebrate other girls, especially in middle school, a time when girls are particularly prone to competitive feelings. Help her focus on doing her best rather than beating someone else. The organization Girls on the Run takes this approach, and Allie Riley, the organization's senior vice president of programming and evaluation, says it works. "At the 5K, the whole team will run in with a struggling girl, or you'll see two girls trying to cross the finish line together." At home, encourage your daughter to articulate a specific goal, then ask, "Did you run more laps today than yesterday?" This is healthier than fixating on whether she ran more laps than everyone else.

When girls are part of a group with a shared goal, they learn to set their egos aside. They also may be more likely to support other women when they enter the work world. "Unfortunately, it's been communicated to us over the years that there are fewer spots for women—a limited inventory," Orender noted, and team sports teach girls to invest in others' success. Girls who aren't interested in sports can join another group with a shared vision. Consultant Jon Gordon, author of *The Power of a Positive Team*, recommends activities such as drama or marching band. "In theatre, you have to make it about what's best for the performance, and in a marching band you have to trust that the person next to you won't hit or step on you," he told me. "It's all about being better for each other—no one achieves greatness in isolation."

Caroline Miller, a positive psychology expert and author of *Getting Grit*, wants middle school girls to grow up understanding that it's counterproductive to undermine one another—either now or when they're adults. When I spoke to her, she had just returned from presenting to women leaders in Québec. She asked them, "Does anyone feel like one of the biggest challenges we face at work is women shooting each other from inside the tent?" Every single woman raised their hand. She started the #Share222 movement after hearing that complaint repeatedly. The moment a woman hears about another woman's achievement, Miller wants her to post the news on two social media outlets. You can model that kind of supportive behavior for your daughter, and also coach her to behave the same way. Instead of posting a party pic or selfie, encourage her to share news about a girlfriend who achieved a meaningful personal goal. This practice kicks off a positive cycle. Girls want to reciprocate, and they learn to focus more on friendship and tenacity than popularity or appearance.

In addition to teaching your daughter to celebrate other girls' successes, you can look for conferences that unite and empower girls. Ashley Eckstein, founder of Her Universe and the voice of Ahsoka Tano in *Star Wars*, recently brought her thirteen-year-old niece to the Girl Up Leadership Summit in Washington, DC. She wanted her to experience what it felt like to be around hundreds of girls celebrating one another. One of the speakers was sixteen-year-old Chanice Lee, editor in chief of the Melanin Diary, a popular online global platform for black teens. "When I introduced Chanice, the cheers from the audience of just other girls literally gave me goosebumps," Eckstein told me. "Something very right was happening in that room."

Learn to navigate conflict and articulate feelings.

Parents can coach girls to solve problems on their own, whether they need academic support or want more responsibility at an internship. Urge your daughter to use her voice, whether she actively contributes to class discussions, writes for the school paper, or champions a cause. Recently, Shipman's daughter was upset that a school activity was offered only to boys, and she summoned the courage to ask administrators to revisit the policy. Although she didn't love the initial result, she felt good about representing all girls. It was a learning experience for Shipman, too. "Halfway through, I realized the outcome didn't matter, because it was such a valuable experience for her to advocate for herself."

Mothers can make a point of speaking up in front of their daughters. "When I was little, my mother would complain at Roy Rogers that her french fries weren't hot," Simmons told me. "I was dying at the time, but when I was about thirty I found myself doing the same thing." You may not know what will make an impact, but your daughter is watching and listening. Orenstein notes that it may be hard for some mothers to express their feelings, ideas, limits, and wants. "Boys have issues around being allowed only happiness and anger, but girls need practice articulating disagreement or boundaries," she explained. "We don't give girls a lot of language, because it feels like you're not being nice. When my daughter was in preschool and needed to be more assertive, my husband would practice with her and say, 'This is what you say, and this is what you do.' I watched and was like, 'Wow, I wouldn't know what to do.'"

Don't let anyone else define her goals.

If you want your daughter to dream big, underscore the importance of a support network, whether it's family, peers, or future colleagues. No one can be successful at everything, so encourage her to stay optimistic and to believe in her intrinsic value even when she stumbles. If she doesn't experience failure or disappointment, she may never discover her inner strength or realize she can triumph after a string of setbacks.

At every step of the way, ask your daughter questions to help her formulate a plan. What does she hope to accomplish? What does she need to do to get there? How can she move forward when things don't go as planned? Whether she follows a choreographed path or takes unexpected detours, her journey will be smoother if she feels confident in the driver's seat.

TOP TIPS FOR PARENTS

- Don't be overly critical of your daughter (or yourself).
- Encourage her to take credit for her work and to seek mentors.
- Define leadership as making a difference.
- Treat your sons and daughters the same. If you teach your son about the stock market, for instance, teach your daughter, too. Boys and girls also should be assigned the same chores and follow the same rules.
- Talk about your personal experiences as a woman, and times you persevered through obstacles (share these with your son, too).
- Encourage your daughter to celebrate other girls' meaningful accomplishments.
- Urge your daughter to use her voice, whether she's ordering a meal in a restaurant, protesting a school policy, or participating in a march.

CONVERSATION STARTERS

- "Do you think others are as hard on you as you are on yourself?"
- "What does being a leader mean to you? What are the different ways someone can be a leader?"
- "What helps you recover after a setback?"
- "What are some ways that girls benefit when they build one another up rather than tear one another down?"
- "Is there anything you'd do differently if you thought no one would judge you?"
- "Can you think of a time when you realized that you were stronger than you thought?"

CHAPTER 16

TAKING RISKS IN A WORLD OF NO'S

> **KEY SKILLS**
>
> 6—Self-advocate
> 7—Self-regulate emotions
> 8—Cultivate passions and recognize
>   limitations
> 9—Make responsible, healthy, and
>   ethical choices
> 10—Create and innovate

*"Why would I try out when there's no way I'll ever get
cast in the play?"*

*"Elliot will get all the votes because he has way more
friends."*

*"I don't know anyone on my new team, so I'm done
with soccer."*

"THERE'S NO WAY I'M SPENDING SUMMER VACATION TRYING
out for tennis," my daughter Emily told me. "I doubt I'll make
the team." She was fourteen and hadn't started high school yet, but the
coaches ran junior varsity tryouts during the summer after eighth grade.

"Do you want to be on the team?" I asked her.

"I do, but I'm going to get cut." Her brother Ben, then fifteen, looked
up from his phone. "Well, you definitely won't make the team if you don't
try out."

As a little girl, Emily had loved to sing songs for strangers and share stories she "wrote" by stringing random letters together. But like many kids, by the time she hit middle school, she had started to become more cautious and less willing to make mistakes. We encouraged her to take risks, own her goals, and learn that she could bounce back from disappointment.

I tried to frame the tryout in a positive light, but I really hoped she'd reach a decision on her own. We were still going in circles several days later when her brother had an epiphany. "You know, you should try out for the varsity team," he told her. This turned out to be a highly inflammatory suggestion.

"Are you out of your mind?" Emily asked. "If I'm worried about making JV, why would I try out for varsity?"

Ben explained that kids who are cut from varsity start out higher on the ladder for JV tryouts. "I wish I'd done that," he told her. "I still would have ended up on JV, but it's a smart strategy." Somehow, he convinced her to tell the coach that she *might* try out for varsity.

The night before varsity tryouts, the coach emailed the players. Apparently, he had missed the critical word "might" in Emily's email. She was listed on his roster and expected to show up the following morning. The coach explained the process. Each day, he wrote, the girls could challenge the person directly above them on the ladder. At the end of the week, the top twelve players would make the team. Emily came downstairs to show me the email, highlighting one data point in particular. "I told you," she said. "I really am ranked the lowest. Number twenty-five out of twenty-five players!"

"Look on the bright side," I said. "You've got nowhere to go but up." I finally got a laugh.

The next morning, I drove her to the school courts and headed to work. She sent her brother a text after she arrived. "Just so you know, I'm going to get crushed," she wrote. "Go down fighting," he told her. And then we heard nothing.

When I picked Emily up that afternoon, she was noticeably calmer. "I beat number twenty-four," she said. Over the course of the week, she continued to challenge up. The following day she beat number twenty-three, then number twenty-two. She beat everyone she played, ultimately land-ing at number nineteen. When I picked her up on the last day, the coach pulled me aside. "She had no business beating the other players," he said. "They're all technically better, but she fought for every ball. If you keep signing her up for lessons, she won't have to work so hard."

Later that day, he cut Emily from varsity, but she didn't care. She had overcome her fear, accomplished more than she expected, and discovered she was pretty scrappy. She transitioned to junior varsity tryouts and landed the third singles spot. That's when I finally exhaled. As a parent, it may be harder to push our kids out of their comfort zone than to take risks ourselves.

As it is, the world tells children, "No, you can't," in endless ways. They hear it from adults, peers, and, as Emily learned, even from themselves. It's so easy for kids to get derailed, to succumb to negativity and internal defeatist voices. At times, I catch myself discouraging my children from chasing ill-fated goals, but I'm doing them no favors. My advice may seem loving, protective, and even sound, but it's equally likely to be premature, misguided, or limiting. I try to check myself, to remember that children are perpetually learning and maturing.

Setbacks build resilience and are a necessary part of that journey. We need to teach kids how to take risks and move forward with optimism. This is a tough task for anyone, but it's especially challenging when you're twelve or thirteen and feel like everyone is watching you. Here are several ways to help your middle schooler summon the courage to fail.

Identify why something feels risky.

Your child may not understand why they fear an activity. Do they worry about being judged? Are they afraid of making a mistake? Does it feel too high-stakes? Sue Ashford, who conducts research on why people avoid leadership roles, explains that there are three categories of risk. "There's image risk. Will I look stupid by stepping up when I see a need? There's interpersonal risk. I could step up and lead, but maybe my friend wanted to lead and it would hurt our relationship." There's also instrumental risk, which relates to real consequences. If a child leads a project and it goes well, they get credit for being the anchor. But if it doesn't go well, they could get blamed.

Instead of offering a generic, "It'll be fine," help your child identify what's giving them pause and validate their concerns. Then work backwards—ask them to envision the end goal, and encourage them to make the attempt. As my son pointed out, you won't win any contests you don't enter, so remind them to let others do the rejecting. If they don't get cast in the play, or they get cut from the baseball team, there's no rule that they can't try out again. It still may not work out in their favor, but they get to decide how many attempts they can tolerate.

You can point out that even Kobe Bryant had to deal with negativity. His school counselor told him his dream of being an NBA player was unrealistic and he should choose something else. Although that may be solid advice for 99.9 percent of kids, someone will grow up to be a Kobe Bryant. No one can predict the future, and your child should do what inspires them. Tell them that although they can't control anyone else's thoughts or behavior, they can count on their own perseverance. They should bet on themselves and expect success, not because they know more than others, but because they care deeply, and they can trust themselves to put in both the time and effort.

Recognize that quitting can feel risky.

Quitting can require bravery, too. A child may stay the course because they've been told they're gifted and shouldn't squander their potential. Or they may be afraid to admit they're miserable because their parents have sunk so much time and money into their pursuit. It can be hard for an adult to shift direction, let alone a middle schooler. Your child may need explicit permission.

Persistence and grit are important, but walking away might help kids lead happier, healthier lives. Several studies, including one by Canadian researchers Gregory Miller and Carsten Wrorsch, have shown that people who let go of unattainable or unwanted goals enjoy better well-being and experience fewer illnesses. Help your child figure out what drives them, what they truly love to do, and what they hope to accomplish. As author and educator Alfie Kohn wrote in the *Washington Post*, "Even if you don't crash and burn by staying the course, you may not fare nearly as well as if you'd stopped, reassessed, and tried something else."

Still, quitting can feel counterintuitive. If your child (or you) needs reassurance, consider the many examples of well-known people who let go of one goal in favor of another. *Business Insider* ran an article on famous career changers. Vera Wang pivoted from professional figure skater to fashion designer. Astronaut John Glenn became a US senator in Ohio. Dwayne "The Rock" Johnson was a backup linebacker for the Canadian Football League before he crossed over to TV and movies.

Your child may know they're done with one activity, but don't know what they'd like to try instead. Create a list of possibilities together and tell your child to pick one. If they can't decide, tell them you'll pick something for them, but reassure them that if they don't like it, they can make a different choice the next time. To maximize the chance of a good match, build the risk-taking around their interests. If your child fears new social situations but loves to draw, an art class might be a good stretch.

Help your child get an accurate read on feedback.

Kids can walk down the hall and get tons of feedback, both good and bad. For a child prone to self-doubt, an incorrect read might stop them in their tracks. It's terrifying to give a presentation or try out for a play in front of a group of peers you believe are judging you. I counseled one sixth-grade student, Summer, who was convinced her teacher had a favorite student—and that it wasn't her. Her mother told me it was interfering with her willingness to contribute to class discussions. She also told me she suspected her daughter was oversensitive and off base.

Some kids are too attentive—someone looks at them funny and they feel belittled. Kids with low self-esteem tend to interpret messages in ways that align with their self-concept. Your child may need to take a step back to gain perspective. Help them look for patterns and question whether they're accurately decoding others' reactions. In Summer's case, I told her I'd observe the classroom dynamic. When I told her that I hadn't seen any evidence of favoritism, she conceded that it was possible her insecurity might be unfounded. We talked about how she could continue to raise her hand, regardless of whether or not she was the "teacher's pet."

Start with small exposures.

Claire Shipman explains to parents that risk-taking and confidence-building are transferrable, and their child can build those muscles by taking "starter risks." If they're trying to summon the courage to try out for the basketball team, but they're terrible, start with a smaller gamble. They could try making an omelet, or introduce themselves to a potential new friend. Those more comfortable actions will put them in the mind-set of taking bigger risks. All anxieties respond to exposure, which is why many kids seem to outgrow their shyness.

Shipman took this gradual approach with her daughter. "She recently wanted to hang out with a new seventh-grade girl, but she was worried about asking her directly," she told me. "She developed this slow strategy of talking to her about weekends and things she might do, then decided to ask her indirectly by saying, 'Do you want to hang out sometime?'" When that went okay, she texted the girl to say, "Do you want to come over this weekend?" "At each step of the way, she actually applauded herself a bit, and I could see that her confidence was building. I didn't understand how big a thing this was, but social interactions are hard."

Small exposures work in the school setting, too. On more than one occasion, I've discovered a seventh-grade girl crying in the bathroom right before her mini TED Talk, a videotaped speech about an important aspect of her identity (an assignment I explain in more detail in Chapter 5). For some students, public speaking is terrifying. When this happens, I scaffold the risk-taking. The student might read the speech to me alone, or to me and a few friends they trust will support them. I've had kids practice by presenting with their back to the crowd. One boy asked me if he could read it really fast without glancing up. A girl wanted to build up to the big moment by literally reading the speech from inside the bathroom stall. Different approaches work for different students, and I'll do whatever I can to keep them from backing out completely.

In a situation like this, ask your child to rate their anxiety on a one-to-ten scale, then talk about what would constitute a risk in the four-through-seven range so you can customize the risk-taking. Look for any motivating factors and come up with contingency plans. If they don't meet with success, don't be overly reactive. Instead, suggest they take a break or try a different strategy. As Quiet Revolution founder Susan Cain told me, "When you imagine the normal fears people have, they're amplified immeasurably in middle school. The boy you have a crush on or the girl who shut you out of her clique might be in the audience, and it's easy for parents to forget how all-consuming those dynamics can be."

It's important to get it right now, while your child is malleable. If you force kids out of their comfort zone during their formative years and they have a traumatic experience but never a successful one, the fear could linger for decades. "For the rest of their life, their amygdala will send the signal, 'Get the hell out of there, don't do this.' It gets encoded, and their brain doesn't move on," Cain explained. At the same time, some discomfort is okay. No one ever died from having a feeling, and you don't want your child to believe they shouldn't do something because it feels scary. That may be adaptive if you're talking about crossing a busy highway at rush hour, but it's less helpful when their fear prevents them from trying out for the school play.

Demonstrate bravery in your own life, too. Talk about your fears and let them see you try to conquer them. If you're afraid of heights, tell them when you braved the balcony of a high-rise. If you're afraid of public speaking, share when you summoned the courage to present to a group. Parents may inadvertently send the opposite message. If you say, "I don't want to invite the neighbor over because the house is a disaster," for example, your child's takeaway will be that you avoid social risks.

There are some kids who have the opposite problem; they go overboard and endanger themselves. Your child will be less inclined to put themselves in harm's way if they have a wide repertoire of strategies to manage stress. (I'll offer tips in Chapter 17.) Sometimes, a child simply has a higher threshold for risk than their parents. When my friend Alison Pion's son was fourteen, he participated in an outdoor program that tracked wolves for weeks at a time, with no cell phone or ability to communicate with the outside world. When he'd head into the wilderness, Pion had to take more than a few deep breaths. "I want him to take reasonable risks, but that means I have to put aside my worries and need to be in control of the situation," she told me. "I have to weigh these opposing responsibilities. I want to keep him safe, but also raise someone who can do things in life and be independent. I feel that's a gift I can give him."

It's hard not to send mixed messages. "Parents will say, 'Take risks,' but at the same time they'll say, 'What were you thinking when you rode that electric scooter across town?'" When I spoke to psychotherapist Amy Morin, she pointed out that children's risk-taking becomes uneven in middle school. "A kid may do a physical stunt without batting an eye, but won't make a presentation. You might gain some street credibility if you take that dare, but if you mess up a science experiment you might fall down a few notches, and for middle schoolers that can feel like the worst thing in the world."

To avoid confusion, help your child understand the difference between a healthy risk and an unsafe risk. Kenneth Ginsburg suggests thinking of your child's behavior as a puzzle with 1,000 pieces. The edges symbolize the power of discipline and modeling. You want your child to understand your boundaries, because that's about their safety. Once you have those edges in place, it's time to consult the cover of the box to get a sense of what the puzzle should look like. You're that cover image, and it's your job to model what it means to take safe risks. At the end, you're left with the irregular pieces in the middle, which represent your child's role. Their job is to fail and recover within those boundaries you've established. Be a consistent presence through their ups and downs, and remember that almost everything that happens within the context of school is a safe risk.

When your child wants to take smart risks, positive reinforcement is key. You may need to challenge a bias toward negativity, in them or in yourself. Rick Hanson, a neuropsychologist who wrote *Resilient: How to Grow an Unshakeable Core of Calm, Strength, and Happiness*, has done research that shows our brains are hard-wired to pay more attention to bad experiences than to good ones, and negative self-talk can get in the way. Be sure to reflect on your child's progress and note any success, no matter how small.

— IDEA FOR EDUCATORS —
SCAFFOLD RISK-TAKING FOR STUDENTS
WHO FEAR PUBLIC SPEAKING

Before presentations, acknowledge to students that public speaking can feel scary. Invite any students with specific concerns to meet with you in advance. Have them rate their anxiety level on a one-to-ten scale, and ask them what would constitute a risk in the four-through-seven range. They may respond that they'd feel better if they presented to a smaller group first, or delivered a shortened version of their presentation. If you push a student too far too fast, it can backfire, and they may develop an even bigger phobia. It's better to offer gradual exposure and praise any incremental improvement. The idea is to scaffold the risk-taking, not allow them to opt out completely.

Look outward instead of inward.

Instead of being reactive to their environment, help your child focus on what they're hoping to create in the world. Middle schoolers have an easier time shedding fear and rising above negativity when they look beyond themselves to the needs of their community. Pose the question, "What might help everyone have a better experience together?"

I've seen how powerful and affirming this outreach can be for students. My former student Emily Axelrod was in eighth grade when she wanted to start a GSA at Pyle Middle School. It would be the school's first student-run club, and its first and only affinity group. I caught up with Axelrod when she was in high school to get her thoughts on the experience a few years removed. "It was unclear what it would look like, if it would be allowed, and if we'd have resistance," Axelrod told me. "Until then, clubs were something your parents signed you up for, and this was something parents wouldn't even necessarily know about. We had to be under the radar."

She met with the principal, Chris Nardi, and me to talk about her idea. She had written a detailed proposal with the club's cofounder that addressed everything from advertising to safety. She also met with me separately to discuss confidentiality, students' well-being, and a few personal concerns. "Part of it was that I knew I could tell people I was the straight part of the GSA, and other founders didn't have that privilege," she recalled. As one of the students setting up the space, she felt responsible for making sure no participants were negatively impacted. She frequently had to defend the club to students who insisted there were no gay people in the school and, therefore, no need for a GSA.

Although she had moments of discomfort, Axelrod told me her closeted and questioning peers were the brave ones. "There were quite a few kids who hadn't come out to their parents, and they had to trust that the kids in the club would maintain confidentiality." They had reason to be wary, she added, because some students were not accepting. "Kids would use slurs, call each other gay as an insult, and make fun of the kids with dyed hair who dressed androgynously. I think we brought some of that to the surface," she added. Three years later, Axelrod says she's most proud of the fact that the GSA is still going strong. "We were worried it would only last a year because most of the vocal members were eighth graders, but it's still thriving. The fact that we started it was a huge step forward."

When kids look outward, they're also less likely to fixate on perceived physical imperfections. Middle schoolers tend to see themselves in a different, and often harsher, light than how others see them. Explain that a negative self-perception may stop them from putting themselves out there, whether they want to reach out to a new friend or audition for a play, and no one is as focused on them as they think they are.

Let them challenge rules.

Let your child see you question or disobey ridiculous rules, or advocate for a group that's being treated unfairly. My kids know that I'll ignore a "No Trespassing" sign on a deserted beach. At times, it's better to seek forgiveness instead of permission. Whether your child wants to defy an overly restrictive dress code or petition for recess, don't negate their concerns. Middle school is the perfect time to emphasize that if you ask enough people, there'll always be someone whose job is to say "no."

If your child's pursuit is worthwhile, ethical, and safe, urge them to take a chance. It's a lot easier to stop something than to create something, so encourage them to make naysayers work hard to put on the brakes. Then have their back. It's okay to be honest about your concerns, but don't let your own discomfort get in their way. If your child's venture goes awry, swing into debrief mode. Ask, "What do you think you'd do differently next time? Do you feel like you made any positive change? How did it feel to take that risk?"

If your child feels they've been treated unfairly or dismissively, be a sounding board and help them maintain their sense of purpose. The world is full of kind, good, and generous people. Let them know, however, that some may treat them with judgment or contempt, especially if they try to change the status quo. Remind them that this has nothing to do with them. Encourage them to take the high road and stay positive.

My friend Genie's eighth-grade daughter and her friends decided to take on a school policy they disliked. The girls were upset that bikinis were forbidden at a school-sponsored pool party. When they asked an administrator for an explanation, they were told it was a long-standing rule. "They kept getting vague answers and grew increasingly frustrated," Genie told me. She didn't direct her daughter, but she listened, validated that kids could challenge an adult's decision, and referenced history. "Not just laws around gender, but ones related to race and sexuality. A rule can be in play for so long, we don't question it, but we need to shake things up sometimes."

The girls wrote a letter in petition format arguing that it was an unfair policy. "They protested on the grounds that it was biased, and explained that it's one thing to say you want to have everyone's stomach covered, but to focus on girls' bellies and suggest it's highly sexualized and would tempt boys is sexist to both sides," Genie said. The school decided to change the policy, only mandating "appropriate and comfortable attire." "I think it was key that I said her grievances were legitimate, but the actions and choices came from her. I did stress respect and taking the time to think through the issues."

TOP TIPS FOR PARENTS

- Ask your child to rate their fear on a one-to-ten scale and help them shoot for risks in the four-through-seven range.
- Give positive reinforcement and don't let your own anxiety get in their way.
- Let your child question ridiculous rules or policies.
- Encourage them to go for what they want and let others do the rejecting.
- For kids who push the envelope, set clear boundaries regarding safety and morality.
- For risks that don't fall into those two categories, allow room for trial, error, and recovery.
- Let them see you take risks.

CONVERSATION STARTERS

- "You know how public speaking makes me nervous? Well, today I gave a presentation in front of my practice group."
- "Here's a list of new activities I think you might like. Which ones look good? You have to try something, but I want it to be something that appeals to you."
- "I know you're not where you want to be yet, but I'm really proud of the progress you've made."
- "If you don't like that rule, is there anything you could do to change it?"

CHAPTER 17

MANAGING SETBACKS AND SHORING UP RESILIENCE

"My parents say they hope my generation will clean up the mess they've made. That's a whole lot of pressure."

"Middle school can be kind of a mess—there's romantic drama, friend drama, and pressure to figure out who you are. Everyone's pretending to know exactly what they're doing, but no one does."

"Everyone thought I was an overachiever and maybe worked a little too hard, but I looked happy, so no one was too concerned until my anxiety went through the roof."

IN EIGHTH GRADE, SOFIA, NOW FIFTEEN, WAS INSANELY BUSY performing in the musical, captaining the handbell choir, prepping for regionals in debate, competing on the math team, singing in chorus, playing the harp, and getting straight A's. On the outside, she looked happy, but internally she was falling apart. Middle school had all the elements of a perfect storm. "It was a build-up where I never realized how anxious I'd been all my life," she told me. "I had trouble focusing on schoolwork, felt my friends' stress on top of my own, and I didn't know how to handle an awkward dating relationship." Still, everyone thought she was happy. "A lot of the time I was, but I was very good at smiling and hiding my stress, even from the people closest to me."

Sofia finally sat her mother down and said she thought she might be depressed. "Since it was so incongruous with how I acted, it took my parents a few weeks to understand," she said. She started meeting with her school counselor and seeing a psychologist, and she learned coping strategies, including mindfulness and self-validation. When she went to high school, the first few months were rough, but she was able to worry a lot less. "I got a seventy-five on a math quiz and I was able to stop thinking about it in two minutes. One math quiz isn't going to determine my future, or whether I go to college, or who's going to be friends with me or like me. I've realized that I'm fifteen, I can't change the world, I can't get 100 percent on every assessment, everyone I like won't like me back, and I have to be okay with that."

Identifying depression or anxiety in middle schoolers isn't always straightforward. They don't always recognize when their behavior has changed or when they need support, and they can appear silly and light in the midst of crushing stress. Between sessions at a middle school conference in Philadelphia, educator William Parker and I talked about how parents are conditioned to expect a fair amount of moodiness from kids this age. As a result, Parker, a father of four, didn't realize his thirteen-year-old daughter was struggling with depression until she admitted she was checking out websites on self-harm. "If she hadn't come to us, I'm not sure I would have noticed anything was wrong, which is scary," he told me.

The National Institutes of Health reported that nearly a third of all adolescents ages thirteen to eighteen will experience an anxiety disorder during their lifetime, with the incidence among girls (38.0 percent) far outpacing that among boys (26.1 percent). According to the *Journal of Developmental & Behavioral Pediatrics*, more than one in twenty kids had current anxiety or depression in 2011–2012. To help spot problems, the American Academy of Pediatrics has issued updated guidelines that call for universal screening for depression for kids age twelve and up. Only about 50 percent of adolescents with depression get diagnosed, and as many as two in three depressed teens don't get treatment.

This finding doesn't surprise me. Every time I give a lesson on anxiety and depression and offer support, at least one student comes to see me right away. Often, they had no idea until I broached the topic that feeling unbearable sadness or anxiety is a valid reason to seek help. I've started encouraging all teachers to self-identify as a safe person to approach for assistance with emotional issues. Every kid needs an adult, and student-counselor ratios are absurdly high. Plus, students may connect more readily with someone other than their school counselor.

For educator Ned Johnson, that person was one of his seventh-grade teachers. He spent three months in a psychiatric hospital when he was thirteen, after walking around for years as a perfectionist, thinking he should kill himself. He'd always assumed his teachers loved him because he got perfect grades. "When I came back from the hospital, I was afraid I'd run a gauntlet of kids saying, 'Here's the crazy kid,' and the teachers saying, 'How could you let us down?'" Ms. Greenberg was his favorite teacher, and he thought she'd ask, "Where are all your assignments?" "But when I poked my head in like a little rat afraid to get its head taken off by a hawk, her face lit up," Johnson recalled. "She said, 'Ned, how are you?' I thought, 'Oh thank god, I can relax.'"

Kids need that kind of support. The American Psychological Association surveyed more than 1,000 teens who said their stress level during the school year far exceeds what they believe to be healthy. In a survey of 22,000 high schoolers conducted by the Yale Center for Emotional Intelligence and Lady Gaga's Born This Way Foundation, 29 percent of students reported feeling stressed. Meanwhile, according to the Centers for Disease Control, the suicide rate among ten- to fourteen-year-olds doubled in the United States from 2007 to 2014. In 2011, for the first time in more than twenty years, more teenagers died from suicide than homicide.

This is not to say we should eliminate every stressor. We've become anxiety phobic—if something feels scary, kids think they shouldn't do it. That "fight or flight" reflex was adaptive when we were cavemen who needed to run from a lion, but it's less helpful today. As I pointed out in the chapter on taking risks, exposure to some anxiety can be good for kids and teach them how to adapt and rebound. Your child is going to face problems they can't readily solve. In those moments, they need to know how to conserve their energy, take care of themselves, and focus on what they can control. Here are several strategies that will help them shore up their resilience so they can navigate the ups and downs of middle school and beyond.

Understand your child's world and help them process troubling events.

Every middle schooler today was born after September 11, 2001, when the world changed in an instant. Ben, my oldest child, was born that summer, and I never would have predicted that in time I'd become wary of exposing him to unfiltered current events, or that I'd largely lose that battle once he got a cell phone and 24-7 news alerts. I never envisioned that in my role as a middle school counselor, I'd need to reassure students concerned about jihadists and school shootings.

Over time, access to new technologies has magnified each new tragedy, repeatedly exposing kids to deeply troubling images. As adolescent social worker Britt Rathbone told me, "They're seeing all kinds of disturbing stuff on the Internet that they don't want to admit they saw, so they can't ask for help. They're finding videos of people getting their heads cut off, and sexual stuff that can be quite unusual." And the more unusual, the more they talk about it. If that information comes from a fellow eighth grader, there's no easy avenue for getting support.

Even without the constant exposure to terrible news, middle schoolers are already a simmering stew of emotions, and for many, fear has been added to the pot. Some of my students have memorized procedures from school emergency handbooks. They know how to shelter in place if there's a chemical or biological attack, and how to lock down their classroom and hide in a closet if a crazed shooter storms the school. This is their normal. One of my eighth graders told me her parents hope her generation will fix the mess they've made. To her, that feels like one more source of pressure. While recent events have turned some kids into activists, others are stuck in a perpetual state of heightened vigilance. From a neurological and physiological perspective, all this fear and anxiety isn't good for them. It hinders their ability to focus and learn, to feel empathy and self-compassion, and to manage their feelings.

To help your child digest the constant stream of information, make sure they know how to sort fact from misinformation. Listen to their fears without minimizing them, and try to discern what they need. Is it information? Context? Perspective? Reassurance? Comfort? Remind them of the helpers doing good, and of the school officials and law enforcement professionals working to keep them safe. While there's no such thing as an "average" middle schooler, most children under age twelve won't be able to handle violent footage. Do your best to limit younger middle schoolers' exposure to upsetting images by monitoring screen time and online exploration, but continue to answer their questions and help them process events. This can be tough for parents, especially when you're asked to explain something you can't make sense of yourself.

Loosen control, but be there to help them recover.

To ensure your child can experience a challenge, recover, and grow from it, make it clear you're there for them and have their back. Michael Meaney's classic rat study on resiliency shows how this works. His researchers would stress out rat pups by reaching into the cage and picking them up with latex gloves. Then they'd return the rat pups to their mother, who would lick and groom them. "Like Teflon, the cortisol would slide right out of their system," Ned Johnson explains, adding, "It's this back and forth of, 'Oh my goodness, thank god, oh my goodness, thank god.'" The rat pups' nervous systems became wired to know that in the presence of a stressor, they could handle it, and that turned them into adventurous, "California laid-back rats." Unlike more typical rats, who hide in corners to avoid predators, these rats would venture out to the middle of the cage for treats or to play.

Recently, Johnson's eighth-grade daughter, Katie, got a fifty-two on a test. He made a point of staying calm and poking fun at the situation. That was his way of "licking and grooming." He asked her if she was surprised, and she said, "I'm really mad. I did well on the long answers, but terrible on the multiple choice." Katie also admitted she had studied the wrong material. A few days later, Johnson asked her if he could make a suggestion, and they talked about how she could prepare differently for the next test, including making sure she had the right handouts. In the end, Katie learned that she could fail a test, survive, and move forward. "It's that sense of control that she doesn't have to be a fifty-two student," Johnson explained. "I'm saying it's hilarious, and that I'm not more upset than she is—that's licking and grooming. Yes, she bombed something, but she's still super bright, the sun will still come up, and Dad still loves her."

To understand how important it is for kids to feel a sense of agency, consider researcher Sonia Lupien's N.U.T.S. model of stress. For something to be stressful, it has to contain novelty and unpredictability, pose a threat to the ego, and undermine one's sense of control. When children understand that the actions they take help determine the outcome, they feel less anxious. After the school shooting at Marjory Stoneman Douglas High School, for example, middle schoolers across the country raised funds, lobbied for better gun control, and helped organize events, including the March for Our Lives. Encourage your child to acknowledge when they've made these kinds of positive contributions. While it never hurts to count your blessings, researchers Adam Grant and Jane Dutton found that focusing on the good you do can be even more powerful and less passive than adopting an attitude of gratitude.

It's not easy to hand over the reins to your child. When women give birth, their brains literally change to help them be more alert to their baby's needs, and it can be hard to let go of that hypervigilance. You don't want to protect your child from all adversity—you want to be there when they experience it. Maybe their boyfriend or girlfriend broke up with them, or their friend lost interest in them, or they didn't make the travel softball team. Once your child has taken steps to recover, ask, "Are you happy with how you handled the situation? Would you do anything differently next time?" Praise them for making the effort to get through a rough patch.

Keep in mind that loosening control doesn't mean handing over all decision-making. Questions such as, "Should Mom or Dad take that new job?" are inappropriate for middle schoolers and give them *too* much power. They can't figure the big stuff out, and you'll only heighten their anxiety. Instead, say, "We care about your opinion, but we'll be making the final call."

Model healthy coping strategies and emotion regulation.

Middle school may be the perfect time to model self-care. Your child is old enough to absorb lessons about healthy habits, but young enough to be watching your every move.

Teach stress-management strategies, such as exercising, reading a book, or listening to music. Make sure they express their emotions, whether that's through crying, laughing, talking, praying, writing, or any other artistic expression. They can experiment to find what works for them, and you can share strategies that work for you. You may discover you'd benefit from meditating yourself, or from taking things off your own plate. Do what you need to do to be a non-anxious presence.

I've found mindfulness to be particularly effective with middle schoolers. Mindfulness—which is simply being aware of your negative thoughts and feelings without judging them—is a form of self-compassion. At an age when kids tend to be mercilessly self-critical, it can help them accept that no one is perfect, and that they're allowed to make mistakes. That mind-set can ward off anxiety. A study in *Health Psychology Open* found that individuals who can respond to their failures with a more forgiving attitude are less stressed and less likely to engage in unhealthy perfectionism or behaviors such as overeating.

Sofia told me that mindfulness has been critical for her. "Especially in the digital age. I can just listen, or sit and watch, and be present in the moment and not feel like I'm procrastinating," she told me. I've tried a number of different methods with students over the years, most of which you can try at home. I've worked in big and small groups, from facilitating large drop-in yoga classes during homeroom, to drinking hot chocolate mindfully with one or two students at a time. They might smell the drink on the inhale, then focus on cooling it off on the exhale. Sometimes, students place stuffed animals on their chests and observe them rise and fall as they practice deep breathing. I also have kids blow bubbles and ask them, "How is your breathing different when you're trying to make lots of little bubbles as opposed to a few big ones?" Or, I'll tell them to imagine blowing their anxiety or anger into the bubbles.

I toss balls with kids to demonstrate that thoughts are transient, or simply to help them calm down and feel rooted in the moment. Many kids find it meditative to count as we throw the ball (and the more competitive kids like to have two balls in play at once, and often come back to beat their own record). My students create and shake jars of glitter and picture their feelings settling along with the glitter pooling at the bottom. They write their concerns in Sharpies on balloons and bat them back and forth, a physical reminder that they can neutrally observe their thoughts and return their focus to the task at hand. I've done mindful eating exercises with everything from raisins to Pop Rocks. I'll have students hold melting ice cubes to demonstrate that they can sit with discomfort. I often ask students to rate their distress on a scale of one to ten before and after an activity. Invariably, they report that the simple acts of playing, moving, and having fun help them feel better.

At home, you can spend fifteen minutes talking in a technology-free zone. If your child seems upset, settle your own thoughts before engaging in discussion. Some kids find it helpful to pretend they have a special remote control that can change the channel on unpleasant thoughts. If they're too frustrated or irritable to concentrate on homework, don't force the issue. Instead, take a walk together or do something meditative, such as playing Jenga or kneading pizza dough. They'll be more productive after a brief break. No matter what you do, your child will benefit from having your undivided attention.

I've found that my students do better when I pair mindfulness strategies with skill-building (see Idea for Educators). When kids feel competent, they gain confidence and feel better-equipped to handle stressful situations. So if you're a baker, teach your child how to make a cake. If you're an amateur carpenter, let them help you with a project. If you like to knit, teach them how to make a scarf.

— IDEA FOR EDUCATORS —
PAIR MINDFULNESS WITH SKILL-BUILDING

If you run mindfulness groups or classes for students, consider simultaneously teaching them a valuable life skill. When kids feel competent, their confidence goes up and their anxiety goes down. Several years ago, I realized that while the students in my mindfulness groups all benefited from learning relaxation strategies, the kids who struggled academically didn't fare as well as the others. I wondered if they'd feel less anxious and more confident if they learned CPR, a life-saving skill that would set them apart from the typical middle schooler.

I decided to test this theory with a new group of students. My principal at the time, Chris Nardi, got certified as a first aid and CPR instructor and trained the kids. I taught them mindfulness while a counseling colleague, Rebecca Best, taught mindfulness strategies to a second group of students who didn't get any CPR training.

Georgetown University clinical health psychologist and professor Ken Tercyak helped us design our protocol. We could only collect data informally, but based on students' pre- and post-assessments, the combined approach seemed to be more effective at reducing anxiety than mindfulness training alone. I attribute this thesis to a couple of factors. One is that middle schoolers—whether or not they're anxious—benefit from believing they have a special strength. The second is related to relationship-building. It's powerful when your principal chooses to invest in you. The students' takeaway was twofold: "My principal cares about me, *and* he thinks we can learn this stuff."

Teach them not to fear emotions.

You don't want your child to fear big emotions. Mindfulness is one approach, but I'm all for mixing and matching strategies. Amy Morin uses the "Friend or Enemy" exercise to help kids understand how to wield emotions constructively. For example, anger might be a friend if you stand up to someone mean, but an enemy if you swear at your mother. To stop rumination, she recommends the "White Bear" activity. First, instruct your child to think about white bears for sixty seconds. For the next minute, tell them they can think about anything they want *except* for white bears. (Of course, they all think about white bears.) Then hand them a deck of cards and instruct them to find all the twos. After they do that, ask them, "How often did you think about white bears while you were searching for the twos?"

Most children will say they didn't think about bears at all. Kids learn they have the ability to redirect their attention and stop obsessing.

Middle schoolers often want to rehash an upsetting situation with a friend, but that can keep them stuck in a bad place. They're usually better off doing something physical, like going for a run or cleaning their room. Your child also can write their worries on index cards, then literally and metaphorically put them aside. Some parents find it helps to put a "worry box" in their kid's bedroom where they can "put the worries to bed." As I mentioned in Chapter 11, you can even set aside short periods of "worry time" when you talk exclusively about their fears and concerns. The rest of the time, encourage your child to practice setting aside intrusive thoughts. You're not dismissing them; you're just not letting them crowd out everything else.

I tell my students I want them to have a "toolbox" of strategies they can access on their own at any time. I might have them write their favorite aphorisms or mantras on "coping cards" they can leave in their desk or binder. They come up with statements like, "Just because my heart is racing doesn't mean I'm in danger," or, "I can handle feeling stressed." If your child always imagines the doomsday scenario, play it out. Ask, "What's the evidence that's true? If you're right, how bad would it really be? Is there any evidence that it's *not* true? If a friend said that, how would you advise them?"

If the catastrophizing relates to something performance-related, try to reframe their anxiety as excitement. A Harvard study found that people who viewed stress as a way to improve performance managed their stress better than those who ignored it. Help them view the situation as an opportunity to become stronger. If all else fails, remind them that emotions are fleeting and no bad feeling lasts at the same magnitude forever.

In other chapters, I've written about the benefits of journaling to understand different perspectives, raise self-awareness, and even come up with new inventions, but expressive writing also helps kids feel better, especially if they journal about difficult experiences. Researchers who asked participants to journal found that those who wrote about upsetting incidents had better psychological outcomes than those who wrote about neutral topics.

Accepting negative emotions, period, is associated with greater psychological health. Researchers wrote in the *Journal of Personality and Social Psychology* that acceptance may keep someone from being overly reactive.

The goal isn't to make sure your child is happy all the time. That's not realistic, or even protective. Studies have shown that having a diversity of emotions may actually prevent specific harmful ones, such as stress or anger, from overwhelming a person. Whether your child writes it out, cries it out, or screams it from the rooftop, let them release their feelings. There are no shortcuts. Emotions are like trains traveling through a tunnel. The only way out is to go all the way through.

Know when to seek therapy.

In the years since I first became a school counselor, I've noticed an increasing openness to therapy. It's a positive shift. More parents are telling their child that they deserve to feel better and *can* feel better. Pediatrician Ken Ginsburg, who provides extensive information about depression and anxiety on the website for the Center for Parent and Teen Communication (parentandteen.com), suggests that parents reassure their child that therapy doesn't "take away" emotions.

"Emotions are good things; the key is to learn to manage this blessing of having emotions in a way that makes you a better person instead of making you miserable," he explained. When one of his patients is in deep emotional distress, he'll tell their parents, "Congratulations for having a child who is sensitive and feels things deeply. We need to get them through this time, but in the long run this will serve them very well."

The key is to make sure your child gets the mental health support they need. As Morin pointed out, "You take your child to the dentist to take care of their teeth; why wouldn't you put that effort into taking care of their mind?" I recognize that for some parents, the decision can feel loaded. One parent told me she worried her daughter would become dependent on the therapist. Another parent feared their child would be labeled or medicated. Cost can be a concern, too. Many mental health–care providers don't accept insurance, but most communities have a crisis center that will conduct a free assessment and provide the names of low-cost professionals.

The decision to seek therapy is clear-cut when a child is cutting themselves or purging after meals, but more often, parents just have a gut sense that something isn't right. Maybe their kid's grades are declining, or they're expressing dark thoughts to strangers on social media, or their friend group has shifted dramatically. That's an important clue—their peer group reflects how they see themselves.

When in doubt, have a professional conduct an evaluation. They can do an assessment without your emotions. Your child might be more likely to be truthful, too. Some kids withhold information because they want to spare their parents pain. In fact, researchers recently reported in the journal *Pediatrics* that while 50 percent of parents are unaware that their eleven- to seventeen-year-old is having suicidal thoughts, younger teens are more likely than older teens to deny they're in distress. "When talking about adolescent suicide, half the time we're talking about kids who are depressed, and half the time we're talking about kids who are impulsive," pediatrician Ken Ginsburg explained over the phone. "Kids this age can't articulate their pain as clearly as older teens, their peers are less mature and don't know how to recognize the signs, and they don't want to snitch." Put this all together, and it's easy to see why parents can be the last to know their child is suffering. Some educators are trying to plug that gap. Cristina Conolly, director of psychological services for Montgomery County Public Schools, implemented the SOS Suicide Prevention Program in every middle school in her district this year. Students learn to recognize the signs of depression, care for struggling friends, and report concerns to adults.

Often, mental health treatment can be done briefly and focus on skill-building. Britt Rathbone shared a typical situation involving a sixth-grade boy who struggles with sleepovers and friend issues. "I may work with him and get it under control in six to eight meetings," he told me. "Then I may ask, 'Do you want to take a break? Do you want to do check-ins?' Sometimes the family will call us back in tenth grade, and then you know them."

— **SOME WARNING SIGNS: TAKE NOTE WHEN YOUR CHILD** —

» Loses interest in once-pleasurable activities
» Becomes excessively angry or irritable

» Cries for no reason
» Experiences intense sadness or feelings of worthlessness or guilt
» Has chronic anxiety
» Has difficulty thinking or concentrating
» Exhibits changes in eating or sleeping behaviors
» Needs excessive reassurance
» Fixates on weight or body image
» Thinks often about death or dying/makes suicidal statements
» Abuses substances
» Self-harms
» Retreats inward
» Can't get offline (addicted to gaming, social media, etc.)

Help them retain optimism, and validate their feelings.

Your middle schooler is prone to big emotions and needs to be taught to challenge extreme or inaccurate thoughts that don't serve them. But it's equally important that they recognize when they're experiencing joy, awe, or contentment, and hold onto those pleasant feelings as long as possible! As psychologist Mary Alvord told me, "Optimistic kids see things as temporary and specific—they failed the math test, they didn't fail life. Pessimistic kids, on the other hand, globalize that to, 'I'm stupid and can't do anything well.'"

Validate your child's feelings even if they make no sense to you. Don't ever say, "Why are you freaking out?" If they tell you, "Kids in school hate me and I'm a loser," you're going to want to respond, "Of course you're not a loser!" Resist that temptation. It won't make them feel better, and it may even hinder their ability to rebound. Validating doesn't mean you agree. It simply communicates, "I can imagine feeling that way." If your son is upset that his teacher embarrassed him in class, for example, you could say, "I'd be mad, too, if my teacher made fun of me." After he's had a chance to calm down, you can then ask, "Do you think he meant it personally?" Sofia has learned how to validate herself, and she says her parents also have worked hard on this skill. She told me it's made a big difference. "When I feel heard, I can get to the real problem-solving without the quintessential teenage moment, 'Mom, you just don't get it.'"

TOP TIPS FOR PARENTS

- Teach your child to talk back to the worry. They can say, "This isn't helpful, so I'm going to ignore you," or, "This will be over soon."
- Help them process troubling events.
- Be there to help them recover from a setback.
- Validate their feelings.
- Help them connect to times they've been successful in the past.
- Create coping cards with their favorite strategies.
- Come up with mantras such as, "I can handle feeling anxious."
- Set aside short periods of designated "worry time," or put a "worry box" in their bedroom where they can "put their fears to bed."
- Model taking a deep breath when you're stressed—and when you do, announce it out loud. Draw on other mindfulness strategies as needed.
- Look for signs that it's time to consider therapy.

CONVERSATION STARTERS

- "What are some situations that make you feel anxious?"
- "If you were in a crisis, who could you go to for help?"
- "What are some coping strategies you can use when you feel stressed or anxious?"
- "I know that experience was unsettling. Do you want to talk about it?"
- "On a scale of one to ten, how big is this worry? What would make it more manageable?"

CHAPTER 18

PREPARING KIDS FOR A CHANGING WORLD

KEY SKILLS

2—Negotiate conflict

5—Consider others' perspectives

6—Self-advocate

8—Cultivate passions and recognize limitations

10—Create and innovate

"I hate group projects because I'm the only one who ever does anything. If I just said, 'Forget it,' we'd get an F."

"I have no idea what I want to do. I'm not really good at anything."

"My parents want me to keep playing violin, but I hate it. They're like, 'If you quit violin, you'll just use that time to draw cartoons.' Well, I might, but it's my life."

IN MIDDLE SCHOOL, KATIE BARRY STRUGGLED TO CONTROL THE heap of tangled papers and books in her locker. She could buy a locker shelf, but they were rigid, expensive, and not very durable. They also couldn't be reused, because lockers varied in size from grade to grade. This was a problem for her classmates, too, and in eighth grade, she decided to design "Katie's Locker Hammock." Her solution—an inexpensive, flexible shelf constructed out of fabric, grommets, and suction cups—won Stanley Black and Decker's 2017 Most Innovative award.

With half of all US jobs at high risk of being automated within the next two years, creative problem solvers like Barry will have an edge, says Roxanne Moore, a research engineer on the faculty at Georgia Tech and director of the K–12 InVenture Challenge. Soft skills such as agility and inventiveness may predict success more than grades, scores, or core knowledge.

Fostering these traits is especially important in middle school because that's when they tend to wane. In his famous Creativity Test in 1968, George Land found that creativity drops from 30 percent to 12 percent between ages ten and fifteen. I spoke to Jeanine Esposito, managing director of Innovation Builders in Westport, Connecticut, who told me she's spent her whole career teaching people how to think the way they did when they were little kids. "Literally 90 percent of four- to five-year-olds are using innovation-type tools to solve a problem—iteration of ideas, no self-censoring, understanding it from a totally different perspective," she said. That drops to 30 percent by age ten and to 2 percent in adulthood. We need to catch kids in middle school and help them retain what they already know how to do.

As these concerns trickle down to schools, they're incorporating more experiential learning. This isn't about dismissing the importance of foundational skills. As Scott Murphy, a director in Montgomery County Public Schools, told me, "You can't interpret information in different contexts if you don't know how to read. Kids can google anything, but they still have to be able to filter what they find for credibility and meaning. The job of schooling and the job of parents isn't just preparing kids for college. College isn't a career."

Executives at cutting-edge companies agree. Novelist Tope Folarin told me that when he worked at Google, his boss let him use 20 percent of his time on creative interests. "They found that their most successful projects came from those moments when engineers and other employees were playing around with concepts and not necessarily trying to complete an assigned task," he said. Laszlo Bock, the former senior vice president of People Operations at Google, Inc., has publicly stated that he doesn't think grade point averages and test scores predict much, and that the best hires like "figuring out stuff where there's no obvious answer." He also has pointed out that top students rarely experience failure, so they don't learn how to learn from failure. More than a dozen companies, including Google, Apple, and IBM, are no longer requiring applicants to have college degrees at all.

These messages are confusing. "People my age with teenage kids walk around saying, 'What do we tell our kids to do?' We don't know," business school professor Sue Ashford told me. "It used to be easy. We'd say, get a business or a law degree if you want to be safe, but no one knows what's safe anymore." Your child's future job may not even exist yet.

Understandably, parents are struggling to adapt to the velocity of change. There's no instruction manual for raising innovative kids who can tolerate ambiguity. To gather clues, I spoke to engineers, artists, doctors, educators, innovators, writers, entrepreneurs, and consultants. While there's no one path to success, here are strategies that will help prepare your child for a rapidly changing work world.

Teach them to innovate.

When she was thirteen, Alexis Lewis invented the Rescue Travois, a wheeled cart that could carry at least two children. "I got the idea from reading about the Somalian famine of 2011," she told me. "Families were forced to walk for weeks, and parents had to leave kids who were too weak to walk by the roadside to die." Her lifesaving, patented product could be air-dropped and easily assembled.

Now eighteen and a student at the University of North Carolina, Lewis told me her family raised her to be curious and to have a sense of agency. Her grandfather, a rocket scientist, encouraged inquiry and questions. "He worked on the Apollo Missions, but he looked at STEM as learning about the world around you, not as super complicated math. You don't have to be conventionally smart to solve a problem and make something really cool," she said.

Researchers have found that exposure to innovation during childhood greatly increases the chance that a child will grow up to be an inventor. Introduce your child to real-life inventors; visit science museums; browse websites such as Wired, Popular Science, and New Scientist; check out educational YouTube channels; or design rockets using the online Kerbal Space Program. Your child can enter science competitions, such as the Annual Global Invent It Challenge, or read about other kids' winning entries. IDEO's Innovator page for DIY.org gives kids badges for completing projects such as improving an existing product, redesigning their neighborhood, or making a pitch to their local community. Kids also can use the SCAMPER checklist to think about how they could improve or replace a product or service. The technique uses idea-spurring questions, such as, "What would happen if you combined this product with something else? How could you make it more fun?"

Use language carefully to free your child's ideas. If they self-censor, Jeanine Esposito suggests turning their negativity around by posing the question, "How might we?" or, "What would have to be true for this to work?" If they're trying to define a problem, encourage them to preface it with the words, "I wish," or, "It would be amazing if." Avoid binary "yes or no" questions, which tend to shut down conversation; say "Yes, and" instead of "Yes, but"; and try responding with the simple question, "Why?" Don't interrupt with preemptive conclusions.

Esposito also likes doing the "worst idea" exercise with middle schoolers because they enjoy playing with rules. First, have your child identify the worst idea possible, then ask them to state two good things about that idea. Original ideas come from identifying the best parts of bad ideas. After they come up with a plan, they can test their ideas.

Look for experiential programs at their school.

Identify any experiential learning opportunities at school, too. Montgomery County Public Schools, for example, partnered with KID Museum for the Invent the Future Challenge. Teams of students from every middle school in the district build prototypes to address an environmental sustainability issue. "It's not just about doing STEM or having a hands-on maker experience," Murphy explained. "We're asking students to become global citizens who can solve global problems."

Middle schools in the West Windsor–Plainsboro Regional School District in New Jersey dedicate a week to solving a real-world action plan, such as global health, education, or gender equality. The district modeled the program on the Harvard Kennedy School Spring Exercise. The Soundings program in the Radnor Township School District challenges eighth graders to work as a class to explore student-selected global issues for an entire year.

Schedule hands-on, "no mistakes time."

To build confidence in creative thinking, Olan Quattro, a painter and art teacher at Sheridan School, recommends that parents keep a "rainy day drawer" full of materials. She'll throw recyclables, bottle caps, paper, glue, popsicle sticks, clay, and yarn on the table, and say to her eleven-year-old son, "What can you make with this?" Emphasize that it's "no mistakes time," she said, noting that middle school is when kids start feeling like art needs to be perfect. "Around fifth grade, there's this developmental desire to make their art look realistic, and if their idea doesn't match what they can do, they say, 'I can't do that, I'm not creative, I'm not an artist.'"

For her son's birthday, Quattro bought him a subscription to a monthly maker kit. The first one came with supplies to build a catapult, but he could build it in different ways. Maker learning, which emphasizes hands-on, self-guided projects, builds kids' technical skills and confidence through tinkering and designing. This was true for Juan Carlos, for whom school had always been a struggle. In sixth grade, his mother, Virginia, a single mother of four, regularly found him asleep with homework in his lap. In seventh grade, however, he was invited to participate in a partnership between Parkland Middle School in Rockville, Maryland, and the KID Museum's Invention Studio. He learned to code, use a 3-D printer, and create something of his own design. Cara Lesser, the museum's founder, explains to parents that maker programming feeds the sense of agency that is missing in many traditional school settings.

At the Invention Studio, Juan Carlos was able to experiment and take risks in ways that didn't always feel as safe at school. "I discovered what interests me," he said. "I may have trouble paying attention in school, but these programs have so many other components, from designing to understanding how things work." He participated in GEMS, an army-sponsored summer STEM enrichment program, joined the Design Apprenticeship

Program at the National Building Museum, and returned to the KID Museum to mentor the new group of seventh graders going through the program. He still finds school challenging, but he knows he has the motivation and intellect to become an engineer. As an added bonus, his mother told me she no longer needs to keep pushing him.

Tony Wagner, author of *Creating Innovators: The Making of Young People Who Will Change the World*, told me that children like Juan Carlos often feel penalized for their mistakes. With maker learning, he said, "We encourage kids—especially those who are not good traditional students—to love learning and to value the process of trial and error rather than fearing it." Lesser has seen this principle play out many times. Invention Studio instructors worked on-site with the lowest-performing students at three public middle schools, helping them build their own boom boxes. "They had to wire speakers and amplifiers and connect the boxes to their cell phones," she told me. "One seventh-grade girl started crying when she saw it working, and the instructor started crying, too. It was such a powerful experience for this girl who hadn't been successful in school."

Maker learning is also a way to deepen accelerated learners' understanding of material. Ari Mindell, who taught programming at KID Museum in high school, told me that two of his advanced young students created a humidity, temperature, and smoke sensor designed to detect house fires. They, too, thrived on the freedom to design something substantive almost entirely on their own.

Develop their curiosity and powers of observation.

Here's more good news about journaling: it builds self-understanding and the ability to consider others' perspectives. As Tope Folarin told me, "It enables you to be genuine and to understand that everyone has this teeming inner life." When he was growing up, he'd feel angry, but he wouldn't investigate the source of his anger. "Something missing in my childhood was constant engagement with what was happening inside."

Quattro uses art to achieve the same goal. She suggests that parents take sketch books and colored pencils with them to museums, then tell their child to pick a work of art to draw. "My eleven-year-old son will sit in front of a piece for twenty minutes instead of zooming through," she told me. Ask your child to reflect on their emotional reaction and to imagine the thoughts of both the artist and subject.

To cultivate intellectual humility and curiosity, teach them that no one person has all the answers. Pediatrician Ken Ginsburg tells kids, "If I think red, and I'm with someone who thinks blue, together we can think purple." Model how to listen to someone nonjudgmentally. If your child comes home upset about a perceived offense, ask, "Why do you think they did that? Where do you think they were coming from?" Help them understand that people are multifaceted and they can learn to engage with people who view the world differently.

If your child can do that, they'll have an easier time understanding the unwritten survival rules of their environment, whether it's middle school or work. When your child comes home with critical feedback, ask, "What can you learn from that?" Teach them to observe others' reactions to them so they can get back on track. They can consult with counselors, teachers, other adults, and friends to make sure they're eliciting the desired response. When they bring up a group project, ask targeted questions. "What did the group do well together? How do you think being part of a group helped the end result? What could have gone better?"

Practice these skills at home, too. If your middle schooler fights with their sibling, encourage them to reflect on how they could have avoided the argument. Point out when they've used a successful strategy, such as taking turns. When I'd drive my two older kids to middle school, they'd fight over who got to sit shotgun. When they tired of the tension, they came up with a complicated but equitable system. Now, when they disagree over whose turn it is to take out the trash or empty the dishwasher, I tell them I know they can figure it out.

— IDEA FOR EDUCATORS —
THINK DIFFERENTLY ABOUT GROUP PROJECTS

Be thoughtful about group projects to ensure that every student is engaged and working on their individual growth edges. We tend to worry about students who don't pull their weight, but kids who dominate groups lose out, too. They may be overly invested in the end result, or struggle to embrace others' ideas. Ask students to discuss what different personality types bring to the table and what they might need in a group member to balance themselves out. Then have them pair with people who aren't just like them.

Make sure everyone feels like they can contribute. Instead of dismissing a teammate's idea, instruct students to ask, "What would have to be true for that to work?" As the project gets underway, use informal peer evaluations at different checkpoints. That way, students have a chance to shift gears if they're acting too domineering or too hands-off. Make fairly evaluating each other part of the grading process, and encourage them to keep a journal. "What bugged them? When and why did they clash with teammates? What strengths and weaknesses did the other students bring to the project? What tendencies did they identify in themselves? Where did they fail? How did they regroup after a setback?"

Consider a hybrid approach to meet the needs of both introverts and extroverts. Before students start collaborating, build in time for individual brainstorming. Then have students exchange ideas in groups of two before sharing their thoughts with the group.

Instill a sense of purpose and cultivate "big likings"

Purpose doesn't have to come from a grand passion. As Susan Cain told me, "A big liking can become a deep source of meaning." As your child explores new interests, they may even pick up some networking skills. "When you become obsessed with a topic, you want to talk about it with other like-minded people, you start to seek those people out, you share what you know with them, and you become valuable to the network you created," Cain explained.

Even a simple project can infuse kids with purpose. Sandy Speicher, partner and managing director of IDEO San Francisco, told me about the time a group of her students were tasked with designing name tags. "I thought, "'Oh man, a name tag feels so small,'" she recalled. But then she interviewed one of the student designers. Andrew, fourteen, said, "I learned to see myself as a leader who could create something that brings joy to others." When she asked him how else he could imagine using those skills, he paused, then said, "I think the state economy of Michigan could use help, and also the school cafeteria." After your child completes a project, ask them what made the experience meaningful, and validate that they made a difference.

Nick Morgan, the president of Public Words and author of *Can You Hear Me?*, recommends asking your child to list their ten most meaningful experiences. Help them make connections so they begin to understand what motivates them. "They might notice that, 'Every time something cool happened to me, I was working on a team,' or, 'I was alone and really competitive,'" he said, adding, "The idea is to identify the elements that need to be in place for them to be awesome." Have this conversation regularly—their answers will keep changing.

Coach rather than control.

Kids can get conflicting messages in middle school. "On the one hand, you're allowed to exhibit autonomy and bike to school, but then you get to school and are micromanaged," Roxanne Moore told me. "There can be a lot of no's and mistrust." The structure of school and activities can make it hard to find ways to give your child freedom. Anne Dickerson, the founder of media training group 15 Minutes, told me she wants her kids to feel confident that they can navigate the world independently, but noted, "Sometimes the best I can do is offer a little more free range." On a recent visit to New York City, she let her eighth-grade daughter take public transportation by herself. When she went the wrong way on the subway, her daughter learned to find the right way by herself.

"Everyone is so overscheduled," The Elements founder Margaret Rietano told me. "Monday is chess, Tuesday is Kumon, Wednesday is soccer, Thursday is violin." To counteract that pressure, she tells her instructors to let kids run with their imagination. They may make a stone bridge, build a fort, or play in the creek. "In the simplest terms, we're getting kids outside and grounded, regulating emotions and stimulating creativity," she explained.

"Children are almost like prisoners today—they're more or less confined to where they're being monitored," notes Peter Gray, a research professor at

Boston College and author of *Free to Learn: Unleashing the Instinct to Play Will Make Our Children Happier, More Self-Reliant, and Better Students for Life*. Parents aren't sending their kids out to play unsupervised the way they did in the past, partly because it seems non-normative and partly because of their fears. To bring unstructured play back into children's lives, Gray founded the Let Grow Foundation with Lenore Skenazy.

Michael Hynes, the superintendent of the Patchogue Medford School District in New York, runs one of the first districts to implement the Let Grow Project. Students at three of his district's middle schools can now engage in one hour of self-directed play before school. "The closest thing to a silver bullet I've ever seen in my twenty-plus years serving children in education is to allow them multiple opportunities every day for free play, a place where adults get out of the way," Hynes told me. "The return on this investment is significant: less anxious, depressed, and upset children." Gray adds that these kids also develop a greater sense of agency. "When children have more control over their play, they learn to create their own agendas, negotiate with other children as equals, and feel less like victims of fate," he told me. You may not be able to influence how much recess your child gets at school, but you can give them time and space to explore on their own, whether they take the Metro to a museum or go for a hike in the woods.

Your child can handle more than you think. When my son Ben was in eighth grade, he went to China on a school trip. After a long day of sightseeing, he fell asleep on the bus. No one noticed when he didn't get off the bus at the hotel. When he woke up, he found himself alone in the middle of the night on a locked bus somewhere in Beijing. He had no phone or money, and he didn't know Mandarin. He yelled and banged on a window until a man finally heard him and called the police. Ben waited for officers to arrive, then cracked open a window so he could tumble out the side of the bus. The police took him to the Beijing police station, where he told them the name of his hotel. As it turned out, it was part of a chain with many locations, so police had to make several calls before they could reunite him with his group. The experience wasn't fun, but he got through it, and he learned that he's resourceful and resilient. Meanwhile, we learned that we could grant him more freedom. (That said, we implemented a new rule: no sleeping on moving vehicles!)

A couple of years ago, I met with a group of middle school parents about cell phones. Several liked that phones made it easy for them to keep tabs on their child's whereabouts. They could text them to make sure they'd arrived safely at their destination, or to remind them what time they needed to be home for a music lesson. The ability to check in alleviated their anxiety. I completely understood their perspective, but I asked them to consider whether they might inadvertently be transmitting the message, "I don't think you can manage on your own." Be reflective and try to recognize when anxiety is driving your behavior, whether it relates to giving your child more freedom or letting them solve problems on their own.

Children need practice making decisions, cleaning up mistakes, and handling unpredictability. Scott Murphy admits that while he spends his days making sure students know how to address global challenges, home is another story. "I'm guilty of trying to solve my kids' problems quickly, whether they can't find their socks or don't know the time of the basketball game," he told me. "My wife stops me in my tracks and makes me let them figure it out."

Allow that discomfort, says Emily Bianchi, assistant professor of organization and management at Emory University's Goizueta School of Business. Her research on forced periods of uncertainty, such as starting work in a recession, has shown that adversity can lead to increased flexibility, gratitude, and satisfaction later in life. Bianchi has three children, and like most parents, her instinct is to shield them from disappointment and keep their lives as predictable and consistent as possible. Instead, she told me, she "tries to let periods of unpredictability in their lives linger a little longer than I otherwise would." Take the long view, and imagine your child as an adult facing obstacles and setbacks.

TOP TIPS FOR PARENTS

- Be careful not to shut down their ideas.
- Cultivate "big likings" rather than passions.
- Make trips to museums, and ask your child to tell you what they think the artist or subject might have been thinking.

- If they fight with a sibling, ask them how they could have avoided the argument.
- Have them keep track of products or experiences that irritate them and think about ways they could improve them.
- Take field trips to local makerspaces to pique your child's interest in hands-on learning and innovation.
- Look for in-school experiential learning opportunities.
- Encourage kids to use different tools for classroom assignments, and provide materials for "no mistakes" creative time at home.
- Visit online do-it-yourself and coding websites with your child.
- Give them the time and space to explore, and don't solve problems for them.

CONVERSATION STARTERS

- "What have you failed at this week?"
- "What experiences have been the most meaningful to you?"
- "How do you think we could improve this product or experience?"
- "What worked—or didn't work—when you did that group project? What did you learn about yourself?"
- "What are some possible ways to solve your problem?"

MOVING FORWARD

"Make mistakes, model self-compassion,
and grow alongside your child."

O NE OF MY FAVORITE PARTS OF WRITING THIS BOOK WAS THE
conversations it generated. Whenever I wrote in public, at least one
teen or young adult would ask me about the topic. At the words "middle
school," they'd have an immediate visceral reaction. David, for example,
was a college student working as a supervisor in the Starbucks where I
often wrote, and his reaction startled me. He yelled to another barista to
cover for him, dragged over a chair, and sat down. "Oh my god," he said.
"Do you want stories? Worst years of my life."

When David, now twenty, was in middle school, his friend Max handed
him a Red Bull and told him to drink it. "As soon as I did, he told me he
had peed in the can," he said. For the rest of middle school, David's classmates called him "Piss Drinker." Not long after that, a teacher tapped him
to be the lead in the play. "We performed for the school, and as I walked
out, a boy called me a faggot and punched me hard. I was called gay a
lot—that seems to be a thing in middle school—and I was made fun of for
being Serbian."

David didn't tell any adults about the bullying. "My father was raising
me alone, and I didn't want him to worry," he told me. "I thought that
school administrators might overreact, so I masked it. I turned to video
games and comic books, but I wish I had told someone."

As a school counselor, I know that he's just one of many students with stories like this—and that parents rarely get the full picture. Early adolescence is a time of inner turmoil and social churn, and many kids shut down when they most need support. It's hard for them to articulate what they need when they're in the thick of it. They're too busy coping with everything from getting dumped by friends to adjusting to their new bodies.

But if you take nothing else away from this book, I want you to realize this: middle school doesn't have to be the worst years of anyone's life. I wrote this book to change that paradigm. Yes, it can be a difficult phase, but you can use the steps I've outlined in chapters on everything from kindness to resiliency to ensure your child emerges more confident, self-aware, accepting, and innovative than when they started. Maybe even more self-directed and organized!

While I've shared my own professional experience and the collective wisdom of middle schoolers, their parents, and experts across diverse fields, I'm including one last set of voices. Relatively recent middle school graduates are young enough to vividly remember their middle school highs and lows, but old enough to have some perspective. After a while, I started asking permission to share these impromptu "coffee shop conversations," because their unique lens makes them perfect middle school tour guides for parents. Here's what they wish their own parents had known, along with their advice for you and your middle schooler.

The social stuff is hard for all of us.

"In middle school, I was embarrassed about being associated with the mean girls," law student Hannah told me as she drank an iced tea. Still, she wanted to be in their social circle and didn't challenge their behavior. "They were gossipy and catty, but I stayed silent." She believes that if she'd shared more with her parents, they would have encouraged her to take a stand.

Then there's Anna, whose classmates alternated between calling her a whale, bulldozer, slut, and whore. I caught up with her during her senior year in high school. She shared that she went through all of eighth grade with just one friend, a girl who is still an important part of her life. She urges parents to tell their middle schoolers, "One good friend can be better than trying to be friends with everyone."

Kelly, a high school junior, leaned over to add her perspective. "Know what I'd tell my middle school self? Popularity is total bullshit. It doesn't matter at all, so stop trying to be something you're not."

The social stuff is hard for everyone, but high schooler Sofia notes that it can be even harder for kids who are LGBTQ+. She advises parents and middle schoolers to adopt an accepting, optimistic attitude. "I have plenty of friends who are out as transgender or LGBTQ+ who are managing it," she said. "There are all sorts of people in the world, and you'll find your place. My friends who are LGBTQ+ had a harder time on the whole, but plenty of straight cisgender kids also have a hard time in middle school."

When I spoke to Elysia, a twenty-two-year-old law student from New York, she said, "Bullying is a huge thing. I was bullied for my weight because I was a little bigger in middle school. If my parents had asked me about my day or got more involved in my school, I might have told them more."

"Parents need to ask a lot of questions," David added. He wishes he had more perspective back then. "I'd tell kids that just because everyone hates you in middle school, it doesn't mean everyone will hate you when you grow up. I can make friends with anyone. The old me wouldn't talk to anyone, but the new me will sit down and tell you my whole life story." He also wants parents to understand how important it is to nip bullying early, explaining that a few years after he was taunted, "I became what I hate." When he asked his boss at Starbucks for a promotion, the answer was a resounding no. "He sat me down and said, 'You can't get promoted if no one wants to work with you. Stop being a dick to everyone.'" David didn't even realize he was being mean. "I was acting out what I had experienced. I had to train myself to be nice, and that conversation set the gears in motion."

You may think it's "just" middle school, but the academic stress is real.

Even though she was a strong student, Elysia worried about grades in middle school. "I wasn't a great test taker, so I'd get especially anxious about that. I don't think my dad realized just how stressed I was." She suggests that parents acknowledge their child's desire to do well, but tamp down the pressure. "Tell your kid one test won't make you or break you. Reiterate that you'll be proud of them no matter what, and you won't think less of them if they do poorly." Sofia adds, "It's really important for parents to let kids know it's normal to be stressed out, and it's okay to ask for help—it's, 'Congratulations, you're a middle schooler, you're a human being.'"

We're not embarrassed *by* you, we're embarrassed to be *with* you.

When Hannah was in seventh grade, she got invited to a high school football game. "Other parents dropped their kids off, and my parents were like, 'Oh, it would be so fun to go to that together,'" she said. "I was hanging out on this big hill with all the eighth graders, and when my parents tried to say hi, I brushed them off. My dad was so disappointed in me for acting too good for them and ignoring them."

They got into a huge argument, and her father couldn't grasp that her behavior had nothing to do with him. "I'm at a high school game around older kids, and I didn't want to look young," she explained. "I love them, but I wanted to feel independent and was embarrassed." She thinks they could have avoided a blow-up if her father had calmly said, "Even if you're embarrassed, you always need to say hi."

I may not share much, but talk to me anyway.

"Kids won't talk if they think they'll get in trouble," Elysia told me. "They'll just sneak out or won't tell you anything." She recommends that parents say, "If I know you're safe, and you tell me what's going on, you won't get in trouble."

That said, Sofia doesn't think parents should force their child to tell them everything. "Just sit down and talk about life, about their social drama, about academics, about whatever is on their mind, and let them know you hear them. Tell them you get that it's difficult, and maybe Mary Jo isn't being the best friend right now—but don't just jump in and give advice."

When all else fails, Hannah wants parents to know that, "Eventually, you'll be friends with your child again. I talk to my dad at least three times a week, and my mother every day."

The good news is that everyone I spoke to is now in a good place. They learned and grew from their middle school experiences. They know how to choose a good friend and be a good friend. They're self-aware and resilient. These skills may not have come easily, but that's okay. Middle schoolers are supposed to make mistakes. That's how they learn and grow. Your job is to love and support your child unconditionally—to offer wisdom, perspective, and boatloads of strategies.

As of this writing, Alex, my youngest child, is just starting middle school. My older two kids are in high school. It's hard to believe. Like many parents, I approach each new developmental phase with a mix of apprehension and nostalgia. It seems like only yesterday that my oldest child graduated from preschool. On that day, I startled myself by bursting into tears in a hallway lined with crayon drawings. A teacher with grown kids stopped to comfort me. From here on out, she noted wistfully, time would fly. I knew my child would transition just fine to kindergarten, but I wasn't so sure about myself.

When I meet with parents whose kids are in transition, I've learned to expect the occasional tears. As I hand over tissues, they often share how surprised they are by their emotional response, believing they left that rawness behind in the baby phase. I get it. It's a feeling that strikes at unexpected times. Like when we bump into a mom from a long-ago baby play group. Or that moment we realize our child is able to avert danger without our help, or suddenly needs to lean down to hug us. Or when we stumble across our child's favorite old pair of Superman overalls in the basement.

As parents, it can seem like we're perpetually readying our child for life's next challenge. We keep a phone next to our bed during that first sleepover. We casually lurk by the school playground to see whether they join the four-square game. We hold our breath at class plays when they pause a bit too long before reciting their lines. When they get knocked down on the soccer field, we resist the urge to instantly run to their side. When they don't receive an invitation or a spot on a sports team, we stand ready to reassure them, knowing we wield little power to shield them from pain. Our ability to protect wanes as they age, but the urge doesn't diminish.

Parenting your child through middle school involves those same familiar feelings, from optimism and pride to protectiveness and fear. Your child wants and needs you now more than ever—even when they say they don't. The constancy of your love and the consistency of your presence will ground them during a phase defined by flux. Your role is to emphasize and demonstrate the importance of empathy, honesty, inclusivity, self-care, and safe, ethical behavior. But for everything else—from homework to house rules—I urge you to adopt an innovator's mind-set. Tinker with strategies and approaches. Make mistakes and model risk-taking, curiosity, self-compassion, collaboration, and creativity. Grow and evolve alongside your child.

Transitions can be hard, but here's the good news. When it comes to coping with change, your child is your best teacher. Their job is to march through life's phases, and they often do it unquestioningly and without a backwards glance. If there's a swimming pool, they're going to jump in—they don't care whether the water is cold. If you follow their lead and just do what's next, the rest will fall into place.

PARENT DISCUSSION GUIDE

INTRODUCTION

RELIVING YOUR OWN MEMORIES. The book starts with this line: "Mention the words 'middle school' and most adults groan." What memories do you bring to the table, and how have they impacted how you feel about your child going through middle school?

DRAWING FROM EXPERIENCE. Do you think you'll give your child specific advice or parent them differently because of your personal experience?

ANTICIPATING THE PHASE. What are your biggest hopes and fears for your child?

CHAPTER 1: WHAT'S THE BIG DEAL ABOUT MIDDLE SCHOOL?

FOSTERING CREATIVITY AND CONFIDENCE. Kids' confidence can start to plummet in middle school. Why do you think that happens? What do you think parents can do to prevent that nosedive?

THINKING ABOUT THE TEN KEY SKILLS. Which of the ten skills do you think your child lacks? Which strengths do they already possess? Which skills do you think have been most essential in your own life? Is there a specific skill on this list that you wish you had developed when you were your child's age?

PART I: Values and Integrity

CHAPTER 2: MAKING RESPONSIBLE, HEALTHY, AND ETHICAL DECISIONS

PROBLEM-SOLVING. Research shows that critical thinking more strongly predicts life events than intelligence. Why do you think critical thinking is so important? How can you teach your child to solve problems on their own?

DEALING WITH TRICKY SITUATIONS. Middle schoolers (and teens in general) are wired to seek novelty. How can you provide your child with fun, safe opportunities to stretch, experiment, and grow?

STARTING WITH TRUST. How can you balance your child's desire for privacy with their need for teaching, coaching, and support? How can you know when to pull back and when to increase your involvement? When your middle schooler breaches your trust, how can you get them back on the right path without damaging your relationship?

INSTILLING PURPOSE. Kids who engage in personally meaningful activities are less likely to make unhealthy or unsafe choices. How can you help your child identify pursuits that matter to them? What gave you purpose as a tween and teen?

SLOWING DOWN. How can you set your child up for success so they're less likely to make impulsive choices? What elements do you think need to be in place to set the stage for good decision-making?

CHAPTER 3: FOSTERING HONESTY

STAYING CALM. Why is it so challenging to stay calm and nonreactive when your child lies? What makes dishonesty such a button pusher?

DETERMINING THE ROOT CAUSE. What are some of the reasons kids lie? Why does the root cause matter? How can you figure out what's going on with your child?

PROVIDING A RUNWAY. How can you make it easier for your child to admit the truth? How can you model honesty? What's the difference between an offensive lie and a defensive lie? Do you remember lying to your parents when you were your child's age?

HAVING IT OUT. It's counterintuitive, but arguing is communicative. What do you think kids are trying to accomplish when they fight with you? Why is it so important to them to know what you're thinking?

TREATING THE LIE & THE TRANSGRESSION SEPARATELY. Experts advise imposing different consequences for a lie and the problematic behavior. Why is it important to separate the two?

CHAPTER 4: ENCOURAGING KINDNESS AND EMPATHY

PRIORITIZING COMPASSION. How can you reinforce your child's image as someone strong enough to do the right thing?

KEEPING IT REAL. How can you underscore the importance of kindness, yet still acknowledge that your child won't like everyone? Why is it so important to be authentic when having these conversations?

ROLE MODELING. How can you model kindness in your own life? What can you do as a family to instill this value? Can you identify any growth areas for yourself? Sometimes your child has strengths that you don't have. What do you admire about how your child treats others?

IDENTIFYING THE CAUSE. What are some of the reasons that kids lash out at peers? What are some strategies to help them cope with negative feelings—such as jealousy or anger—that may be preventing them from being their best selves?

SETTING EXPECTATIONS AROUND BEHAVIOR. You can't legislate feelings, but you can be firm about behavior. Why is shaming a child ineffective? Why is it important that they view themselves as a good person?

CHAPTER 5: EMBRACING DIFFERENCE IN SELF AND OTHERS

ENCOURAGING AUTHENTIC INCLUSION. What's the difference between true social engagement and acts of charity? How can you model inclusion in your own life? What can you do to help kids move beyond fear to understanding?

PROVIDING WINDOWS AND MIRRORS. Why is it important for kids to see visual representations of themselves? How can you expand their worldview?

EXAMINING BIAS. No one is immune from bias. Do you think it's important for parents to acknowledge their own attitudes and associations? If so, why? How can you help your child put themselves in other people's shoes?

EXPLORING IDENTITY. Why is it important to talk about your family's traditions and their identity? How does building your child's sense of self help them accept their own and others' uniqueness? What is most significant to you about your own identity?

CHAPTER 6: MANAGING SHIFTING FRIENDSHIPS

CHASING POPULARITY. When your child desperately wants to be popular, how can you redirect their energy elsewhere? What's the downside to chasing "likes" and "follows" on social media? What questions can you ask your child to get them thinking about the difference between ephemeral popularity and enduring friendship? Was popularity important to you in middle school? How has your attitude toward friendship evolved over the years?

CULTIVATING GOOD MATCHES. How can you leverage your child's strengths and interests to help them find right-fit friends? Why is it protective to have friends from settings other than school? How can you give your kid an assist if they're struggling to make friends? Can you recall a time in middle school when you felt insecure about your place in the pecking order?

GIVING THEM A PATH FORWARD. If your child is acting mean, how can you break that pattern? Why is it important to criticize their behavior as opposed to their character?

TAMPING DOWN MELODRAMA. It can be tough for kids to extract themselves from social drama. How can you teach them to disengage when they're not a core player?

CHAPTER 7: DEALING WITH BULLYING

STAYING SAFE. How can you help your child stay safe and stand up for themselves? How can you gather information about what's happening at school? When should you betray your child's confidence, and how can you explain your reasoning to them?

REGAINING FOOTING. How can you help your child recover emotionally when they've been bullied? How can you change the narrative so they don't let the bullying experience define them? How can you help your child stop intrusive thoughts from getting in their way? When should you seek outside professional help for them?

DEFINING BULLYING. What's the difference between a kid who's acting mean and a kid who's bullying someone? Why is that distinction important? What could happen if a parent moves too fast to demand consequences? Why should schools tread carefully before bringing a bullied child and their aggressor together?

HELPING THE CHILD DOING THE BULLYING. What are the potential long-term negative consequences for the aggressive child? How do you think you'd react if the school told you your child was targeting a classmate?

BEING AN UPSTANDER. Not every child feels comfortable standing up to a bully. What are some other steps they can take to support a classmate who's been wounded? Why do you think it's so hard for kids to simply say, "That's wrong," or, "That's mean?"

CHAPTER 8: COPING WITH GOSSIP AND SOCIAL TURMOIL

CONTAINING GOSSIP. What makes gossip such a hard-to-remedy and painful form of relational aggression? How is it different from other forms of bullying?

FEELING RAW. How can you help your child when they come home devastated that people are gossiping about them?

ADDRESSING YOUR OWN ANXIETY. What personal issues do you bring to the table? Do you think gossip is different today than when you were growing up?

SPREADING THE MEANNESS. Why do you think many kids feel compelled to tell their friends about mean comments others make about them? What do you think they should be doing with the information? How can a child avoid engaging in gossip in the first place?

PROTECTING THEIR REPUTATION. How can you mitigate the damage once a rumor has been spread? If you went through a similar experience, what were the takeaways for you?

CHAPTER 9: GROWING UP SEXUALLY HEALTHY

ADMITTING DISCOMFORT. What do you think makes it difficult for some parents to broach sexuality with their child? How can you move beyond that awkwardness? Do you think you have a good sense of what your child knows about sex? How much information (or misinformation) did you have at their age?

TALKING ABOUT VALUES. How does articulating your family's values provide a framework for talking about sexuality and relationships? If you had to name your family's top five values, what would they be? How does each one relate to healthy sexuality?

EXPLAINING CONSENT AND SEXUAL HARASSMENT. Given what you know about middle schoolers, how might they approach issues such as consent or harassment differently than adults? How can parents broach this topic?

ADDRESSING STEREOTYPES AND GENDER DIFFERENCES. What gender stereotypes do you think your child has internalized? What are the different norms and expectations for boys and girls? How can parents avoid perpetuating stereotypes?

CHAPTER 10: PREPARING FOR LOVE

SHARING YOUR WISDOM. What life lessons have you learned from both good and bad relationships that you'd like to share with your child? What are your own memories of middle school crushes or first dating experiences?

FACTORING IN OUTSIDE INFLUENCES. How can you use the media to bring up love? What realistic and unrealistic portrayals of love do you think your child has picked up from the media? What was your attitude toward dating or relationships when you were a teen?

PREPARING KIDS FOR EMOTIONAL RISKS. What do you want your child to understand about heartbreak and emotional vulnerability?

IMPARTING THE NUANCES. Do you think your child knows the difference between a crush, physical attraction, and enduring love? What do you wish you had known growing up that you'd like to share with them?

CHAPTER 11: ENCOURAGING BALANCE AND SETTING REASONABLE EXPECTATIONS

ENCOURAGING BALANCE. What makes it difficult for a middle schooler today to lead a balanced life? How can you help your child recognize when their plate is full? Do you think you struggle with balance in your life?

EASING PERFORMANCE PRESSURE. One middle school principal recommends that you "grow the tree you've got." What does that mean to you in regard to your child? Do you think your expectations are clear and reasonable? Did you prioritize pleasing your parents when you were your child's age?

COMBATING PERFECTIONISM. How can you help your child set realistic, attainable goals? How can you keep the mood light when tensions run high? Are you hard on yourself? How can you model self-compassion?

CHAPTER 12: TACKLING HOMEWORK

DEALING WITH AVOIDANCE. What are some of the reasons a middle schooler might avoid homework?

GIVING KIDS AGENCY. How can you avoid a power struggle with your child? What kinds of choices can you give them so they feel a sense of control?

ENGAGING WITH SCHOOL. When should you get the school involved? Why is the school better equipped to deal with quality control and accountability?

NAMING NEGATIVE VOICES. How can you depersonalize the struggle so kids stay positive and maintain a growth mind-set? Was homework a struggle for you?

CHAPTER 13: INTERVENING WHEN SCHOOL IS A STRUGGLE

QUESTIONING VERSUS ACCUSING. One educator is quoted as saying, "Most questions are really accusations with a question mark at the end." What does that statement mean to you? What are some questions you can ask that get at the root of your child's struggle and also treat them as the expert in their own lives?

PARTNERING WITH THE SCHOOL. What are some effective strategies for working with the school? How can educators help you identify the underlying issues? Did any learning, attentional, or emotional issues get in your way when you were a student?

COPING WITH SOCIAL REPERCUSSIONS. A learning or attentional issue can impact a child's friendships. How can parents help kids explain or compensate for their social difficulties?

LEVERAGING STRENGTHS. How can teachers help a struggling child maintain their reputation in the classroom? What's the upside to spending more time focusing on a child's strengths instead of their deficits?

CHAPTER 14: CONNECTING WITH BOYS AND HELPING THEM CONNECT WITH OTHERS

CHALLENGING MASCULINE EXPECTATIONS. What are some of the pressures boys face today? Do you think the middle school environment makes it easier or harder for boys to buck stereotypes? Do you think it's important to challenge these norms? What role can fathers play? What are some myths about boys that you think society perpetuates?

ACCEPTING YOUR CHILD FOR WHO THEY ARE. Why is a parent's acceptance and unwavering love so critical during this developmental phase? What are "high-yield" conversations, and how do they give boys a sense of security?

CONNECTING AND CONVERSING. What are some tips and tricks for initiating meaningful dialogue with your son, especially if he's reserved?

NORMALIZING EMOTIONAL INTIMACY. One expert notes that boys are quicker to walk away when there's a hiccup in a relationship. Do you think that's true? How can you teach your son to repair a rift in a friendship?

NURTURING CURIOSITY. How can you teach your son the art of listening and asking questions? How does curiosity help boys forge relationships?

CHAPTER 15: RAISING STRONG, EMPOWERED GIRLS

BUILDING CONFIDENCE. Surveys show that girls take a bigger hit to their confidence than boys during the middle school years. How can you help your daughter continue to take risks and maintain her sense of self? When we tell girls to be strong and brave, are we layering on yet another set of expectations?

STRENGTHENING FATHER-DAUGHTER BONDS. Why do you think fathers tend to pull back when girls enter puberty? Research shows that might be when they need them most. What's different or unique about the father-daughter relationship?

DEFINING LEADERSHIP. Many teen boys and girls (along with their parents) are biased against female leaders. How can we define leadership more broadly so both extroverted and introverted girls feel they can make a difference?

IDENTIFYING SOURCES OF SUPPORT. What role can mentors play in your daughter's life? Have mentors been impactful in your life?

DREAMING BIG. Do you think girls are less likely to take credit for their work? If so, how can parents encourage them to own their success?

How can parents convey that nice, kind girls also can be competitive, ambitious, and goal-oriented?

CHAPTER 16: TAKING RISKS IN A WORLD OF NO'S

DEALING WITH SETBACKS. Recovering from failure is hard for anyone, but it's especially hard at twelve or thirteen when you feel like the world is watching you. How can you help your child move forward with optimism after hitting a bump in the road? What makes middle school the perfect time to develop resilience?

QUITTING REQUIRES BRAVERY. Why is quitting often viewed in a negative light? Are there times when quitting makes sense? Why do some parents have a hard time letting their child drop an activity? What have you quit in your own life, and how do you feel about those choices now?

INTERPRETING FEEDBACK. What might make a middle schooler more likely to misread feedback? How can you help your child accurately interpret social cues?

SCAFFOLDING RISK. You and your child might have very different ideas about what constitutes a risk. How can you help your child tackle a fear, and how can you model risk-taking in your own life?

CHAPTER 17: MANAGING SETBACKS AND SHORING UP RESILIENCE

IDENTIFYING DEPRESSION OR ANXIETY. Do you think you'd know if your child were struggling emotionally? How can parents maximize the chance their child will reach out for help if they're suffering?

PROCESSING EVENTS IN THE NEWS. From school shootings to terrorism, kids are barraged with the 24-7 news cycle. How can you help your child process upsetting events, particularly those you may be having difficulty making sense of yourself?

LOOSENING CONTROL. How much freedom do you feel comfortable giving your middle schooler? What are the signs that your child is ready for more autonomy? How much freedom did you have at their age? How is the world different today?

REGULATING EMOTIONS. Middle schoolers can have intense highs and lows. How can you help your child build a "toolbox" of coping strategies? What approaches have worked for them in the past, and what works best for you?

CHAPTER 18: PREPARING KIDS FOR A CHANGING WORLD

CREATING INNOVATORS. How can you expose your child to innovation and give them opportunities to practice creative problem-solving?

CULTIVATING "BIG LIKINGS." What's the benefit of fanning the flames on "big likings" rather than focusing on passions?

DEVELOPING CURIOSITY. It can be hard to know how to prepare kids for such a rapidly changing and uncertain world. What skills do you think your child will need most?

COACHING VERSUS CONTROLLING. What's the difference between the two parenting approaches? Why is coaching more likely to produce kids who can resolve conflict or solve problems? What style do you use most often?

CONCLUSION

ADAPTING TO CHANGE. Is change hard for you? What have you learned from watching your child adapt to new routines, expectations, and friend groups?

EDUCATOR DISCUSSION GUIDE

INTRODUCTION

DRAWING FROM PERSONAL EXPERIENCE. The book starts with this line: "Mention the words 'middle school' and most adults groan." What memories do you bring to the table, and how do they impact your teaching? What do you think makes this phase unique?

ENGAGING WITH KIDS. Do you think you engage with students differently because of your own experience? What initially drew you to work with this age group?

ADDRESSING CHALLENGES. What are middle schoolers' biggest social and academic challenges? How can educators ease students' transition to middle school?

CHAPTER 1: WHAT'S THE BIG DEAL ABOUT MIDDLE SCHOOL?

PRESERVING CREATIVITY AND CONFIDENCE. Surveys show that kids' confidence can plummet in middle school. Have you seen any evidence that this is true? Have you observed differences in confidence between male and female students? How does this impact your teaching?

ACQUIRING THE TEN KEY SKILLS. Which of the ten skills do you think students most need in middle school? Which ones do you think will be most critical to their success and happiness? Which of these skills do you think have been most essential in your own life?

CHAPTER 2: MAKING RESPONSIBLE, HEALTHY, AND ETHICAL DECISIONS

PROBLEM-SOLVING. Research shows that critical thinking more strongly predicts life events than intelligence. How can teachers impart problem-solving skills?

HELPING STUDENTS STRETCH. Middle schoolers (and teens in general) are wired to seek novelty. How can educators help students feel grounded and purposeful? What are ways students can stretch, experiment, and grow at school?

STARTING WITH TRUST. How can teachers build a trusting relationship with students who break rules or push the envelope? How can they get them back on the right track without damaging their relationship? What is your school's approach to discipline, and do you think it's effective? When do you think it's helpful to share your own mistakes with students?

CHAPTER 3: FOSTERING HONESTY

STAYING CALM. What's your approach when students lie or plagiarize? What do you wish parents understood about this age group when it comes to making mistakes?

DETERMINING THE ROOT CAUSE. What are some of the reasons your students lie? Why does the root cause matter?

CHAPTER 4: ENCOURAGING KINDNESS AND EMPATHY

KEEPING IT REAL. How can you build a positive school climate? How can you encourage kindness while acknowledging that middle schoolers will choose their own friends and won't like everyone?

ROLE MODELING. Like parents, teachers are role models. How can you set a positive example? What are effective ways to respond when you notice that a child is targeting others?

SETTING EXPECTATIONS AROUND BEHAVIOR. You can't legislate feelings, but you can be firm about behavior. Why is shaming a student ineffective? How can you use homeroom or advisory time to build understanding among classmates, or to solve sensitive interpersonal issues?

BUILDING EMPATHY. The book mentions the Shadow a Student exercise, which is designed to help educators understand students' experience. Why is it so important for educators to have empathy for their students? What does having empathy look like in the classroom? Can you recall a time when you made an incorrect assumption about a student?

CHAPTER 5: EMBRACING DIFFERENCE IN SELF AND OTHERS

ENCOURAGING AUTHENTIC INCLUSION. What's the difference between true social engagement and acts of charity? How can educators help children move beyond fear to understanding? What can they do to promote inclusion everywhere from the classroom to the cafeteria?

PROVIDING WINDOWS AND MIRRORS. Why is it important for kids to see visual representations of themselves? Does your curriculum expand students' worldview? How can teachers help kids take pride in their identity?

EXAMINING BIAS. No one is immune to bias. As an educator, how often do you think about your own biases? What steps do you take to address them?

CHAPTER 6: MANAGING SHIFTING FRIENDSHIPS

FINDING THEIR PLACE. How can educators give an assist to students who are struggling to find their place in the social hierarchy?

CULTIVATING GOOD MATCHES. What should teachers consider when forming groups or assigning team projects? What role can teachers play in clique busting or disrupting negative social dynamics?

CHAPTER 7: DEALING WITH BULLYING

EXAMINING SCHOOL CLIMATE. Is bullying a problem in your school? How does your school approach the issue? How can educators help a student who has been targeted?

RESOLVING CONFLICT. Why is it so important that administrators tread lightly before bringing an aggressor and target together?

DEFINING BULLYING. Do you think parents understand the difference between a child who's acting mean and one who's bullying someone? Why is that distinction important?

CHAPTER 8: COPING WITH GOSSIP AND SOCIAL TURMOIL

CONTAINING GOSSIP. What makes gossip such a hard-to-remedy and painful form of relational aggression, and how can it leak into the school setting? What role can schools play when it comes to putting a stop to it or helping students return to normalcy?

ADDING SOCIAL MEDIA TO THE MIX. How has social media changed your job? Why do you think students feel so powerless when they're the subject of gossip? Have you had to deal with any relational aggression in your own life? If so, how has that experience informed your teaching and the way you relate to middle schoolers?

CHAPTER 9: GROWING UP SEXUALLY HEALTHY

GIVING OUT INFORMATION. Does your school offer sex education or health and wellness classes? Do you think students are getting the information they need to make good choices? What do you see as the school's role, and what do you see as the parents' role?

EXPLAINING CONSENT AND SEXUAL HARASSMENT. Does it surprise you that middle schoolers struggle with many of the same issues surrounding consent and harassment as adults? Are you seeing any evidence of this in your school?

ADDRESSING STEREOTYPES AND GENDER DIFFERENCES. When you were growing up, what ideas did you absorb about gender expectations? Do you think societal norms are different today? How can educators avoid perpetuating stereotypes in the school setting?

CHAPTER 10: PREPARING FOR LOVE

SHARING YOUR WISDOM. Do students ever ask you for romantic advice or pose questions about your own relationships? What are their biggest concerns? What do you think is appropriate to disclose about yourself? What are your own memories of middle school crushes or first dating experiences?

INCORPORATING RELATIONSHIP TENETS INTO THE CURRICULUM. Do you think teachers should be talking about healthy relationships with students? If so, how can you find natural extensions in the curriculum?

CHAPTER 11: ENCOURAGING BALANCE
AND SETTING REASONABLE EXPECTATIONS

SEEKING BALANCE. What factors make it difficult for students to lead balanced lives? How can you help students manage perfectionist tendencies? In your community, what are the norms around achievement? Do you think they need to be reexamined? How can educators keep the mood light?

MANAGING EXPECTATIONS. How can educators help students set reasonable, attainable goals? How does your own temperament influence how you advise students?

CHAPTER 12: TACKLING HOMEWORK

GIVING KIDS AGENCY. How can teachers work with students who avoid homework? How can they depersonalize the struggle so kids stay positive and solution-oriented?

ENGAGING WITH PARENTS. What do you do when your student is battling their parents over homework? What do you think are parents' biggest misconceptions about homework?

CHAPTER 13: INTERVENING WHEN SCHOOL IS A STRUGGLE

IDENTIFYING THE RIGHT ISSUES. What are some questions you can ask to get at the root of a student's difficulties? What do you think it means to treat kids as the expert in their own lives?

PARTNERING WITH PARENTS. What's the role of the school in addressing learning issues, and what's the role of parents? What factors might strain that parent/school partnership?

GIVING STRUGGLING STUDENTS A BOOST. How can teachers leverage struggling students' strengths, especially when their classmates grow impatient with them?

CHAPTER 14: CONNECTING WITH BOYS AND HELPING THEM CONNECT WITH OTHERS

CHALLENGING MASCULINE EXPECTATIONS. What are some of the pressures middle school boys face today? Do you think the school environment makes it easier or harder for them to buck stereotypes? How can educators tackle stereotypes about masculinity?

SETTING BOUNDARIES. Middle school boys can be physical or flippant, and not every boy enjoys those kinds of interactions. How can educators help boys recognize and respect their classmates' boundaries?

NURTURING CURIOSITY. Researchers have found that teaching boys interviewing skills helps them forge relationships. How does showing curiosity help boys connect with others more intimately? How can you foster that trait in the classroom?

CHAPTER 15: RAISING STRONG, EMPOWERED GIRLS

BUILDING CONFIDENCE. Why do you think girls take a bigger hit to their confidence than boys during middle school? How can educators help them maintain a strong sense of self?

DEFINING LEADERSHIP. Many teen boys and girls are biased against female leaders. How can schools encourage girls to take on leadership roles?

How can they convey that leaders come in many different forms, and that reserved girls can make a difference too?

DREAMING BIG. How can educators encourage girls to take credit for their work and to own their success? How can they convey that nice, kind girls also can be ambitious, competitive, and goal-oriented?

CHAPTER 16: TAKING RISKS IN A WORLD OF NO'S

TAKING RISKS. Recovering from failure is hard for anyone, but it's especially hard at twelve or thirteen when you feel like the world is watching you. What makes middle school such a prime time to develop resilience?

SCAFFOLDING RISK. How can teachers help students tackle fears? How can they make it safe to take risks in the classroom?

CHAPTER 17: MANAGING SETBACKS AND SHORING UP RESILIENCE

IDENTIFYING DEPRESSION OR ANXIETY. How can educators normalize help-seeking behavior so students don't suffer in silence? Do you feel equipped to support students who present as anxious or depressed? Does your school have enough resources to address students' mental health needs? How do students' emotional challenges impact their performance or behavior at school?

BUILDING COMMUNITY. How can schools establish a caring community in which students look out for one another? How can educators incorporate social-emotional learning into the curriculum?

REGULATING EMOTIONS. Middle schoolers can have intense highs and lows. How can teachers help students identify and utilize positive coping strategies?

CHAPTER 18: PREPARING KIDS FOR A CHANGING WORLD

CREATING INNOVATORS. How can middle schools give students opportunities to solve problems and engage in experiential learning? How can teachers encourage kids to be inventive?

TEACHING COLLABORATION. When it comes to group projects, loud voices can drown out quieter contributors. What can teachers do to make sure that everyone plays a role and has the chance to work on skills such as teamwork and conflict resolution?

CONCLUSION

ADAPTING TO CHANGE. Is change hard for you personally? What have you learned from watching your students adapt to new routines, expectations, and friend groups?

RESOURCES

CHAPTER 1
Social and Academic Maturity

"Can Creativity Be Taught? Results from Research Studies." *Creativity at Work*. August 25, 2017. https://www.creativityatwork.com/2012/03/23/can-creativity-be-taught/.

Caskey, Micki, and Vincent A. Anfara, Jr. "Developmental Characteristics of Young Adolescents." AMLE—Association for Middle Level Education. https://www.amle.org/BrowsebyTopic/WhatsNew/WNDet/TabId/270/ArtMID/888/ArticleID/455/Developmental-Characteristics-of-Young-Adolescents.aspx.

Duchesne, Stéphane, Catherine F. Ratelle, and Bei Feng. "Psychological Need Satisfaction and Achievement Goals: Exploring Indirect Effects of Academic and Social Adaptation Following the Transition to Secondary School." *The Journal of Early Adolescence* 37, no. 9 (2016): 1280–308. doi:10.1177/0272431616659561.

MacIver, Douglass J., with Robert W. Dodd. 2018. "Semi Self-Contained Learning Communities in Grade 6: Bringing New Evidence to Bear on Middle Grades Education." Johns Hopkins School of Education Center for Social Organization of Schools. http://www.jhucsos.com/2018/01/semi-self-contained-learning-communities-in-grade-6-bringing-new-evidence-to-bear-on-middle-grades-education/.

Schwartz, Amy Ellen, Leanna Stiefel, and Michah W. Rothbart. "Do Top Dogs Rule in Middle School? Evidence on Bullying, Safety, and Belonging." *American Educational Research Journal* 53, no. 5 (2016): 1450–484. doi: 10.3102/0002831216657177.

Middle School and Confidence

Monitor on Psychology. http://www.apa.org/.

"Poll | The Confidence Code for Girls." The Confidence Code for Girls with Ypulse. 2017 https://www.confidencecodegirls.com/poll.

CHAPTER 2

Nicotine Use

Audrain-Mcgovern, Janet, Matthew D. Stone, Jessica Barrington-Trimis, Jennifer B. Unger, and Adam M. Leventhal. "Adolescent E-Cigarette, Hookah, and Conventional Cigarette Use and Subsequent Marijuana Use." *Pediatrics*, 2018. doi:10.1542/peds.2017-3616.

Dai, Hongying, Delwyn Catley, Kimber P. Richter, Kathy Goggin, and Edward F. Ellerbeck. "Electronic Cigarettes and Future Marijuana Use: A Longitudinal Study." *Pediatrics*. April 23, 2018. http://pediatrics.aappublications.org/content/early/2018/04/19/peds.2017-3787.

Miech, Richard, Megan E. Patrick, Patrick M. Omalley, and Lloyd D. Johnston. "What Are Kids Vaping? Results from a National Survey of US Adolescents." *Tobacco Control* 26, no. 4 (2016): 386–91. doi:10.1136/tobaccocontrol-2016-053014.

Monitoring the Future: A Continuing Study of American Youth. http://www.monitoringthefuture.org/.

Risk-Taking Behavior

"High School YRBS." Centers for Disease Control and Prevention. https://nccd.cdc.gov/Youthonline/App/Default.aspx.

Kann, Laura, Tim Mcmanus, William A. Harris, Shari L. Shanklin, Katherine H. Flint, Joseph Hawkins, Barbara Queen, Richard Lowry, Emily O'Malley Olsen, David Chyen, Lisa Whittle, Jemekia Thornton, Connie Lim, Yoshimi Yamakawa, Nancy Brener, and Stephanie Zaza. "Youth Risk Behavior Surveillance United States, 2015." *MMWR. Surveillance Summaries* 65, no. 6 (2016): 1–174. doi:10.15585/mmwr.ss6506a1.

"SIECUS Sexuality Information and Education Council of the United States." SIECUS—Home. https://siecus.org/.

Brain Development/Maturity

"Brain Maturity Extends Well Beyond Teen Years." *NPR*. October 10, 2011. https://www.npr.org/templates/story/story.php?storyId=141164708.

Butler, Heather A., Christopher Pentoney, and Mabelle P. Bong. "Predicting Real-World Outcomes: Critical Thinking Ability Is a Better Predictor of Life Decisions than Intelligence." *Thinking Skills and Creativity* 25 (2017): 38–46. doi:10.1016/j.tsc.2017.06.005.

Johnson, Sara B., Robert W. Blum, and Jay N. Giedd. "Adolescent Maturity and the Brain: The Promise and Pitfalls of Neuroscience Research in Adolescent Health Policy." *Journal of Adolescent Health* 45, no. 3 (2009): 216–21. doi:10.1016/j.jadohealth.2009.05.016.

Trustworthy Faces

Li, Qinggong, Gail D. Heyman, Jing Mei, and Kang Lee. "Judging a Book by Its Cover: Children's Facial Trustworthiness as Judged by Strangers Predicts Their Real-World Trustworthiness and Peer Relationships." *Child Development*, 2017. doi:10.1111/cdev.12907.

Slepian, Michael. "Uncovering the Secrets of a Trustworthy Face." *Scientific American*. August 08, 2017. https://www.scientificamerican.com/article/uncovering-the-secrets-of-a-trustworthy-face/.

Anxiety

Hartley, Catherine A., and Elizabeth A. Phelps. "Anxiety and Decision-Making." *Biological Psychiatry* 72, no. 2 (2012): 113–18. doi:10.1016/j.biopsych.2011.12.027.

"Taking Center Stage Act II: Middle Grades Success." Early Warning Signs of Violent Student Behavior—Taking Center Stage-Act II (TCSII) (CA Dept of Education). http://pubs.cde.ca.gov/tcsii/documentlibrary/characteristicsmg.aspx.

Ethical Dilemmas

"Ethical Dilemmas Archive." Character Education—The Six Pillars of Character—Citizenship. http://www.goodcharacter.com/dilemma/archive.html.

CHAPTER 3
Lying/Cheating and Technology

"Academic Cheating Fact Sheet." Cheating Is a Personal Foul. http://www.glass-castle.com/clients/www-nocheating-org/adcouncil/research/cheatingfactsheet.html.

Common Sense Media. Kids & Teen Media. "35% of Teens Admit to Using Cell Phones to Cheat." News release, June 18, 2009. Common Sense Media. https://www.commonsensemedia.org/about-us/news/press-releases/35-of-teens-admit-to-using-cell-phones-to-cheat.

Noguchi, Sharon. "Nearly a Third of U.S. Teens Use Electronics to Cheat, Survey Says." *The Mercury News*, August 06, 2017. https://www.mercurynews.com/2017/08/06/nearly-a-third-of-u-s-teens-use-electronics-to-cheat-survey-says/.

Wormeli, Rick. "Cheating and Plagiarizing." *AMLE—Association for Middle Level Education*, August 2017, www.amle.org/BrowsebyTopic/WhatsNew/WNDet/TabId/270/ArtMID/888/ArticleID/833/undefined.

Lying and Success

Josephson Institute. "Josephson Institute's 2012 report card on the ethics of American youth." 2012, Los Angeles. Retrieved from http://charactercounts.org/pdf/ reportcard/2012/ReportCard-2012-DataTables.pdf.

Brain Development

"Brain Maturity Extends Well Beyond Teen Years." *NPR*. October 10, 2011. https://www.npr.org/templates/story/story.php?storyId=141164708.d.

CHAPTER 4
Kindness

Greater Good, July 2010, greatergood.berkeley.edu/video/item/happiness_for_a_lifetime.

Jones, Damon E., Mark Greenberg, and Max Crowley. "Early Social-Emotional Functioning and Public Health: The Relationship Between Kindergarten Social Competence and Future Wellness." *American Journal of Public Health* 105, no. 11 (2015): 2283–290. doi:10.2105/ajph.2015.302630.

"Kind Communities—A Bridge to Youth Mental Wellness." Born This Way Foundation. https://bornthisway.foundation/research-survey/kind-communities-survey/.

Layous, Kristin, S. Katherine Nelson, Eva Oberle, Kimberly A. Schonert-Reichl, and Sonja Lyubomirsky. "Kindness Counts: Prompting Prosocial Behavior in Preadolescents Boosts Peer Acceptance and Well-Being." *PLOS ONE* 7, no. 12 (2012). doi:10.1371/journal.pone.0051380.

Lyubomirsky, Sonja, Kennon M. Sheldon, and David Schkade. "Pursuing Happiness: The Architecture of Sustainable Change." *Review of General Psychology* 9, no . 2 (2005): 111-31. doi:10.1037/1089-2680.9.2.111.

"The Children We Mean to Raise." *Making Caring Common*. 2014. https://mcc
.gse.harvard.edu/the-children-we-mean-to-raise.

Danish School System

Alexander, Jessica. "Teaching Kids Empathy: In Danish Schools, It's . . . Well,
It's a Piece of Cake." *Salon*. August 11, 2016. https://www.salon.com/2016
/08/09/teaching-kids-empathy-in-danish-schools-its-well-its-a-piece-of
-cake/.

Stoltzfus, Kate. "Lessons from Denmark: Teachers Can Incorporate Empathy
in the Curriculum." *Education Week—Teacher Beat*. August 15, 2016. http://
blogs.edweek.org/teachers/teaching_now/2016/08/lessons_from_denmark
_teachers_can_incorporate_empathy_in_the_curriculum.html.

Empathy

"Books That Teach Empathy." *Common Sense Media: Ratings, Reviews, and Advice*. January 01, 1970. https://www.commonsensemedia.org/lists/books-that
-teach-empathy.

"Can Fiction Stories Make Us More Empathetic?" *ScienceDaily*. August 11,
2014. https://www.sciencedaily.com/releases/2014/08/140811151632.htm.

Krevans, J., and J. C. Gibbs. "Parents' Use of Inductive Discipline: Relations to
Children's Empathy and Prosocial Behavior." *Advances in Pediatrics*. December 1996. https://www.ncbi.nlm.nih.gov/pubmed/9071781.

Swanbrow, Diane. "Empathy: College Students Don't Have as Much as
They Used To." *University of Michigan News*. May 27, 2010. https://news
.umich.edu/empathy-college-students-don-t-have-as-much-as-they-used
-to/.

Vedantam, Shankar. "Does Reading Harry Potter Have an Effect on Your Behavior?" *NPR*. May 01, 2015. https://www.npr.org/2015/05/01/403474870/
does-reading-harry-potter-have-an-effect-on-your-behavior.

Vezzali, Loris, Sofia Stathi, Dino Giovannini, Dora Capozza, and Elena Trifiletti.
"The Greatest Magic of Harry Potter: Reducing Prejudice." *Journal of Applied
Social Psychology* 45, no. 2 (2014): 105–21. doi:10.1111/jasp.12279.

Meditation

Condon, Paul, Gaëlle Desbordes, Willa B. Miller, and David Desteno. "Meditation Increases Compassionate Responses to Suffering." *Psychological Science*
24, no. 10 (2013): 2125–127. doi:10.1177/0956797613485603.

"San Francisco Schools Transformed by the Power of Meditation." *NBCNews
.com*. December 29, 2014. https://www.nbcnews.com/nightly-news/san
-francisco-schools-Transformed-power-meditation-n276301. updated 01 Jan.
2015.

Awe and Social Behaviors

Piff, Paul K., Pia Dietze, Matthew Feinberg, Daniel M. Stancato, and Dacher Keltner. "Awe, the Small Self, and Prosocial Behavior." *Journal of Personality and Social Psychology* 108, no. 6 (2015): 883–99. doi:10.1037/pspi0000018.

Rudd, Melanie, Kathleen D. Vohs, and Jennifer Aaker. "Awe Expands People's Perception of Time, Alters Decision Making, and Enhances Well-Being." *Psychological Science* 23, no. 10 (2012): 1130–136. doi:10.1177/0956797612438731.

Cognitive Benefits from Physical Activity and Nature

Berman, Marc G., John Jonides, and Stephen Kaplan. "The Cognitive Benefits of Interacting with Nature." *Psychological Science* 19, no. 12 (2008): 1207–212. doi:10.1111/j.1467-9280.2008.02225.x.

Parker-Pope, Tara. "How to Manage Stress Like an Olympic Biathlete." *New York Times*. February 21, 2018. https://www.nytimes.com/2018/02/21/sports/olympics/biathalon-clare-egan-biathlete-training.html.

"Physical Activity Helps Improve Social Skills." *Psych Central*. October 06, 2015. https://psychcentral.com/news/2010/03/15/physical-activity-helps-improve-social-skills/12120.html.

"Research Shows Link Between Physical Activity and Social Skills in Children." Transparent Tape Test for Pinworms | Michigan Medicine. March 14, 2010. https://www.uofmhealth.org/news/1513link-between-physical-activity-and-social-skills.

Activism and Gratitude

Emmons, Robert. "Why Gratitude Is Good." *Greater Good*. November 16, 2010. https://greatergood.berkeley.edu/article/item/why_gratitude_is_good.

Gopnik, Alison, Shaun O'Grady, Christopher G. Lucas, Thomas L. Griffiths, Adrienne Wente, Sophie Bridgers, Rosie Aboody, Hoki Fung, and Ronald E. Dahl. "Changes in Cognitive Flexibility and Hypothesis Search Across Human Life History from Childhood to Adolescence to Adulthood." *PLOS Biology*. July 25, 2017. https://doi.org/10.1073/pnas.1700811114.

CHAPTER 5

Awareness

Mascareñaz, Lauryn. "Five Things for Educators to Keep in Mind After March for Our Lives." *Teaching Tolerance*. March 26, 2018. https://www.tolerance.org/magazine/five-things-for-educators-to-keep-in-mind-after-march-for-our-lives.

Inclusion

Bi, Xuan, Carol Quirck, Selene Almazon, and Michele Valenti. "Inclusive Education Research & Practice." *Maryland Coalition for Inclusive Education*, 2010. https://www.csuchico.edu/lref/pols/chicagoad.pdf.

Hehir, Thomas, Todd Grindal, Brian Freeman, Renée Lamoreau, Yolanda Borquaye, and Samantha Burke. "A Summary of the Evidence on Inclusive Education." August 2016. https://alana.org.br/wp-content/uploads/2016/12/A_Summary_of_the_evidence_on_inclusive_education.pdf.

"IAN Research Report: Bullying and Children with ASD." IAN Research Report: Bullying and Children with ASD | Interactive Autism Network. October 07, 2014. https://www.iancommunity.org/cs/ian_research_reports/ian_research_report_bullying.

Stereotypes and Empathy

Lick, David J., Adam L. Alter, and Jonathan B. Freeman. "Superior Pattern Detectors Efficiently Learn, Activate, Apply, and Update Social Stereotypes." *Journal of Experimental Psychology: General* 147, no. 2 (2018): 209–27. doi:10.1037/xge0000349.

"Projects." Virtual Human Interaction Lab. https://vhil.stanford.edu/projects/.

"What Does 'White Privilege' Mean to You? We Asked 18 People to Discuss Terms About Race." *The Seattle Times*. June 20, 2016. https://projects.seattletimes.com/2016/under-our-skin/.

Representation and Positive Role Models

Adichie, Chimamanda Ngozi. TED: Ideas Worth Spreading. July 2009. https://www.ted.com/talks/chimamanda_adichie_the_danger_of_a_single_story#t-3952.

"Andrea Cleveland and Monica Harwell." *StoryCorps*. August 13, 2015. https://storycorps.org/listen/monica-harwell-and-andrea-cleveland-150814/#.

Wilson, Wendy. "Little Girl in Awe of Michelle Obama's Portrait Goes Viral." *TheGrio*. March 05, 2018. https://thegrio.com/2018/03/05/little-girl-awe-michelle-obamas-portrait-goes-viral/.

CHAPTER 6

Transitioning Friendships

Hartl, Amy C., Brett Laursen, and Antonius H. N. Cillessen. "A Survival Analysis of Adolescent Friendships." *Psychological Science* 26, no. 8 (2015): 1304–315. doi:10.1177/0956797615588751.

Kamper, Kimberly E., and Jamie M. Ostrov. "Relational Aggression in Middle Childhood Predicting Adolescent Social-Psychological Adjustment: The

Role of Friendship Quality." *Journal of Clinical Child & Adolescent Psychology* 42, no. 6 (2013): 855–62. doi:10.1080/15374416.2013.844595.

Ostrov, Jamie M., Stephanie A. Godleski, Kimberly E. Kamper-Demarco, Sarah J. Blakely-Mcclure, and Lauren Celenza. "Replication and Extension of the Early Childhood Friendship Project: Effects on Physical and Relational Bullying." *School Psychology Review* 44, no. 4 (2015): 445–63. doi:10.17105/spr -15-0048.1.

Robb, Alice. "The Enduring Influence of Your Middle-School Best Friend." *The Cut.* October 24, 2017. https://www.thecut.com/2017/10/the-enduring -influence-of-your-Middle-school-best-friend.html.

Coping Mechanisms

Williams, Lisa A., and Monica Y. Bartlett. "Warm Thanks: Gratitude Expression Facilitates Social Affiliation in New Relationships via Perceived Warmth." *Emotion* 15, no. 1 (2015): 1-5. doi:10.1037/emo0000017.

Yeager, David S., Hae Yeon Lee, and Jeremy P. Jamieson. "How to Improve Adolescent Stress Responses." *Psychological Science* 27, no. 8 (2016): 1078–091. doi:10.1177/0956797616649604.

CHAPTER 7
Self-Bullying

Grandclerc, Salome, Diane De Labrouhe, Michel Spodenkiewicz, Jonathan Lachal, and Marie-Rose Moro. "Relations Between Nonsuicidal Self-Injury and Suicidal Behavior in Adolescence: A Systematic Review." *Plos One* 11, no. 4 (2016). doi:10.1371/journal.pone.0153760.

Patchin, Justin W., and Sameer Hinduja. "Digital Self-Harm Among Adolescents." *Journal of Adolescent Health* 61, no. 6 (2017): 761–66. doi:10.1016 /j.jadohealth.2017.06.012.

Roos, David. "Startling Number of Teens Cyberbully Themselves." *HowStuff Works.* November 13, 2017. https://lifestyle.howstuffworks.com/family/parenting /tween-teens.

Coping Mechanisms

Bruehlman-Senecal, Emma L. "This Too Shall Pass: Temporal Distance and the Regulation of Emotional Distress." PhD diss., University of California, Berkeley, 2015. Spring 2015. http://digitalassets.lib.berkeley.edu/etd/ucb/text /BruehlmanSenecal_berkeley_0028E_15071.pdf.

Sutton, Robert. "How to Survive a Jerk at Work." *The Wall Street Journal.* August 10, 2017. https://www.wsj.com/articles/how-to-survive-a-jerk-at-work -1502373529.

CHAPTER 8

Cyberbullying

Hurley, Katie. "Helping Kids Navigate a Virtual World Where Cyberbullying Is Common." *U.S. News & World Report.* October 13, 2017. Accessed August 13, 2018. https://health.usnews.com/wellness/for-parents/articles/2017-10-13/helping-kids-navigate-a-virtual-world-where-cyberbullying-is-common.

"New National Bullying and Cyberbullying Statistics." Cyberbullying Research Center. July 31, 2017. https://cyberbullying.org/new-national-bullying-cyberbullying-data.

Sydell, Laura. "Kyle Quinn Hid at a Friend's House After Being Misidentified on Twitter as a Racist." *NPR.* August 17, 2017. https://www.npr.org/sections/alltechconsidered/2017/08/17/543980653/kyle-quinn-hid-at-a-friend-s-house-after-being-misidentified-on-twitter-as-a-rac?utm_term=nprnews&utm_content=bufferdca42&utm_medium=social&utm_source=twitter.com&utm_campaign=buffer.

Technology and Social Media

Anderson, Monica, and Jingjing Jiang. "Teens, Social Media & Technology 2018." Pew Research Center: Internet, Science & Tech. May 31, 2018. http://www.pewinternet.org/2018/05/31/teens-social-media-technology-2018/.

Salm, Lauren. "70% of Employers Are Snooping Candidates' Social Media Profiles." *CareerBuilder.* June 15, 2017. https://www.careerbuilder.com/advice/social-media-survey-2017.

"The 'Wait Until 8th' Pledge—Let Kids Be Kids a Little Longer . . ." Westport Moms.com. August 1, 2017. https://westportmoms.com/wait-until-8th-pledge-let-kids-be-kids-a-little-longer/.

Twenge, Jean M. "Have Smartphones Destroyed a Generation?" *The Atlantic.* March 19, 2018. https://www.theatlantic.com/magazine/archive/2017/09/has-the-smartphone-destroyed-a-generation/534198/.

Twenge, Jean M. "Perspective | Teenage Depression and Suicide Are Way up—and so Is Smartphone Use." *The Washington Post.* November 19, 2017. https://www.washingtonpost.com/national/health-science/teenage-depression-and-suicide-are-way-up—and-so-is-smartphone-use/2017/11/17/624641ea-ca13-11e7-8321-481fd63f174d_story.html?utm_term=.91ccb165b6fc.

Twenge, Jean M., Thomas E. Joiner, Megan L. Rogers, and Gabrielle N. Martin. "Increases in Depressive Symptoms, Suicide-Related Outcomes, and Suicide Rates Among U.S. Adolescents After 2010 and Links to Increased New Media Screen Time." *Clinical Psychological Science* 6, no. 1 (2017): 3–17. doi:10.1177/2167702617723376.

CHAPTER 9

Youth Sex Statistics

"SIECUS Sexuality Information and Education Council of the United States." SIECUS—Home. https://siecus.org/.

"Youth Risk Behavior Surveillance—United States, 2009." *PsycEXTRA Dataset*, 2010. doi:10.1037/e661322010-001.

Sexual Harassment

Espelage, Dorothy L., Jun Sung Hong, Sarah Rinehart, and Namrata Doshi. "Understanding Types, Locations, & Perpetrators of Peer-to-Peer Sexual Harassment in U.S. Middle Schools: A Focus on Sex, Racial, and Grade Differences." *Children and Youth Services Review* 71 (December 2016): 174–83. doi:10.1016/j.childyouth.2016.11.010.

Johnston, Abby. "Meet India's Electric Shock Anti-Rape Bra." *Bustle*. April 25, 2018. https://www.bustle.com/articles/29655-indias-electric-shock-anti-rape-bra-society-harnessing-equipment-is-terrifying-and-necessary.

Simmons, Rachel. "When Middle Schoolers Say #MeToo." *The Huffington Post*. December 15, 2017. https://www.huffingtonpost.com/entry/sexual-harassment-in-schools_us_5a32b145e4b00dbbcb5bb530.

Weissbourd, Richard, Trish Ross Anderson, Alison Cashin, and Joe McIntyre. "The Talk: How Adults Can Promote Young People's Healthy Relationships and Prevent Misogyny and Sexual Harassment." *Making Caring Common*. 2017. https://mcc.gse.harvard.edu/thetalk.

Pornography

Damour, Lisa. "Teenagers, Stop Asking for Nude Photos." *New York Times*. January 02, 2018. https://www.nytimes.com/2018/01/02/well/family/teenagers-stop-asking-for-nude-photos.html.

Jones, Maggie. "What Teenagers Are Learning from Online Porn." *New York Times*. February 07, 2018. https://www.nytimes.com/2018/02/07/magazine/Teenagers-learning-online-porn-literacy-sex-education.html.

"Pornography Is the Public Health Crisis of the Digital Age." *Culture Reframed*. Accessed August 13, 2018. https://www.culturereframed.org/.

"Talking to Your Child About Pornography." *Break the Cycle*. April 27, 2017. https://www.breakthecycle.org/talking-your-child-about-pornography-0.

Thomas, Sara E. "'What Should I Do?': Young Women's Reported Dilemmas with Nude Photographs." *Sexuality Research and Social Policy* 15, no. 2 (2017): 192–207. doi:10.1007/s13178-017-0310-0.

Wolak, J., K. Mitchell, and D. Finkelhor. "Unwanted and Wanted Exposure to Online Pornography in a National Sample of Youth Internet Users." *Pediatrics* 119, no. 2 (2007): 247–57. doi:10.1542/peds.2006-1891.

Technology and Self-Esteem/Body Image

Field, Alison E., Kendrin R. Sonneville, Ross D. Crosby, Sonja A. Swanson, Kamryn T. Eddy, Carlos A. Camargo, Nicholas J. Horton, and Nadia Micali. "Prospective Associations of Concerns About Physique and the Development of Obesity, Binge Drinking, and Drug Use Among Adolescent Boys and Young Adult Men." *JAMA Pediatrics* 168, no. 1 (2014): 34. doi:10.1001/jamapediatrics.2013.2915.

Mujezinovic, Damir. "'The Selfie Generation' Study Explores the Effects of Social Media on Adolescent Body Image." *The Inquisitr*. May 30, 2018. https://www.inquisitr.com/4920082/the-selfie-generation-study-explores-the-effects-of-social-media-on-adolescent-body-image/.

Salomon, Ilyssa, and Christia Spears Brown. "The Selfie Generation: Examining the Relationship Between Social Media Use and Early Adolescent Body Image." *The Journal of Early Adolescence*, 2018, 027243161877080. doi:10.1177/0272431618770809.

Weissbourd, Richard, Trish Ross Anderson, Alison Cashin, and Joe McIntyre. "The Talk: How Adults Can Promote Young People's Healthy Relationships and Prevent Misogyny and Sexual Harassment." *Making Caring Common*. 2017. https://mcc.gse.harvard.edu/thetalk.

LGBTQ+

K., Joseph G., Emily A. G., Noreen M. G., Christian V., and David D. "The 2015 National School Climate Survey: The Experiences of Lesbian, Gay, Bisexual, Transgender, and Queer Youth in Our Nation's Schools." GLSEN. 2016. https://www.glsen.org/article/2015-national-school-climate-survey.

"Pansexual | Definition of Pansexual in English by Oxford Dictionaries." Oxford Dictionaries | English. Accessed August 20, 2017. https://en.oxforddictionaries.com/definition/pansexual.

CHAPTER 10
Youth Want More Emotional Information

Weissbourd, Richard, Trish Ross Anderson, Alison Cashin, and Joe McIntyre. "The Talk: How Adults Can Promote Young People's Healthy Relationships and Prevent Misogyny and Sexual Harassment." *Making Caring Common*. 2017. https://mcc.gse.harvard.edu/thetalk.

Online Manipulation

Cutbush, S. L., Williams, J., Miller, S., Gibbs, D., & Clinton-Sherrod, M. (2012, October). *Electronic Dating Aggression Among Middle School Students: Demographic Correlates and Associations with Other Types of Violence.* Presented at APHA 2012, San Francisco; https://www.rti.org/publication/electronic-dating-aggression-among-middle-school-students-demographic-correlates-and.

Healthy Relationship Skills

"10 Tips on Talking About Healthy Relationships with Teens." *Futures Without Violence.* 2015. https://s3.amazonaws.com/fwvcorp/wp-content/uploads/20160121110131/10Tips_healthyrelationships2.pdf.

Lattimore, Kayla. "4-H Is Helping Kids Plant the Seeds for Healthy Relationships." *NPR.* August 11, 2017. https://www.npr.org/sections/ed/2017/08/11/540618626/4-h-is-helping-kids-plant-the-seeds-for-healthy-relationships?utm_campaign=storyshare&utm_source=twitter.com&utm_medium=social.

The Dibble Institute. Accessed January 12, 2017. https://www.dibbleinstitute.org/.

CHAPTER 11

Academic Pressure and Stress

Conner, Jerusha O., and Denise C. Pope. "Not Just Robo-Students: Why Full Engagement Matters and How Schools Can Promote It." *Journal of Youth and Adolescence* 42, no. 9 (2013): 1426–442. doi:10.1007/s10964-013-9948-y.

"Kids and Stress, How Do They Handle It?" *KidsHealth KidsPoll*, October 12, 2005. National Association of Health Education Center. https://kidshealth.org/media/kidspoll/worry.html.

"Morbidity and Mortality Weekly Report (MMWR)." Centers for Disease Control and Prevention. August 17, 2017.https://www.cdc.gov/mmwr/volumes/65/wr/mm6543a8.htm?s_cid=#suggestedcitation.

Soenens, Bart, Koen Luyckx, Maarten Vansteenkiste, Bart Duriez, and Luc Goossens. "Clarifying the Link Between Parental Psychological Control and Adolescents' Depressive Symptoms: Reciprocal Versus Unidirectional Models." *Merrill-Palmer Quarterly*, 2nd ser., 54, no. 4 (2008). https://digitalcommons.wayne.edu/mpq/vol54/iss4/2/.

Spencer, Kyle. "A New Kind of Classroom: No Grades, No Failing, No Hurry." *New York Times.* August 11, 2017. https://www.nytimes.com/2017/08/11/nyregion/mastery-based-learning-no-grades.html.

"The Children We Mean to Raise." Making Caring Common. 2014. https://mcc.gse.harvard.edu/the-children-we-mean-to-raise.

It's OK to Fail

Cook, Henrietta. "The School Teaching Students That It's OK to Fail." *Brisbane Times*. August 28, 2017. https://www.brisbanetimes.com.au/national/victoria/the-school-teaching-students-that-its-ok-to-fail-20170827-gy4zo1.html.

Warrell, Margie. "Have You Learnt How to Fail Forward? The Lesson We Can't Learn Soon Enough." *Forbes*. September 11, 2017. https://www.forbes.com/sites/margiewarrell/2017/08/31/why-schools-are-teaching-kids-to-fail/#586ff6d11645.

CHAPTER 12

Homework and Technology

Bowman, Laura L., Laura E. Levine, Bradley M. Waite, and Michael Gendron. "Can Students Really Multitask? An Experimental Study of Instant Messaging While Reading." *Computers & Education* 54, no. 4 (2010): 927–31. doi:10.1016/j.compedu.2009.09.024.

Lee, Seungyeon, Myeong W. Kim, Ian M. Mcdonough, Jessica S. Mendoza, and Min Sung Kim. "The Effects of Cell Phone Use and Emotion-Regulation Style on College Students Learning." *Applied Cognitive Psychology* 31, no. 3 (2017): 360–66. doi:10.1002/acp.3323.

Thornton, Bill, Alyson Faires, Maija Robbins, and Eric Rollins. "The Mere Presence of a Cell Phone May Be Distracting." *Social Psychology* 45, no. 6 (2014): 479–88. doi:10.1027/1864-9335/a000216.

Take a Break

Adam, Hajo, and Adam D. Galinsky. "Enclothed Cognition." *Journal of Experimental Social Psychology* 48, no. 4 (2012): 918–25. doi:10.1016/j.jesp.2012.02.008.

"Five Ways to Shift Teaching Practice So Students Feel Less Math Anxious." KQED. April 05, 2017. https://www.kqed.org/mindshift/47907/five-ways-to-shift-teaching-practice-so-students-feel-less-math-anxious.

White, Rachel E., Emily O. Prager, Catherine Schaefer, Ethan Kross, Angela L. Duckworth, and Stephanie M. Carlson. "The 'Batman Effect': Improving Perseverance in Young Children." *Child Development* 88, no. 5 (2016): 1563-571. doi:10.1111/cdev.12695.

CHAPTER 13
Gifted Children

Callahan, Carolyn M., Tonya R. Moon, and Sarah Oh. "Describing the Status of Programs for the Gifted." *Journal for the Education of the Gifted* 40, no. 1 (2017): 20–49. doi:10.1177/0162353216686215.

"National Association for Gifted Children." What It Means to Teach Gifted Learners Well | National Association for Gifted Children. http://www.nagc .org/.

Rakow, Susan. "That Was Then, This Is Now: Gifted in the Middle." *AMLE Magazine*, August 2017, 34.

"Rethinking Giftedness Film." *YouCubed*, November 7, 2017, www.youcubed .org/rethinking-giftedness-film/.

"Students Share the Downside of Being Labeled 'Gifted'." *KQED*, 13 Nov. 2017, www.kqed.org/mindshift/49653.

"Supporting the Emotional Needs of the Gifted." SENG. http://sengifted .org/.

Attention Disorders

Hallowell, Edward. "ADHD: Ferrari Engine for a Brain, with Bicycle Brakes— Dr Hallowell ADHD and Mental and Cognitive Health." Drhallowell. com. February 20, 2018. http://www.drhallowell.com/adhd-ferrari-engine -for-a-brain-with-bicycle-brakes/.

O'neill, Meaghan. "Eight Things I Wish Teachers Knew About My Child with ADHD—*The Boston Globe*." BostonGlobe.com. August 09, 2018. https:// www.bostonglobe.com/magazine/2018/08/09/eight-things-wish-teachers -knew-about-kid-with-adhd/X0f6MF2yVldZ12ZK3nQ2AO/story.html ?s_campaign=8315.

"The State of LD: Understanding Learning and Attention Issues." National Center for Learning Disabilities. Accessed March 29, 2018. https://www.ncld .org/understanding-learning-and-attention-issues.

CHAPTER 14
Communication and Boys

Aznar, Ana, and Harriet R. Tenenbaum. "Spanish Parents Emotion Talk and Their Children's Understanding of Emotion." *Frontiers in Psychology* 4 (2013). doi:10.3389/fpsyg.2013.00670.

Borelli, Jessica L., Leslie Ho, and Lane Epps. "School-Aged Children's Psycho- biological Divergence as a Prospective Predictor of Health Risk Behaviors in Adolescence." *Journal of Child and Family Studies* 27, no. 1 (2017): 47–58. doi:10.1007/s10826-017-0870-x.

"NYU Steinhardt Receives Spencer Foundation Grant to Address Societal Divisions in NYC Middle Schools." *NYU*, November 02, 2017. www.nyu .edu/about/news-publications/news/2017/november/nyu-steinhardt-receives -spencer-foundation-grant-to-address-soci.html.

Reiner, Andrew. "Boy Talk: Breaking Masculine Stereotypes," *New York Times*. October 24, 2018.

Reiner, Andrew. "Teaching Men to Be Emotionally Honest." *New York Times*. April 04, 2016. https://www.nytimes.com/2016/04/10/education/edlife /teaching-men-to-be-emotionally-honest.html.

Reiner, Andrew. "Talking to Boys the Way We Talk to Girls." *New York Times*. June 15, 2017. https://www.nytimes.com/2017/06/15/well/family/talking-to -boys-the-way-we-talk-to-girls.html?mtrref=www.google.com&gwh =6E9778C3EA6E6D2909FD6C6852C31292&gwt=pay.

Danger of Stereotypes

Bennett, Jessica. "A Master's Degree in . . . Masculinity?" *New York Times*. August 08, 2015. https://www.nytimes.com/2015/08/09/fashion/masculinities -studies-stonybrook-michael-kimmel.html.

Love, Kevin. "Everyone Is Going Through Something | By Kevin Love." *The Players' Tribune*. March 6, 2018. https://www.theplayerstribune.com/en-us /articles/kevin-love-everyone-is-going-through-something.

CHAPTER 15
Girls and Confidence

Cain, Susan. "Unlocking the Power of Introverts." Quiet Revolution. https:// www.quietrev.com/.

"How Girls Can Develop 'Critical' Confidence." *Good Morning America*. March 30, 2018. https://www.goodmorningamerica.com/family/story /captureconfidence-girls-develop-critical-confidence-metoo-era-54106629.

Nielsen, Leslie. "Strengthening Father-Daughter Relationships." *Our Children*. March 2005. http://users.wfu.edu/nielsen/PTA.pdf.

"Poll | The Confidence Code for Girls." The Confidence Code for Girls with YPulse. 2018. https://www.confidencecodegirls.com/poll.

Leadership and Empowerment

"2018 Leadership Summit." *Girl Up*. https://www.girlup.org/leadership-summit /#sthash.bhKFMFLt.dpbs.

Marshall, Ava, Chanice Lee, Nateya Taylor, and Alexia Morrison. "The Melanin Diary." *The Melanin Diary*. http://www.themelanindiary.com/.

Walsh, Bari. "Confronting Gender Bias at School." Harvard Graduate School of Education. September 8, 2015. https://www.gse.harvard.edu/news/uk/15/09/confronting-gender-bias-school.

CHAPTER 16
Letting Go

Gillett, Rachel, and Richard Feloni. "19 Highly Successful People Who Prove It's Never Too Late to Change Careers." *Business Insider*. April 16, 2016. http://www.businessinsider.com/successful-people-who-made-a-big-career-change-2016-4/#long-before-ronald-reagan-became-the-40th-president-of-the-united-states-at-69-he-was-a-young-up-and-coming-hollywood-actor-in-film-and-tv-8.

Kohn, Alfie. "The Downside of 'Grit' (Commentary)." Alfie Kohn. November 30, 2014. https://www.alfiekohn.org/article/downside-grit/.

Wells, Jane. "Someone Told Kobe Bryant He Shouldn't Play Basketball." CNBC. March 31, 2016. https://www.cnbc.com/2016/03/30/someone-told-kobe-bryant-he-shouldnt-Play-basketball.html.

Wrosch, Carsten, Michael F. Scheier, Gregory E. Miller, Richard Schulz, and Charles S. Carver. "Adaptive Self-Regulation of Unattainable Goals: Goal Disengagement, Goal Reengagement, and Subjective Well-Being." *Personality and Social Psychology Bulletin* 29, no. 12 (2003): 1494–508. doi:10.1177/0146167203256921.

Wrosch, Carsten, Gregory E. Miller, Michael F. Scheier, and Stephanie Brun De Pontet. "Giving Up on Unattainable Goals: Benefits for Health?" *Personality and Social Psychology Bulletin* 33, no. 2 (2007): 251–65. doi:10.1177/0146167206294905.

CHAPTER 17
Anxiety and Depression

"Anxiety Disorders." National Institute of Mental Health. https://www.nimh.nih.gov/health/topics/anxiety-disorders/index.shtml.

Aubrey, Allison. "Pediatricians Call for Universal Depression Screening for Teens." *NPR*. February 26, 2018.https://www.npr.org/sections/health-shots/2018/02/26/588334959/pediatrians-Call-for-universal-depression-screening-for-teens.

Bitsko, Rebecca H., Joseph R. Holbrook, Reem M. Ghandour, Stephen J. Blumberg, Susanna N. Visser, Ruth Perou, and John T. Walkup. "Epidemiology and Impact of Health Care Provider–Diagnosed Anxiety and Depression Among US Children." *Journal of Developmental & Behavioral Pediatrics* 39, no. 5 (2018): 395–403. doi:10.1097/dbp.0000000000000571.

Morin, Amy. "10 Reasons Teens Have So Much Anxiety Today." *Psychology Today*. November 03, 2017. https://www-psychologytoday-com.cdn.ampproject.org/c/s/www.psychologytoday.com/blog/what-mentally-strong-people-dont-do/201711/10-reasons-why-todays-teenagers-are-so-anxious?amp.

Nutt, Amy Ellis. "Why Kids and Teens May Face Far More Anxiety These Days." *The Washington Post*. May 10, 2018. https://www.washingtonpost.com/news/to-your-health/wp/2018/05/10/why-kids-and-teens-may-face-far-more-anxiety-these-days/?utm_term=.b1d719e890cc.

Schwarz, Nicole. "13 Powerful Phrases Proven to Help an Anxious Child Calm Down." *Lemon Lime Adventures*. December 11, 2017. http://lemonlimeadventures.com/what-to-say-to-calm-an-anxious-child/.

Zuckerbrot, R. A., A. H. Cheung, P. S. Jensen, R. E. K. Stein, and D. Laraque. "Guidelines for Adolescent Depression in Primary Care (GLAD-PC): I. Identification, Assessment, and Initial Management." *Pediatrics* 120, no. 5 (2007): E1299–1312. doi:10.1542/peds.2007-1144.

Stress

"#EmotionRevolution Summit and Survey." Born This Way Foundation. https://bornthisway.foundation/emotionrevolution/summit/.

Jamieson, Jeremy P., Matthew K. Nock, and Wendy Berry Mendes. "Mind over Matter: Reappraising Arousal Improves Cardiovascular and Cognitive Responses to Stress." *Journal of Experimental Psychology: General* 141, no. 3 (2012): 417–22. doi:10.1037/a0025719.

National Survey of Children's Health—Data Resource Center for Child and Adolescent Health. http://childhealthdata.org/learn/NSCH.

"N.U.T.S.—Understanding Stress." *Heart-Mind Online*. January 14, 2015. https://heartmindonline.org/resources/nuts-understanding-stress.

"Stress in America 2009." *American Psychological Association*. 2009. http://www.apa.org/news/press/releases/stress/2009/stress-exec-summary.pdf.

Toppo, Greg. "Our High School Kids: Tired, Stressed and Bored." *USA Today*. October 23, 2015. https://www.usatoday.com/story/news/nation/2015/10/23/survey-students-tired-stressed-bored/74412782/.

Suicide

Carroll, Aaron E. "Preventing Teen Suicide: What the Evidence Shows." *New York Times*. August 17, 2017. https://www.nytimes.com/2017/08/17/upshot/preventing-teen-suicide-what-the-evidence-shows.html.

"QuickStats: Suicide Rates* for Teens Aged 15–19 Years, by Sex—United States, 1975–2015." *MMWR. Morbidity and Mortality Weekly Report* 66, no. 30 (2017): 816. doi:10.15585/mmwr.mm6630a6.

Encouraging Resiliency

Bridges, Frances. "5 Ways to Build Resilience, from Sheryl Sandberg and Adam Grant's New Book 'Option B'." *Forbes*. May 30, 2017.https://www.forbes.com/sites/francesbridges/2017/05/27/5-ways-to-build-resilience-from-sheryl-sandberg-and-adam-grants-new-book-option-b/.

Hoekzema, Elseline, Erika Barba-Müller, Cristina Pozzobon, Marisol Picado, Florencio Lucco, David García-García, Juan Carlos Soliva, Adolf Tobeña, Manuel Desco, Eveline A. Crone, Agustín Ballesteros, Susanna Carmona, and Oscar Vilarroya. "Pregnancy Leads to Long-Lasting Changes in Human Brain Structure." *Nature Neuroscience* 20, no. 2 (2016): 287–96. doi:10.1038/nn.4458.

Leckman, James F. "Nurturing Resilient Children." *Revista Brasileira De Psiquiatria* 29, no. 1 (2007): 5–6. doi:10.1590/s1516-44462007000100003.

Liu, Dong, Josie Diorio, Beth Tannenbaum, Christian Caldji, Darlene Francis, Alison Freedman, Shakti Sharma, Deborah Pearson, Paul M. Plotsky, and Michael J. Meaney. "Maternal Care, Hippocampal Glucocorticoid Receptors, and Hypothalamic-Pituitary-Adrenal Responses to Stress." *Science* 277, no. 5332 (1997): 1659–662. doi:10.1126/science.277.5332.1659.

Wallace, Jennifer Breheny. "How to Raise More Grateful Children." *The Wall Street Journal*. February 23, 2018. https://www.wsj.com/articles/how-to-raise-more-grateful-children-1519398748.

Coping Strategies and Emotion Regulation

Baikie, Karen A., and Kay Wilhelm. "Emotional and Physical Health Benefits of Expressive Writing." *Advances in Psychiatric Treatment* 11, no. 5 (2005): 338–46. doi:10.1192/apt.11.5.338.

Grohol, John M. "15 Common Cognitive Distortions." *Psych Central*. April 12, 2018. https://psychcentral.com/lib/15-common-cognitive-distortions/.

Homan, Kristin J., and Fuschia M. Sirois. "Self-Compassion and Physical Health: Exploring the Roles of Perceived Stress and Health-Promoting Behaviors." *Health Psychology Open* 4, no. 2 (2017). doi:10.1177/2055102917729542.

Jamieson, Jeremy P., Matthew K. Nock, and Wendy Berry Mendes. "Mind over Matter: Reappraising Arousal Improves Cardiovascular and Cognitive Responses to Stress." *Journal of Experimental Psychology: General* 141, no. 3 (2012): 417–22. doi:10.1037/a0025719.

Li, Qing. "Effect of Forest Bathing Trips on Human Immune Function." *Environmental Health and Preventive Medicine* 15, no. 1 (2009): 9–17. doi:10.1007/s12199-008-0068-3.

"Mindfulness for Your Students, Teachers, and School Community." Mindful Schools. https://www.mindfulschools.org/.

Pruess, Angela. "25 Mindfulness Practices Your Kids Will Actually Want to Do." *Parents with Confidence.* June 20, 2018. https://parentswithconfidence.com /25-mindfulness-practices-for-kids-who-cant-sit-still/.

Fostering Diverse Emotions

Anwar, Yasmin. "Feeling Bad About Feeling Bad Can Make You Feel Worse." *Greater Good Magazine.* August 18, 2017. https://greatergood.berkeley.edu /article/item/feeling_bad_about_feeling_bad_can_make_you_feel_worse.

Ford, Brett Q., Phoebe Lam, Oliver P. John, and Iris B. Mauss. "The Psychological Health Benefits of Accepting Negative Emotions and Thoughts: Laboratory, Diary, and Longitudinal Evidence." *Journal of Personality and Social Psychology,* July 13, 2017. doi:10.1037/pspp0000157.

Gopnik, Alison, Shaun O'Grady, Christopher G. Lucas, Thomas L. Griffiths, Adrienne Wente, Sophie Bridgers, Rosie Aboody, Hoki Fung, and Ronald E. Dahl. "Changes in Cognitive Flexibility and Hypothesis Search Across Human Life History from Childhood to Adolescence to Adulthood." *Proceedings of the National Academy of Sciences* 114, no. 30 (2017): 7892–899. doi:10.1073/pnas.1700811114.fsdf.

McGlaughlin, Katie M. "This Train Analogy Will Completely Change How You See Your Crying Child." *Pick Any Two.* August 07, 2017. http:// pickanytwo.net/the-train-analogy-that-will-change-how-you-see-your -crying-child/?utm_campaign=shareaholic&utm_medium=facebook&utm _source=socialnetwork.

Ong, Anthony D., Lizbeth Benson, Alex J. Zautra, and Nilam Ram. "Emodiversity and Biomarkers of Inflammation." *Emotion* 18, no. 1 (2018): 3–14. doi:10.1037/emo0000343.

Orloff, Judith. "The Health Benefits of Tears." *Psychology Today.* July 27, 2010. https://www.psychologytoday.com/us/blog/emotional-freedom/201007 /the-health-benefits-tears.

CHAPTER 18

Creativity

Bryant, Adam. "In Head-Hunting, Big Data May Not Be Such a Big Deal." *New York Times.* June 20, 2013. http://www.nytimes.com/2013/06/20/business /in-head-hunting-big-data-May-not-be-such-a-big-deal.html.

"Can Creativity Be Taught? Results from Research Studies." *Creativity at Work.* August 25, 2017. https://www.creativityatwork.com/2012/03/23/can-creativity -be-taught/.

Connley, Courtney. "Google, Apple and 13 Other Companies That No Longer Require a College Degree." *CNBC*. August 16, 2018. https://www.cnbc.com/2018/08/16/15-companies-that-no-longer-require-employees-to-have-a-college-degree.html.

Hess, Ed. "In the AI Age, 'Being Smart' Will Mean Something Completely Different." *Harvard Business Review*. June 19, 2017. https://hbr.org/2017/06/in-the-ai-age-being-smart-will-mean-something-completely-different.

Nisen, Max. "Why Google Doesn't Care About Hiring Top College Graduates." *Quartz*. February 24, 2014. https://qz.com/180247/why-google-doesnt-care-about-hiring-top-college-graduates/.

"Stanley Black & Decker Awards Locker Hammock Most Innovative Award." STEMIE Coalition. June 7, 2017. http://www.stemie.org/stanley-black-decker-awards-locker-hammock-innovative-award/.

Experiential Learning

"Compass Points Activity." National School Reform Faculty. 2014. https://www.nsrfharmony.org/sites/all/themes/NSRFtheme/assets/ProtocolsA-Z/C/CompassPoints-N.pdf.

Frank, Robert. "Spanx Billionaire's Secret to Success: Failure." *CNBC*. October 16, 2013. https://www.cnbc.com/2013/10/16/billionaire-sara-blakely-says-secret-to-success-is-failure.html.

Frey, Carl Benedikt, and Michael A. Osborne. "The Future of Employment: How Susceptible Are Jobs to Computerisation?" *Technological Forecasting and Social Change* 114 (2017): 254–80. doi:10.1016/j.techfore.2016.08.019.

Gopnik, Alison, Shaun O'Grady, Christopher G. Lucas, Thomas L. Griffiths, Adrienne Wente, Sophie Bridgers, Rosie Aboody, Hoki Fung, and Ronald E. Dahl. "Changes in Cognitive Flexibility and Hypothesis Search Across Human Life History from Childhood to Adolescence to Adulthood." *Proceedings of the National Academy of Sciences* 114, no. 30 (2017): 7892–899. doi:10.1073/pnas.1700811114.

Gottfried, Adele Eskeles, Kathleen Suzanne Johnson Preston, Allen W. Gottfried, Pamella H. Oliver, Danielle E. Delany, and Sirena M. Ibrahim. "Pathways from Parental Stimulation of Children's Curiosity to High School Science Course Accomplishments and Science Career Interest and Skill." *International Journal of Science Education* 38, no. 12 (2016): 1972–995. doi:10.1080/09500693.2016.1220690.

Kashdan, Todd B., and Paul J. Silvia. "Curiosity and Interest: The Benefits of Thriving on Novelty and Challenge." *Oxford Handbooks Online*, 2009. doi:10.1093/oxfordhb/9780195187243.013.0034.

Kaufman, Scott Barry. "Schools Are Missing What Matters About Learning." *The Atlantic*. July 26, 2017. https://www.theatlantic.com/education/archive/2017/07/the-underrated-gift-of-curiosity/534573/.

Leibowitz, Glenn. "If Robots Are Going to Take Our Jobs, Do Grades Still Matter?" *LinkedIn*. August 20, 2017. https://www.linkedin.com/pulse/robots-going-take-our-jobs-do-grades-still-Matter-glenn-leibowitz.

Miller, Claire Cain. "Tech's Damaging Myth of the Loner Genius Nerd." *New York Times*. August 12, 2017. https://www.nytimes.com/2017/08/12/upshot/techs-damaging-myth-of-the-Loner-genius-nerd.html.

Miller, Claire Cain, and Quoctrung Bui. "Switching Careers Doesn't Have to Be Hard: Charting Jobs That Are Similar to Yours." *New York Times*. July 27, 2017. https://www.nytimes.com/2017/07/27/upshot/switching-careers-is-hard-it-doesnt-have-to-be.html.

"Radnor Township School District." Radnor Township SD Homepage. https://www.rtsd.org/.

Vander Ark, "Proposal for an Innovation Diploma." *Getting Smart*. August 17, 2017. http://www.gettingsmart.com/2017/08/proposal-for-an-innovation-diploma/.

WW-P Middle School Challenge. http://markwise8.wixsite.com/globalchallenge.

WEBSITES

Amaze. Amaze.org

"Beyond Differences." Beyond Differences. https://www.beyonddifferences.org/.

Center for Parent and Teen Communication. https://parentandteen.com

"Character.org." Character.org. http://character.org/.

Choose2Matter. http://www.choose2matter.org/.

Design for Change USA. http://www.designforchange.us/pages/aboutus.

DIY. https://diy.org/.

Kerbal Space Program. https://www.kerbalspaceprogram.com/en/?page_id=7.

Mind Tools. "SCAMPERImproving Products and Services." From MindTools.com. April 04, 2018. https://www.mindtools.com/pages/article/newCT_02.htm.

"National Invention Convention and Entrepreneurship Expo (NICEE)." STEMIE Coalition. http://stemie.org/nicee/.

Quiet Revolution. https://www.quietrev.com/.

The Jigsaw Classroom. http://www.jigsaw.org/.

Veritasium. YouTube. https://www.youtube.com/user/1veritasium/featured.

Vsauce. YouTube. https://www.youtube.com/user/Vsauce/featured.

Young Scientist Lab. https://www.youngscientistlab.com/challenge.

BIBLIOGRAPHY

Alvord, Mary Karapetian, and Anne McGrath. *Conquer Negative Thinking for Teens: A Workbook to Break the Nine Thought Habits That Are Holding You Back*. Oakland, CA: Instant Help Books, 2017.

Angello, Michele, and Alisa Bowman. *Raising the Transgender Child: A Complete Guide for Parents, Families & Caregivers*. Berkeley, CA: Seal Press, 2016.

Bennett, Howard J. *The Fantastic Body: What Makes You Tick & How You Get Sick*. Emmaus, PA: Rodale Kids, 2017.

Borba, Michele. *Unselfie: Why Empathetic Kids Succeed in Our All-About-Me World*. New York: Touchstone, 2016.

Bronson, Po, and Ashley Merryman. *Nurtureshock: New Thinking About Children*. New York: Twelve, 2009.

Cain, Susan. *Quiet: The Power of Introverts in a World That Can't Stop Talking*. New York: Crown Publishers, 2012.

Cain, Susan, Gregory Mone, and Erica Moroz. *Quiet Power: The Secret Strength of Introverts*. Penguin Random House, 2016.

Damour, Lisa. *Untangled: Guiding Teenage Girls Through the Seven Transitions Into Adulthood*. London: Atlantic Books, 2017.

Dawson, Peg, and Richard Guare. *Smart but Scattered: The Revolutionary "Executive Skills" Approach to Helping Kids Reach Their Potential*. New York: Guilford Press, 2009.

Dintersmith, Ted. *What School Could Be: Insights and Inspiration from Teachers Across America*. Princeton University Press, 2018.

Fox, Annie. *Middle School Confidential*. Minneapolis, MN: Free Spirit, 2008–2010.

Ginsburg, Kenneth R., and Martha Moraghan Jablow. *Building Resilience in Children and Teens: Giving Kids Roots and Wings*. American Academy of Pediatrics, 2014.

Ginsburg, Kenneth R. *Raising Kids to Thrive: Balancing Love with Expectations and Protection with Trust*. American Academy of Pediatrics, 2015.

Grant, Adam M. *Originals: How Non-Conformists Move the World*. New York: Viking, 2016.

Hanson, Rick, and Forrest Hanson. *Resilient: How to Grow an Unshakable Core of Calm, Strength, and Happiness*. New York: Harmony Books, 2018.

Ignotofsky, Rachel. *Women in Science: 50 Fearless Pioneers Who Changed the World*. New York: Ten Speed Press, 2016.

Johnson, Ned, and William Stixrud, Ph.D. *The Self-Driven Child: The Science and Sense of Giving Your Kids More Control over Their Lives*. Viking, 2018.

Kay, Katty, and Claire Shipman. *The Confidence Code for Girls: Taking Risks, Messing Up, & Becoming Your Amazingly Imperfect, Totally Powerful Self*. New York: HarperCollins, 2018.

Kennedy-Moore, Eileen, and Christine McLaughlin. *Growing Friendships: A Kid's Guide to Making and Keeping Friends*. Aladdin/Beyond Words, 2017.

Kindlon, Dan, and Michael Thompson. *Raising Cain: Protecting the Emotional Life of Boys*. New York: Ballantine, 1999.

Kivel, Paul. *Mens Work: How to Stop the Violence That Tears Our Lives Apart*. Center City, MN: Hazelden, 1999.

Lahey, Jessica. *The Gift of Failure: How the Best Parents Learn to Let Go So Their Children Can Succeed*. New York: Harper, 2016.

Land, George, and Beth Jarman. *Breakpoint and Beyond: Mastering the Future-Today*. New York: HarperBusiness, 1993.

Lythcott-Haims, Julie. *How to Raise an Adult: Break Free of the Overparenting Trap and Prepare Your Kid for Success*. New York: Henry Holt and Co., 2015.

Martinez, Sylvia Libow, and Gary Stager. *Invent to Learn: Making, Tinkering, and Engineering in the Classroom*. Torrance, CA: Constructing Modern Knowledge Press, 2013.

Meyer, Pamela. *Liespotting: Proven Techniques to Detect Deception*. New York: St. Martins Griffin, 2011.

Morgan, Nick. *Can You Hear Me? How to Connect with People in a Virtual World*. Harvard Business Review Press, 2018.

Morin, Amanda. *The Everything Parent's Guide to Special Education*. Avon, MA: Adams Media, 2014.

Morin, Amy. *13 Things Mentally Strong People Don't Do*. New York: William Morrow, 2015.

Orender, Donna. *Wowsdom! The Girls Guide to the Positive and the Possible*. Herndon, VA: Mascot Books, 2018.

Orenstein, Peggy. *Don't Call Me Princess: Essays on Girls, Women, Sex, and Life*. New York: Harper Paperbacks, 2018.

Orenstein, Peggy. *Girls and Sex: Navigating the Complicated New Landscape*. New York: Harper, 2016.

Pearlman, Catherine. *Ignore It! How Selectively Looking the Other Way Can Decrease Behavioral Problems and Increase Parenting Satisfaction*. New York: TarcherPerigee, 2017.

Pennebaker, James W. *Opening Up: The Healing Power of Expressing Emotions*. New York: Guilford Press, 1997.

Pope, Denise Clark, Maureen Brown, and Sarah Miles. *Overloaded and Underprepared: Strategies for Stronger Schools and Healthy, Successful Kids*. San Francisco: Jossey-Bass, 2015.

Prinstein, Mitchell J. *Popular: The Power of Likability in a Status-Obsessed World*. New York: Viking, 2017.

Rayne, Karen. *Girl: Love, Sex, Romance, and Being You*. Washington, DC: Magination Press, 2017.

Rendall, David J. *The Freak Factor: Discovering Uniqueness by Flaunting Weakness*. Charleston, SC: Advantage, 2015.

Rendall, David J. *The Freak Factor for Kids*. SEADS Publishing, 2013.

Robbins, Alexandra. *The Overachievers: The Secret Lives of Driven Kids*. New York: Hyperion, 2006.

Roffman, Deborah M. *Sex and Sensibility: The Parent's Guide to Talking Sense About Sex*. Boston: Da Capo Press, 2001.

Roffman, Deborah M. *Talk to Me First: Everything You Need to Know to Become Your Kids' Go-to Person About Sex*. Boston: Da Capo Press, 2012.

Sandberg, Sheryl, and Adam Grant. *Option B: Facing Adversity, Building Resilience, and Finding Joy*. New York: Knopf, 2017.

Scheff, Sue, and Melissa Schorr. *Shame Nation: The Global Epidemic of Online Hate*. Naperville, IL: Sourcebooks, 2017.

Simmons, Rachel. *The Curse of the Good Girl: Raising Authentic Girls with Courage and Confidence*. New York: Penguin Press, 2009.

Simmons, Rachel. *Enough as She Is: How to Help Girls Move Beyond Impossible Standards of Success to Live Healthy, Happy, and Fulfilling Lives*. New York: Harper, 2018.

Wagner, Tony. *Creating Innovators: The Making of Young People Who Will Change the World*. New York: Scribner, 2012.

Wagner, Tony, and Ted Dintersmith. *Most Likely to Succeed: Preparing Our Kids for the Innovation Era*. New York: Scribner, 2015.

Weissbourd, Richard. *The Parents We Mean to Be: How Well-Intentioned Adults Undermine Children's Moral and Emotional Development*. Boston: Houghton Mifflin Harcourt, 2010.

Wilkinson, Karen, and Mike Petrich. *The Art of Tinkering: Meet 150 Makers Working at the Intersection of Art, Science & Technology*. San Francisco: Weldon Owen, 2017.

Wiseman, Rosalind. *Queen Bees & Wannabes: Helping Your Daughter Survive Cliques, Gossip, Boys, and the New Realities of Girl World*. 3rd ed. New York: Harmony, 2016.

Wiseman, Rosalind. *Owning Up: Empowering Adolescents to Confront Social Cruelty, Bullying, and Injustice*. 2nd ed. Thousand Oaks, CA: Corwin, 2017.

Wormeli, Rick. *Fair Isn't Always Equal: Assessing & Grading in the Differentiated Classroom*. Stenhouse Publishers, and National Middle School Association, 2006.

ACKNOWLEDGMENTS

THE POWER OF GRATITUDE IS A RECURRENT THEME IN THIS book and in my life. I have so many people to thank, starting with my family. A huge thank you to Steve, the most supportive husband on the planet; and to my kids, Ben, Emily, and Alex, who are my best teachers. I'm grateful to my parents, David and Sharon Steinberg, lifelong learners who taught me to look for the good in everyone. I also want to thank my siblings and in-laws: Michael, Daniel, Jane, Tammy, Adam, and Jacqueline. You've been incredible cheerleaders!

There are so many people to thank, especially Amy Joyce, my talented and kind editor at the *Washington Post*. Amy was the first to take a chance on me—and the first to suggest that I expand my ideas into a book. Thank you to my amazing *Middle School Matters* editors—Miriam Riad, Dan Ambrosio, and Claire Schulz—and to the rest of my fabulous team at Hachette Book Group and Da Capo Press, including Michael Giarratano, Lissa Warren, Cisca Schreefel, and Anna Hall. They all believe that middle school really does matter.

I'm fortunate to have a fantastic literary agent, Jill Marsal, who makes everything joyful and easy. And I've been lucky to have Jessica Lahey, Michele Borba, and Claire Shipman as wise and generous guides on this journey. I've written here about raising girls who support and celebrate one another, and that's exactly what these three incredible women do. I'm also grateful to my wonderful school counseling mentor and friend Gloria Silverberg. She's been an important part of my life since my days as her intern.

Thank you to Josh Starr, the CEO of PDK International and my former superintendent, for continuing to bet on me. I've worked with many great organizations and editors, including Rafael Heller at PDK; April Tibbles at the Association for Middle Level Educators; and Sharon Holbrook and Susan Borison at *Your Teen Magazine*. My lovely friend, the writer Alison Pion, belongs in this category. She's been my trusted "first reader" for years. I also want to express my gratitude to everyone at Character dot Org; Nick Morgan, Emma Wyatt, and the team at Public Words; and my close friend and colleague Judy Liss at the Chrysalis Group. A special thank-you to the many Montgomery County Public Schools students, parents, and former colleagues who shared their reflections, ideas, and stories with me. And to my Sheridan School family—thank you for inspiring me! I'm so lucky I get to collaborate with caring, passionate, innovative educators every day.

I can't thank my friends enough for always being there for me, and for being willing to talk about their personal and parenting middle school experiences at dinner, over coffee, while jogging, on the phone, in the carpool line, at sports events—even while bowling! Thank you, too, to the hundreds of students, parents, teachers, psychologists, writers, principals, physicians, researchers, and other experts I interviewed for this book. You're *my* King Arthur's Round Table.

INDEX

Abdur-Ra'oof, Aziz, 171, 175
academic achievement
   autonomy, 134–136
   balance and expectations, 4,
     131–140
   cognitive-behavioral therapy, 139
   college admissions, 133
   conversation starters, 140
   grades, 131–133, 134–136
   ideas for educators–celebrate
     "Failure Week," 137
   perfectionism, 137–139
   sharing experiences, 138
   tips for parents, 139
academic identity, 4
Adichie, Chimamanda Ngozi, 55, 59
*Al Capone Does My Shirts: A Tale from
   Alcatraz* (Choldenko), 56
alcohol, 13, 17–18
Alvord, Mary, 136, 139, 217
*American Educational Research
   Journal*, 2
AMLE Magazine, 156
Anderson, Nancy, 183–184
Apert syndrome, 52–53
Applied Cognitive Psychology, 144

Ashford, Sue, 183, 184, 185, 195, 221
The Asshole Survival Guide (Sutton), 87
The Atlantic magazine, 59, 100
attention deficit disorder (ADD),
   151–152, 159
attention deficit hyperactivity
   disorder (ADHD), 157, 159
Auerbach, Melanie, 25, 153, 159
authentic inclusion, 52–54
autism, 49–50, 53–54, 61–62
automation, 220
autonomy, 134–136
Axelrod, Emily, 201–202

The Bachelor (TV show), 124–125
Barry, Katie, 219–220
Bazelon, Emily, 94, 99
Bell, W. Kamau, 59–60
Bennett, Howard, 152
Best, Rebecca, 73
Beyond Differences, 52
Bianchi, Emily, 229
bias, 56–57
"big likings," 226–227
Biological Psychiatry, 19
Blackmon, Laurel, 156, 157

Bock, Laszlo, 220–221
body image, 111–112, 182–183
Borba, Michele, 36–37, 59, 81, 82,
    85, 88
The Boston Globe, 185–186
boundaries, your own and others',
    107, 176–177
Bowman, Alisa, 115–116, 174
Boyle, Brendan, 17
boys
    art of curiosity, 177
    bullying, 167
    classmates' boundaries, 176–177
    connecting with, 165–179
    conversation starters, 178
    conversations in cars, 171
    crying, 177–178
    emotional intimacy, 167–168,
        175–177
    emotional vocabulary, 177–178
    friendships, 175
    grades, 173
    ideas for educators–"man box"
        activity, 173, 174–175
    loving interactions, 168–170
    masculinity, 167, 172–174
    myths regarding, 166
    physical conflicts, 175–176
    physical interactions, 176–177
    self-awareness, 167
    sensations and emotional state, 178
    shared experiences with, 170–171
    showing interest in, 170
    silence and, leaving room for,
        165–166, 168
    Snapchats of private parts, 176
    stereotypes about, 166–167, 172–174
    tips for parents, 178

    transgender, 174
    video games and, 171
brain development, 1–2, 13
    online time/electronics and, 100
bravery, 199
Break the Cycle reports, 110, 111
Briar, Jay, 29–30, 117
Bryant, Kobe, 196
bullying, 35–37, 54, 61–62, 79–90,
    92, 167, 231–233
    anxiety and, 85–86
    boys and girls, 88–89
    bullies, 35, 50, 62, 87–89
    changing the narrative, 80, 83–84
    consulting advisors, real and
        fictional, 84
    conversation starters, 90
    creating emotional distance, 87
    cyberbullying, 82, 95, 123
    emotional recovery, 80
    ideas for educators–conflict
        resolution, 86
    imagining the future after, 87
    practical strategies to deal with,
        80–83
    problem-solving skills and, 81–82
    rumination and mantras, 84–85
    safety and changing schools, 86
    self-harming behavior and, 82–83
    social status and, 89
    tips for parents, 90
Business Insider, 197

Cain, Susan, 186, 199
Campbell, Kim, 143, 145, 148
Can You Hear Me? (Morgan), 227
CaptureConfidence campaign, 182
CareerBuilder survey, 97

caring for others, 126. *See also* Making Caring Common Project
Carlos, Juan, 223–224
Carlos, Virginia, 223
cell phones, 229
  in the classroom, 144
  grades and, 144
  homework and, 144–145
  mental health and, 99–100
  See also technology
Centers for Disease Control, 207
Chan, Alexander, 125
changing world, preparing kids for, 219–230
  coaching vs. controlling and, 227–229
  college degrees, 220, 221
  conversation starters, 230
  creative thinking, 219–220, 223–224, 226, 227–228
  curiosity, 224–225
  empowerment and resilience, 219–230
  experiential learning programs, 220, 222–223
  ideas for educators–thinking differently about group projects, 225–226
  innovation and invention, 219–220, 221–222, 223–224, 236
  powers of observation, 224–225
  problem-solving, 219–220, 221–222, 229
  sense of purpose and "big likings," 226–227
  tips for parents, 229–230
Child Development, 19, 41, 145
Choldenko, Gennifer, 56

cigarettes/e-cigs, 13
"The Class's Hour," 41
Clinton, Hillary, 185
coaching vs. controlling, 227–229
code words, 16
Cohen, Joanna, 12
college admissions
  grades and, 133
  Making Caring Common Project, 39, 108, 112, 121, 133, 184–185
college degrees, 220, 221
Common Sense Media survey, 27
community, 38
  service work, 46–47
Computers and Education, 145
Computers in Human Behavior, 123
confidence, 4, 180, 181–182, 188–189
The Confidence Code for Girls (Shipman), 43, 181–182
conflict negotiation, 5
Conolly, Cristina, 216
Conquer Negative Thinking, 136
consent, sexual harassment and, 108–109
consulting advisors, real and fictional, 84
controlling vs.coaching, 227–229
conversations in cars, 171
cranial facial differences, 52–53
Creating Innovators: The Making of Young People Who Will Change the World (Wagner), 224
creativity/creative thinking, 4, 6–7, 219–220, 223–224, 226, 227–228
critical thinking. *See* problem-solving/ critical thinking
Cuddy, Amy, 189
cultural differences, 56, 58, 60–61

Cunningham, Bob, 155–156, 157
curiosity, 177, 224–225
Curry, Parker, 54
cyberbullying. *See under* bullying

DACA. *See* Deferred Action for
    Childhood Arrivals, 51
Damour, Lisa, 44, 112–113
"The Danger of a Single Story"
    (Adichie), 59
Dawson, Peg, 141–142, 143–144
Debrief, 101
deep breathing, 45
Deferred Action for Childhood
    Arrivals (DACA), 51
depression, 17, 37, 68, 70, 80, 87–88,
    100, 205–208, 215, 216. *See also*
    mental health
Design Apprenticeship Program of
    the National Building Museum,
    223–224
Diary of a Mom blog (Wilson), 49
Dickerson, Anne, 227
difference in self and others, 49–63
    authentic inclusion, 52–54
    awareness, 51–52
    bullying, 50
    conversation starters, 63
    fear and bias, 56–57
    global connections, 56
    ideas for educators–global
        connections, 56
    intolerance, 50–51
    power of words, 57–59
    self-concept, 50
    "single story" danger, 59–62
    tips for parents, 62–63
    windows and mirrors, 54–55

Dodd, Robert, 3
Dog Whisperer (TV show), 20
Dolin, Ann, 153, 159
Donovan, Jessica, 94, 187
dress codes, 113–114
drugs, 13
Duke University study, 36
Dutton, Jane, 210
Dweck, Carol, 149
dysgraphia, 159
dyslexia, 155, 157–158, 159, 160

early adolescence, 1–2
Eckstein, Ashley, 190
Eckstein, David, 62
Educational Testing Service survey, 27
educators, ideas for
    academic achievement: balance
        and expectations–celebrate
        "Failure Week," 137
    boys, connecting with–"man box"
        activity, 173, 174–175
    bullying–conflict resolution, 86
    difference in self and others–global
        connections, 56
    ethical decisions–ethical dilemmas
        during advisory, 16
    friendships–creative lunch time, 71
    girls, strong, empowered–speakers
        at career lunches, 188
    gossip–student-led discussions,
        96–97
    homework–team meetings, 147
    honesty–teaching parents about
        developmental phase, 30
    intervention for learning
        challenges–accommodations,
        154–155

kindness and empathy–"Shadow a Student" challenge, 42

love–tie-ins in all subjects, 125–126

preparing kids for changing world–thinking differently about group projects, 225–226

risk-taking–scaffold risk-taking and public speaking, 198–199, 201

setbacks and resilience–mindfulness and skill-building, 212–213

sexual health–Gender and Sexuality Alliance, 117–118

emotional intimacy, 167–168, 175–177

emotional regulation strategies, 6, 211–215

empathy. *See* kindness and empathy

empowerment and resilience, 165–230
boys, connecting with, 165–179
girls, strong, empowered, 179–192
preparing kids for a changing world, 219–230
risk-taking, 193–204
See also resilience; setbacks and resilience

endangerment, 199–200

Enough As She Is (Simmons), 44

Esposito, Jeanine, 222

ethical decisions, 6, 11–23
conversation starters, 23
hypothetical and real-world examples, 19–20
ideas for educators–present ethical dilemmas during advisory, 16
plans for tricky situations, 15–16
problem-solving/critical thinking, 13–14
risky behavior, 11–14

sense of purpose, 20

sharing missteps, 21

sleep habits and self-care habits, 17–18

technology and, 21–22

tips for parents, 22

trust and expectations, 18–19

The Everything Parent's Guide to Special Education (Morin), 153

expansive body language, 189

experiential learning programs, 220, 222–223

Facebook, 19, 97. *See also* technology

Fair Isn't Always Equal (Wormeli), 32

family values, 107

The Fantastic Body (Bennett), 152

Faris, Robert, 69, 70, 87, 88

father-daughter relationship, 183

fear, 56–57, 193–195, 195–196, 208–209

flexibility, 73

Folarin, Tope, 220, 224

FOMO (fear of missing out), 69

Fox, Annie, 84, 85–86

The Freak Factor (Rendall), 62, 83

Free to Learn: Unleashing the Instinct to Play Will Make Our Children Happier, More Self-Reliant, and Better Students (Gray), 228

"Friend or Enemy" exercise, 213

friendships, 4–5, 39, 66–78
boys, 175
conversation starters, 78
focusing on what can be control, 70–71
ideas for educators–creative lunch time, 71

friendships *(continued)*
  love and, 122
  meanness and path forward, 75–77
  peer group match, 72–75
  popularity and, 68–70, 70–71, 73–74
  tips for parents, 78
  unbalanced relationships, 69
Frugo, Julie, 125

Gay Straight Alliance (GSA), 26,
    116–117, 117–118, 201–202.
    See also gender identity
GEMS, 223–224
gender differences
  dress codes, 113–114
  stereotypes, 111–114
gender identity, 114–117
  resources, 168
  support, 115–117
  See also Gay Straight Alliance;
    LGBTQ+; transgender
Getting Grit (Miller), 190
The Gift of Failure (Lahey), 134
gifted learners, 156
Ginsburg, Kenneth, 1–2, 13, 16, 126,
    166, 168, 169, 200, 215, 216, 225
girls
  articulating feelings, 191
  body image, 182–183
  celebrating other girls' successes,
    189–190
  confidence, 4, 180, 181–182,
    188–189
  conversation starters, 192
  criticism and, 182–183
  defining goals, 191
  expansive body language, 189
  father-daughter relationship, 183
  ideas for educators–speakers at
    career lunches, 188
  leadership skills, 184–186
  mentors and role models, 186–188
  messaging and, 183–184, 184–185
  owning success, 188–189
  perfection, 181–182
  self-advocacy, 180, 190–191
  strong, empowered, 179–192
  support network, 191
  timidity, 179–180
  tips for parents, 192
Girls & Sex (Orenstein), 112
Girls on the Run, 189
Glasgow, Rodney, 51–52, 55, 57, 113
Glenn, John, 197
global connections, 56
GLSEN school climate survey, 116
Gomez, Selena, 84
Goodall, Jane, 187
Goodstein, Jennifer, 145–146
Goodwin, Alan, 132–133
Gordon, Jon, 43, 189–190
Gordon, Michael, 2, 18, 20
gossip, 91–102
  conservation starters, 102
  countering meanness, 95–96
  ideas for educators–student-led
    discussions, 96–97
  regaining normalcy, 92–95
  reputational damage, 97–101
  resilience and, 101
  seeking help, 100–101
  self-reflection, 101
  Smartphones and, 98–100
  social media and, 92–93, 97–101
  tips for parents, 101–102
grades, 146, 233–234

balance and expectations, 131–133, 134–136
boys, 173
cell phones and, 144
college admissions, 133
inconsistencies and limitations, 133
myths regarding, 132–133
Grant, Adam, 38, 210
gratitude journal, 73. *See also* journaling
Gray, Peter, 227–228
Greater Good Magazine, 36
Growing Friendships: A Kid's Guide to Making and Keeping Friends (Kennedy-Moore), 67
GSA. *See* Gay Straight Alliance (GSA)
Guillen Williams, Julia, 92–93, 98
gun control, 210

Hall, G. Stanley, 1
Hallowell, Edward, 159
Hampton, Natalie, 85
Hanson, Rick, 200
Harry Potter series, 42, 83
Harvard Graduate School of Education study, 53. *See also* Making Caring Common Project
Harvard Kennedy School Spring Exercise, 223
Harvard study, 38, 214
Harwell, Monica, 59
"Have Smartphones Destroyed a Generation?" (*The Atlantic*), 100
Health Psychology Open study, 211
Heitner, Devorah, 100
Hinduja, Sameer, 21, 22, 82, 95, 97, 123

homework, 5, 141–150
after-school support, 146
avoidance, 141–142
cell phones and, 144–145
conversation starters, 150
evaluate and modify, 147–148
ideas for educators–team meetings, 147
independence and, 144
negative voices and, 148–149
physical movement and, 148
reward system, 145–146
routines, 143–144
school as the bad guy, 146–147
self-advocacy skills, 144
sense of agency and, 143–145
study experience, 145–146
task initiation, 141–142
tips for parents, 150
uncomfortable emotions and, 149
honesty, 24–34
conversation starters, 34
ideas for educators–teach parents about developmental phase, 30
lying and, 24–34
modeling, 31–32
tips for parents, 34
values and, 32–33
See also lying
honor, 7–8
Hughes, Eileen, 42
Hurley, Katie, 37, 95, 96, 138, 172–173
Hynes, Michael, 228

IEP (individualized education plan), 153, 154, 157–158
iGen, 99
Ignore It (Pearlman), 114

Ignotofsky, Rachel, 187
immersive virtual reality (IVR) goggles, 58–59
immigrants, 51
inclusion. *See* authentic inclusion
innovation and invention, 6–7, 219–220, 223–224, 236
resources, 221–222
Inside Out (movie), 149
integrity. *See* values and integrity
Interactive Autism Network survey, 62
Internet, 27, 208, 209
online and offline social life, 69
online manipulation, love and, 123–124
online time/electronics, 100
pornography, 110
See also technology
intervention for learning challenges, 151–161
attention deficit disorder, 151–152, 159
attention deficit hyperactivity disorder, 157, 159
change for the better, 157–158
child as expert, 152–153
consulting with professionals, 152
conversation starters, 160–161
directness and sensitivity, 159–160
dysgraphia, 159
dyslexia, 155, 157–158, 159, 160
gifted and twice-exceptional learners, 156
ideas for educators–accommodations, 154–155
IEP (individualized education plan), 153, 154, 157–158
independence, 158

learning disabilities, 155–156
school support, 153–154
Section 504 Plan, 152, 154
sharing information and strategies, 159
tips for parents, 160
invention. *See* innovation and invention

JAMA *Pediatrics*, 112
Jensen, Edyn, 52–53
Jivani, Sanah, 61
Johns, Christina, 17–18
Johnson, Dwayne, 197
Johnson, Katherine, 187
Johnson, Ned, 134, 152, 207, 209–210
Jones, Maggie, 110
Josephson Institute study, 32
Journal of Adolescent Health, 82
Journal of Applied Social Psychology, 42
Journal of Development & Behavioral Pediatrics, 206
Journal of Early Adolescence, 3, 111
Journal of Experimental Psychology, 57
Journal of Personality and Social Psychology, 215
Journal of Youth and Adolescence, 136
journaling, 13, 73, 214, 224
Jovanovic, Ana, 145, 148–149

Karr, Doug, 60
Kay, Katty, 182
Kecmanovic, Jelena, 109
Keltner, Dacher, 40–41, 45
Kennedy-Moore, Eileen, 67, 72–73, 96
Kiang-Spray, Wendy, 58, 135–136
KID Museum, 222, 223, 224

kindness and empathy, 4, 14, 35–48, 70–71, 75, 85, 109
  acts of kindness, 35–37
  community service work, 46–47
  conversation starters, 48
  ideas for educators–"Shadow a Student" challenge, 42
  jealousy and, 43–44
  meanness and, 37–38, 43–44
  mindfulness and, 44–46
  modeling, 39–41
  movement and, 46
  perspectives, 41–42
  tips for parents, 47
Kohn, Alfie, 197

Lady Gaga, 36, 207
Lager, Karen, 53–54
Lahey, Jessica, 134, 138
Land, George, 220
Langdon, Matt, 83, 84
leadership skills, 184–186
learning, 131–161
  academic achievement: balance and expectations, 131–140
  challenges, intervention for, 151–161
  homework and, 141–150
learning disabilities, 155–156
Lee, Chanice, 190
Lesser, Cara, 223, 224
Let Grow Project, Patchogue Medford School District, New York, 228
Lewis, Alexis, 174, 187, 221
LGBTQ+, 114–115, 116–117, 117–118, 233. *See also* gender identity
Lickona, Thomas, 124, 125

LieSpotting (Meyer), 27
The Listening Project, New York University, 166, 177
love, 7–8, 120–127, 168–170, 236
  caring for others, 126
  conversation starters, 127
  emotional risks, 126
  friendships and, 122
  heartbreak and, 120–121, 126
  ideas for educators–tie-ins in all subjects, 125–126
  media literacy, 124–125
  online manipulation, 123–124
  outside influences, 124–125
  sexual health, 126
  sharing experiences, 121–123
  tips for parents, 126
Love, Kevin, 173–174
Lupien, Sonia, 210
lying, 24–34
  arguing and, 33–34
  the long view, 28–29
  offensive vs. defensive, 27
  punishment for, 33–34
  root cause and reasons for, 25, 29–30
  See also honesty
Lyubomirsky, Sonya, 36

maker learning, 223, 224
Making Caring Common Project, Harvard Graduate School of Education, 39, 108, 112, 121, 133, 184–185
mantras, 84–85
marijuana, 13
Maryland Coalition for Inclusion Education report, 53

Mascareñaz, Lauren, 52
masturbation, 106
Meaney, Michael, 209
meanness, 37–38, 43–44
    countering, and gossip, 95–96
    friendship and, 75–77
    See also kindness and empathy
Meet the Robinsons (movie), 149
menstruation, 106
mental health, 99–100. *See also*
    depression; suicide; therapy
Merrill-Palmer Quarterly, 134
Merryman, Ashley, 25–26, 28, 29,
    33–34
messaging, 183–184, 184–185
Meyer, Pamela, 27, 31
Middle School Confidential series (Fox),
    84
middle school models, 2–4
military children, 73, 74
Millan, Cesar, 20
millennials, 99
Miller, Caroline, 190
Miller, Chris, 61–62
Miller, Gregory, 196
Mindell, Ari, 224
mindfulness, 44–46
    strategies, 45, 211–213
Mohan, Manisha, 109
Montgomery County Public Schools,
    Maryland, program, 222
Moore, Roxanne, 220, 227
Morgan, Nick, 227
Morin, Amanda, 153, 158
Morin, Amy, 181, 200, 213, 215
Murphy, Scott, 158, 220, 229
mutuality and reciprocity, 112–113
Myers, Alex, 116

Nardi, Chris, 116, 153–154, 213
National Institutes of Health study,
    100, 206
Nelson, Joseph Derrick, 167, 172,
    175–176
New York Times, 112–113, 133, 173
The New York Times Magazine, 110
Nielson, Linda, 183
No More Mean Girls (Hurley), 37
Noll, Kathy, 88
Northeastern University study, 45
Northwestern University study, 145
*NurtureShock: New Thinking About
    Children*, 25–26
N.U.T.S. model of stress, 210

Obama, Michelle, 54
Ohlrichs, Yuri, 111, 112
Orender, Donna, 187–188, 189
Orenstein, Peggy, 112, 181, 182, 183,
    191
Ostrov, Jamie, 67–68, 101
Owning Up (Wiseman), 81

parents
    academic achievement: balance
        and expectations tips for parents,
        139
    authoritarian vs. authoritative, 41
    bullying tips for, 90
    difference tips for, 62–63
    embarrassed *by* you vs. to be *with*
        you, 234
    ethical-decision tips for, 22
    friendship tips for, 78
    gossip tips for, 101–102
    homework tips for, 150
    honesty tips for, 34

honor and, 7–8

intervention for learning
  challenges tips, 160

kindness and empathy tips for, 47

love and, 7–8, 236

love tips for, 126

parenting through middle school,
  234–236

primary job of, 7–8

as safety net, 8

sexual health tips, 119

sharing missteps, 21

Parker, Jack, 174

Parker, William, 174, 206

Patchin, Justin, 82

Peake, David, 116

Pearlman, Casey, 114

Pearlman, Catherine, 114

peer group match, 72–75

Penn State study, 36

Pennies of Time, 46

perfectionism, 137–139, 181–182

Pew Research Center report, 98

Piaget, Jean, 1

Pion, Alison, 199–200

The Players Tribune (Love), 173

Pletter, Adam, 171

PNAS, 46

Pope, Denise, 135

*Popular: The Power of Likeability
  in a Status-Obsessed World*
  (Prinstein), 68

Popular (Prinstein), 87–88

popularity, 68–70, 70–71, 73–74

pornography, 109–111

The Power of a Positive Team
  (Gordon), 43, 189

power of words, 57–59

powers of observation, 224–225

*Presence: Bringing Your Boldest Self to
  Your Biggest Challenges* (Cuddy),
  189

Prinstein, Mitch, 68, 69, 72, 73, 77,
  87–88

problem-solving/critical thinking,
  13–14, 41, 81–82, 94, 134, 135,
  144, 219–220, 221–222, 229

Project SUCCESS, 3

Psychological Science, 67

public speaking, 198–199, 201

Purple Hibiscus (Adichie), 55

Quattro, Olan, 223, 224–225

*Quiet: The Power of Introverts in a
  World that Can't Stop Talking*
  (Cain), 186

Quinn, Kyle, 97

quitting, 196–197

race, 51, 54–55, 56, 58–59, 59–60

Radnor Township School District
  Soundings program, 223

*Raising Cain: Protecting the Emotional
  Life of Boys* (Thompson), 170

Raising Kids (Ginsburg), 2

Raising the Transgender Child
  (Bowman), 115

Rakow, Susan, 156

Rathbone, Britt, 43, 208, 216

Rayne, Karen, 113–114

reciprocity and mutuality, 112–113

Reiner, Andrew, 167, 173, 177

Rendall, Dave, 62, 83–84

Report Card on the Ethics of
  American Youth study
  (Josephson Institute), 32

reputational damage, 97–101

Rescue Travois, 221

resilience, 101, 209. *See also* empowerment and resilience; setbacks and resilience

Resilient: How to Grow an Unshakeable Core of Calm, Strength, and Happiness (Hanson), 200

Rietano, Margaret, 45–46, 227

Riley, Allie, 189

Rip, Pernille, 56

risk-taking, 193–204

    categories of risk, 195

    challenging rules, 202–203

    confidence-building, 198

    conversation starters, 204

    demonstrating bravery, 199

    endangerment, 199–200

    fear and self-doubt, 193–195

    feedback, 197–198

    gradual exposure, 198–200

    healthy vs. unsafe, 200

    ideas for educators–scaffold risk-taking and public speaking, 198–199, 201

    looking outward, 201–202

    mixed messages, 200

    positive reinforcement, 200

    quitting, 196–197

    tips for parents, 204

    understanding fear of an activity, 195–196

risky behavior, 11–14

Roffman, Deborah, 103, 104, 107, 108, 118

Rottenberg, Sarah, 18

RTI International study, 122

Rudd, Melanie, 45

rule-generation, 18

rumination, 84–85, 213, 214

safety, schools and, 86

safety net, 8

Sandberg, Sheryl, 186

Scheff, Sue, 69, 97, 98

Schilpp, Ali, 56

schools, safety and, 86

Screenwise (Heitner), 100

The Seattle Times, 57

Section 504 Plan, 152, 154

Selby, Sally, 3, 135

self-advocacy, 6, 143, 144, 180, 190–191

The Self-Driven Child (Johnson), 134

self-fulfilling prophecy, 19

self-harming behavior, 82–83

sense of agency, 71, 112–113, 143–145, 209–210, 221, 223, 228

sense of purpose, 20, 226–227

sense of self, 7, 44, 51

setbacks and resilience, 195, 205–218

    anxiety, 206–208, 215

    conversation starters, 218

    coping strategies, 211–212

    depression, 205–208, 215

    emotional distress warning signs and when to seek therapy, 215–217

    emotional regulation strategies, 211–215

    fear, 208–209

    ideas for educators–mindfulness and skill-building, 212–213

    loosening control, 210

    mindfulness strategies, 211–213

    optimism, 217–218

self-compassion, 211

sense of agency, 209–210

stress-management strategies, 211

suicide, 207, 216

technology-free zone, 212

tips for parents, 218

troubling events, processing,
208–209

validating feelings, 217–218

See also empowerment and
resilience; resilience

sexism, 51

sexts, 112–113

sexual harassment, 108–111, 113

sexual health, 103–119

body image, 111–112

books and online resources, 105–106

conversations/conversation starters,
118–119

discussions about sex, 103–104,
105–107

family values, 107

gender identity and sexual identity,
114–117

ideas for educators–Gender and
Sexuality Alliance, 117–118

love, 126

masturbation, 106

menstruation, 106

mutuality and reciprocity, 112–113

myths, 106

sexts, 112–113

sexual activity, 13–14

sexual harassment, 108–111, 113

sexual intercourse, 13–14, 103, 104

sharing experiences, 107

stereotypes and gender differences,
111–114

tips for parents, 119

sexual identity, 114–117

Shame Nation (Scheff), 69, 97

"SHE" (Society Harnessing
Equipment), 109

Shelffo, Janine, 184, 187

Shipman, Claire, 43, 181–182, 188,
191, 198

"Shock Bra," 109

Silverman, Mary Alice, 26

Simmons, Dena, 55

Simmons, Rachel, 44, 181, 182–183,
184, 191

"single story" danger, 59–62

Sit with Us app, 85

Sixteen Candles (movie), 120–121

Sjolseth, Sheila, 46

sleep habits, 17–18

Smart but Scattered (Dawson), 141

Smartphones, 98–100. *See also*
technology

Smith, Hannah, 82

social isolation, 99

social life, online and offline, 69

social media

block, unfollow, unfriend,
97–98

consumption, 98–100

gossip, 92–93, 97–101

sexual harassment, 109

sleep habits, 17

Social Psychology, 144

social skills, 66–127

bullying, 79–90

friendships, 66–78

gossip, 91–102

love, 120–127

sexual health, 103–119

SOS Suicide Prevention Program, 216

Special Olympics, 57

Speicher, Sandy, 226–227

Stakem, Ricky, 176

Stefani, Gwen, 95

Steinberg, Laurence, 13

STEM (science, technology, engineering, and mathematics), 187, 221, 222, 223–224

Sticks and Stones (Bazelon), 94

StoryCorps, 59

The Strength Switch (Waters), 44

stress, academic, 233–234

stress-management strategies, 211

student-teacher mismatch, 5

suicide, 17–18, 82–83, 98–100, 207, 216. *See also* mental health

Sullivan, Megan, 77

Supporting the Emotional Needs of the Gifted, 156

Sutton, Robert, 87

Swift, Taylor, 95

Tager, Ella, 155, 157–158, 159, 160

Tager, Miriam, 157–158

Taking the Bully by the Horns (Noll), 88

Talmus, Laura, 52

Talmus, Lily, 52

TASH, 53–54

teacher-student mismatch, 5

Teaching Tolerance magazine, 52

technology, 21–22, 171. *See also* cell phones; Facebook; Internet; Smartphones

technology-free zone, 212

TED Talk, 59

Tercyak, Ken, 213

terrorist attack, September 11, 2001, 208

texting while driving, 14

therapy
  cognitive-behavioral therapy, 139
  when to seek, 215–216
  See also mental health

Thinking Skills and Creativity, 13

13 Things Mentally Strong Parents Don't Do (Morin), 181

Thompson, Michael, 170, 171

thrive, skills needed to, 4–8

transgender, 115–116, 168, 233. *See also* gender identity

Tubman, Harriet, 84

Twenge, Jean, 99, 100

twice-exceptional learners, 156

Under Our Skin Project, 57

University of California at Berkeley study, 46, 87

University of Florida survey, 108

University of Michigan study, 13, 42, 45

University of New Hampshire study, 109–110

University of Pennsylvania program, 18

University of Pennsylvania study, 13

University of Southern California study, 13

University of Texas at Austin study, 70

UnSelfie (Borba), 36–37, 81

Untangled (Damour), 44

US Weekly, 95

values and integrity, 9–63
  differences in self and others, 49–63
  ethical decisions, 11–23

focus on values, 32–33
honesty, 24–34
kindness and empathy, 35–48
Vernacchio, Al, 112
Virtual Human Interaction Lab,
    Stanford University, 58
Visitacion Valley School mindfulness
    program, 45
Volpitta, Donna, 158

Wagner, Tony, 224
"Wait Until 8th" pledge, 99
The Wall Street Journal, 87
Wang, Vera, 197
The Washington Post, 197
Waters, Lea, 44
Way, Niobe, 166–167, 175, 177
Webster, Jennifer, 74
Weissbourd, Richard, 121, 133
West Windsor Plainsboro Regional
    School District, New Jersey, real-
    world action plan, 222–223

"White Bear" activity, 213–214
white supremacist rallies,
    Charlottesville, Virginia, 97
Williams, Julia Guillen, 76
Wilson, Brooke, 49–50
Wilson, Jess, 49–50, 53
Wiseman, Rosalind, 81, 85, 86
*Women in Science: 50 Fearless
    Pioneers Who Changed the World*
    (Ignotofsky), 187
Wormeli, Rick, 32, 142, 147–148
*Wowsdom: The Girls Guide to
    the Positive and the Possible*
    (Orender), 187–188
Wrorsch, Carsten, 196

Yale Center for Emotional
    Intelligence survey, 207
You and Your Adolescent (Steinberg), 13
Youth Risk Behavior Survey, 13–14,
    103–104
YPulse study, 4, 180

ABOUT THE AUTHOR

PHYLLIS L. FAGELL, LCPC, is the counselor at Sheridan School, a psychotherapist at The Chrysalis Group, and a frequent contributor to *The Washington Post* and other national publications. She is also a regular columnist for the *Association for Middle Level Education* and *Kappan* magazines, and she consults and speaks throughout the country. Phyllis graduated with honors from Dartmouth College and received a master's degree in journalism from the Medill School at Northwestern University. She began her career as a magazine editor before earning her master's degree in counseling from Johns Hopkins University. Phyllis lives in Bethesda, Maryland with her husband and three children.